NIRVANA.

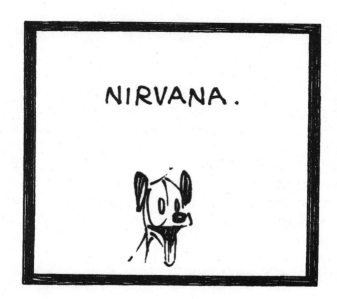

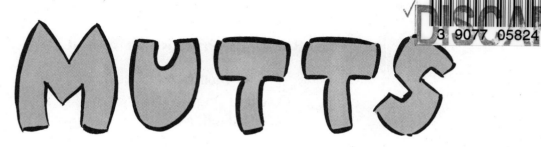

MUTTS

PATRICK McDONNELL

WHAT NOW

**Andrews McMeel
Publishing**

Kansas City

Other Books by Patrick McDonnell

Mutts is distributed internationally by King Features Syndicate, Inc. For information write King Features Syndicate, Inc., 888 Seventh Avenue, New York, New York 10019.

02 03 04 05 06 BAH 10 9 8 7 6 5 4 3 2 1

ISBN: 0-7407-2321-9

Library of Congress Control Number: 2002103638

What Now is printed on recycled paper.

──── **ATTENTION: SCHOOLS AND BUSINESSES** ────

Andrews McMeel books are available at quantity discounts with bulk purchase for educational, business, or sales promotional use. For information, please write to: Special Sales Department, Andrews McMeel Publishing, 4520 Main Street, Kansas City, Missouri 64111.

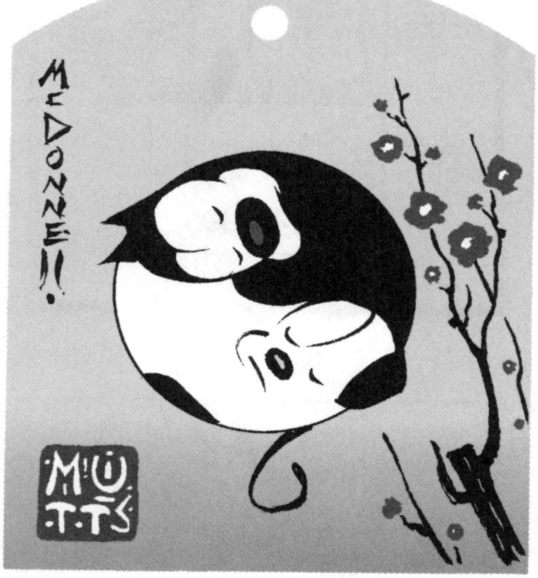

McDONNELL
MUTTS

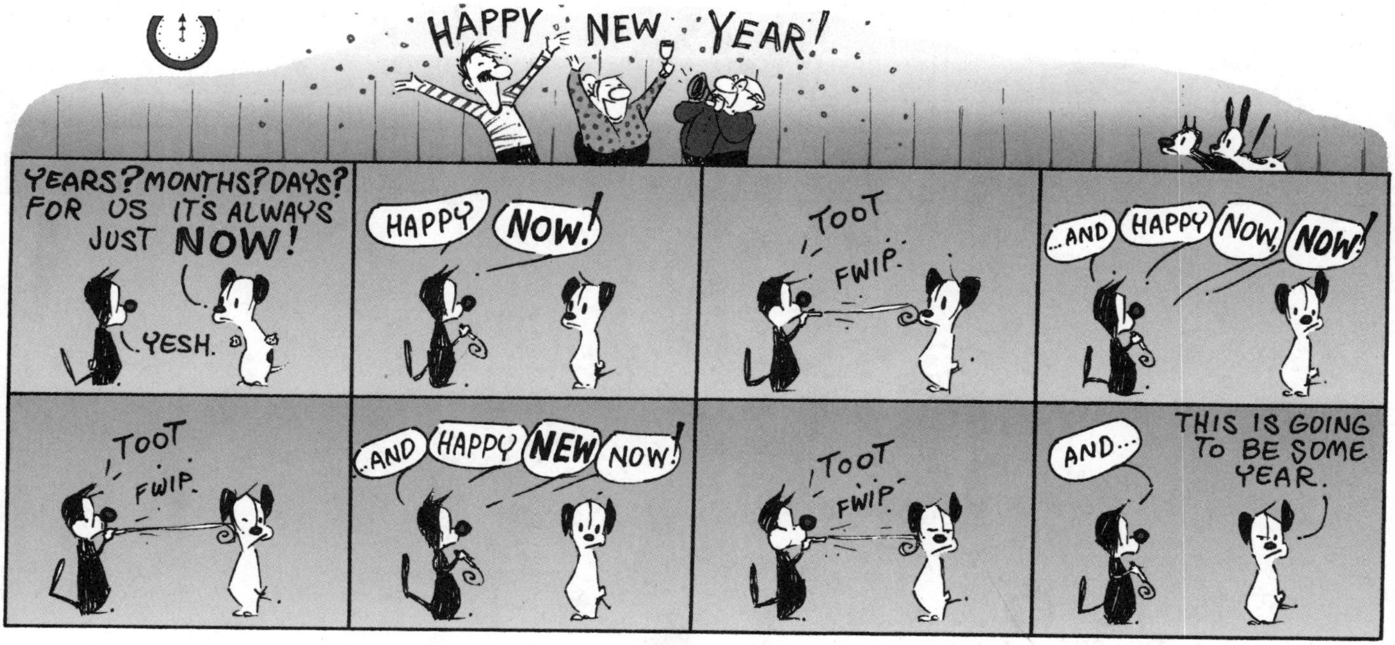

HAPPY NEW YEAR!
YEARS? MONTHS? DAYS? FOR US IT'S ALWAYS JUST NOW!
YESH.
HAPPY
NOW!
TOOT
FWIP.
...AND
HAPPY
NOW,
NOW!
TOOT
FWIP.
...AND
HAPPY
NEW
NOW!
TOOT
FWIP.
AND...
THIS IS GOING TO BE SOME YEAR.

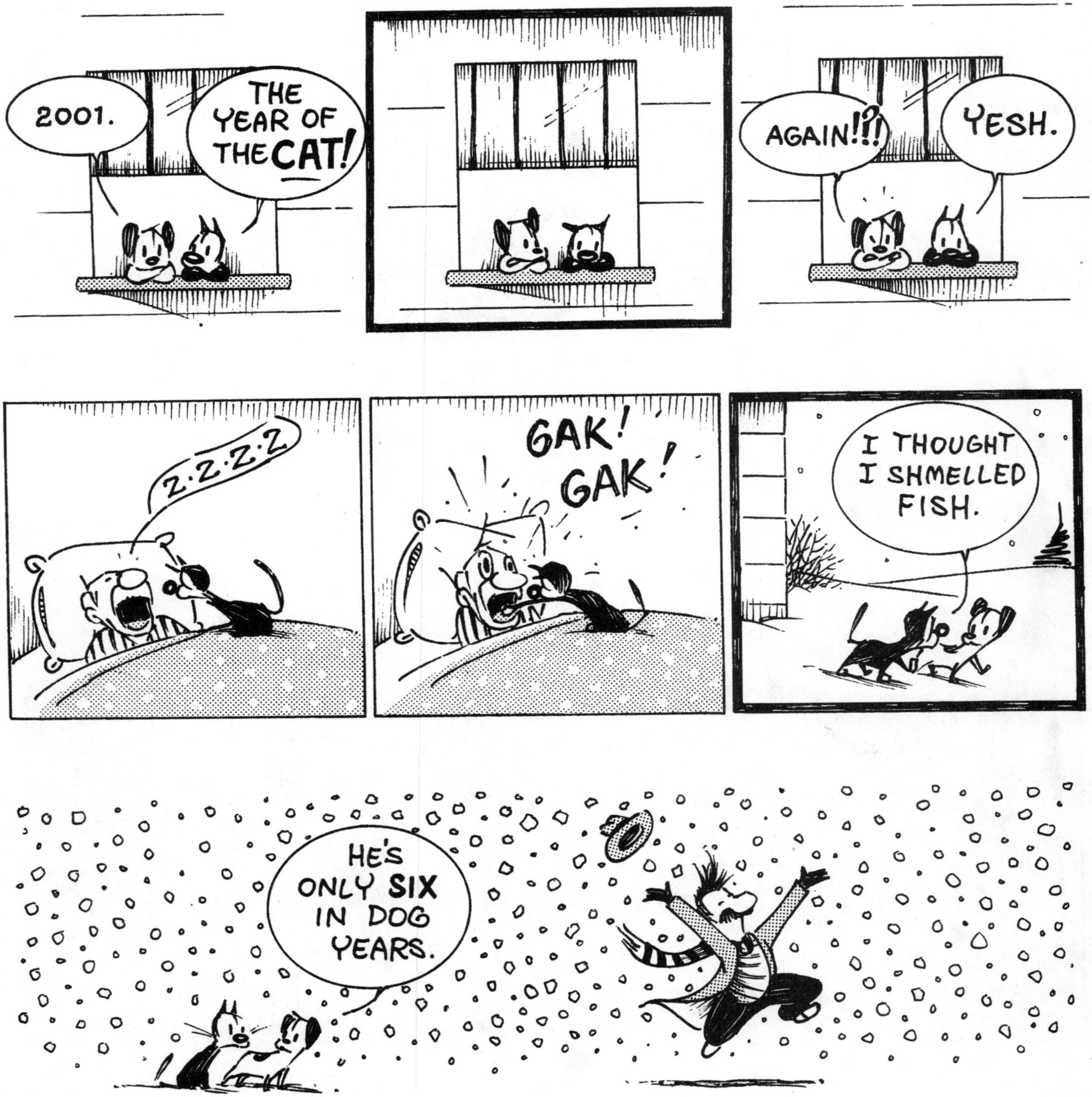
2001.
THE YEAR OF THE CAT!
AGAIN!?!
YESH.
Z·Z·Z·Z
GAK! GAK!
I THOUGHT I SHMELLED FISH.
HE'S ONLY SIX IN DOG YEARS.

MUTTS

OOOOOH... MY NOSE IS ALL SHTUFFED UP...
AAACHOOEY.
OOOOOOH... I HAVE DA SHNIFFLES...
OOOOOO NUTHIN'S SADDER THAN A LI'L SHICK KITTY...
MOMMY.
OOOOOH... I COULD REALLY USE SHOME CHICKY SHNOODLE.
OOOOH... POOR PO MOOCHIE... OOOOOH... POOR PO PUDDY...
OOOOOH, EARL, ARE YOU PRAYING FOR ME TO GET BETTER...?
YES...
THAT... OR LARYNGITIS.

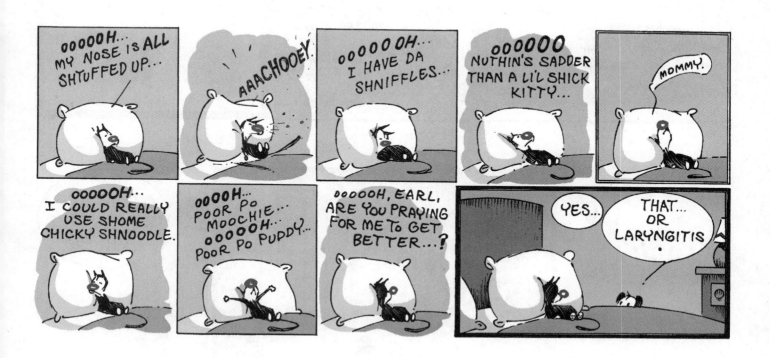

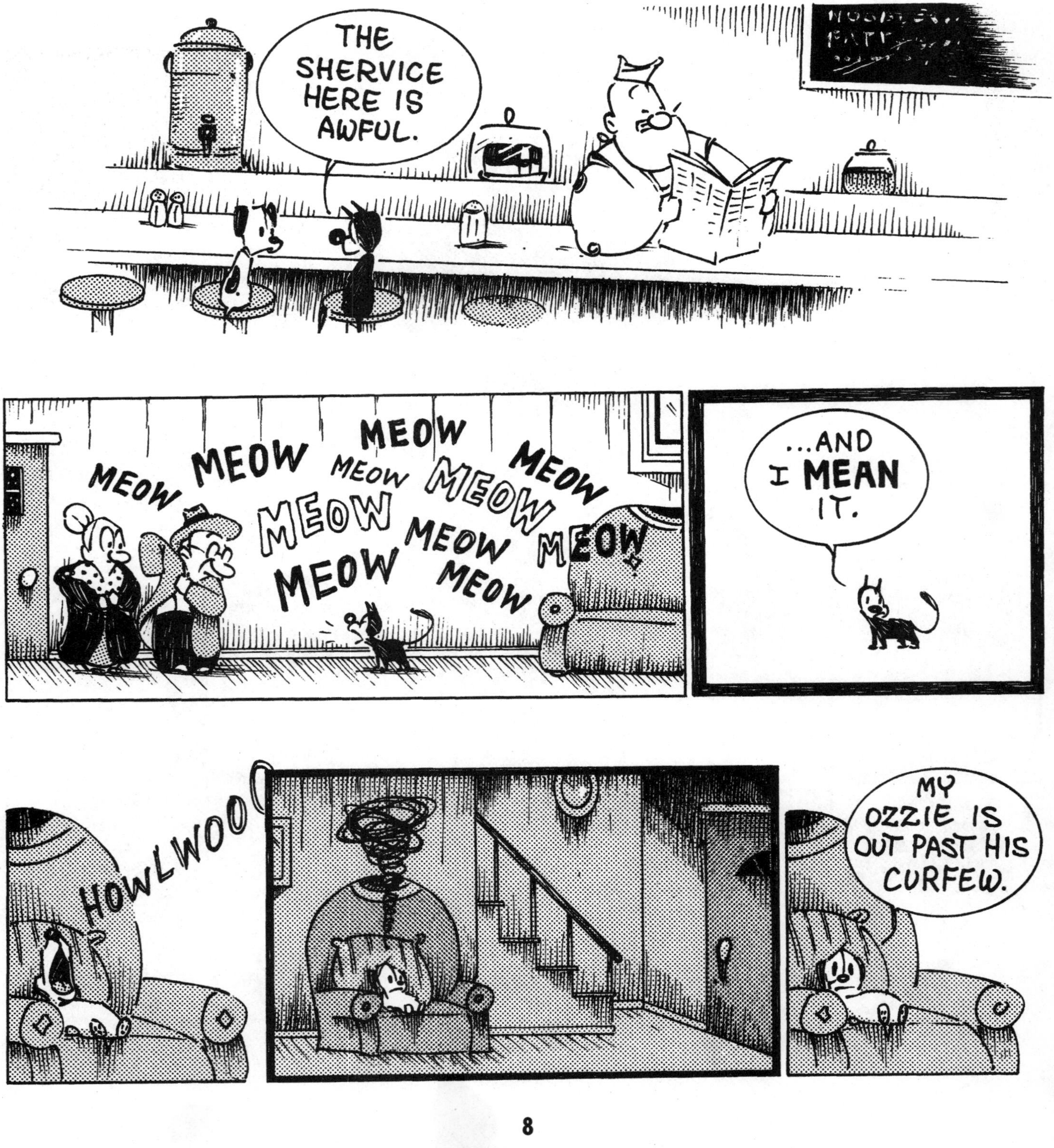
THE SHERVICE HERE IS AWFUL.
MEOW MEOW MEOW MEOW MEOW MEOW MEOW MEOW MEOW MEOW MEOW MEOW
...AND I MEAN IT.
HOWLWOO
MY OZZIE IS OUT PAST HIS CURFEW.

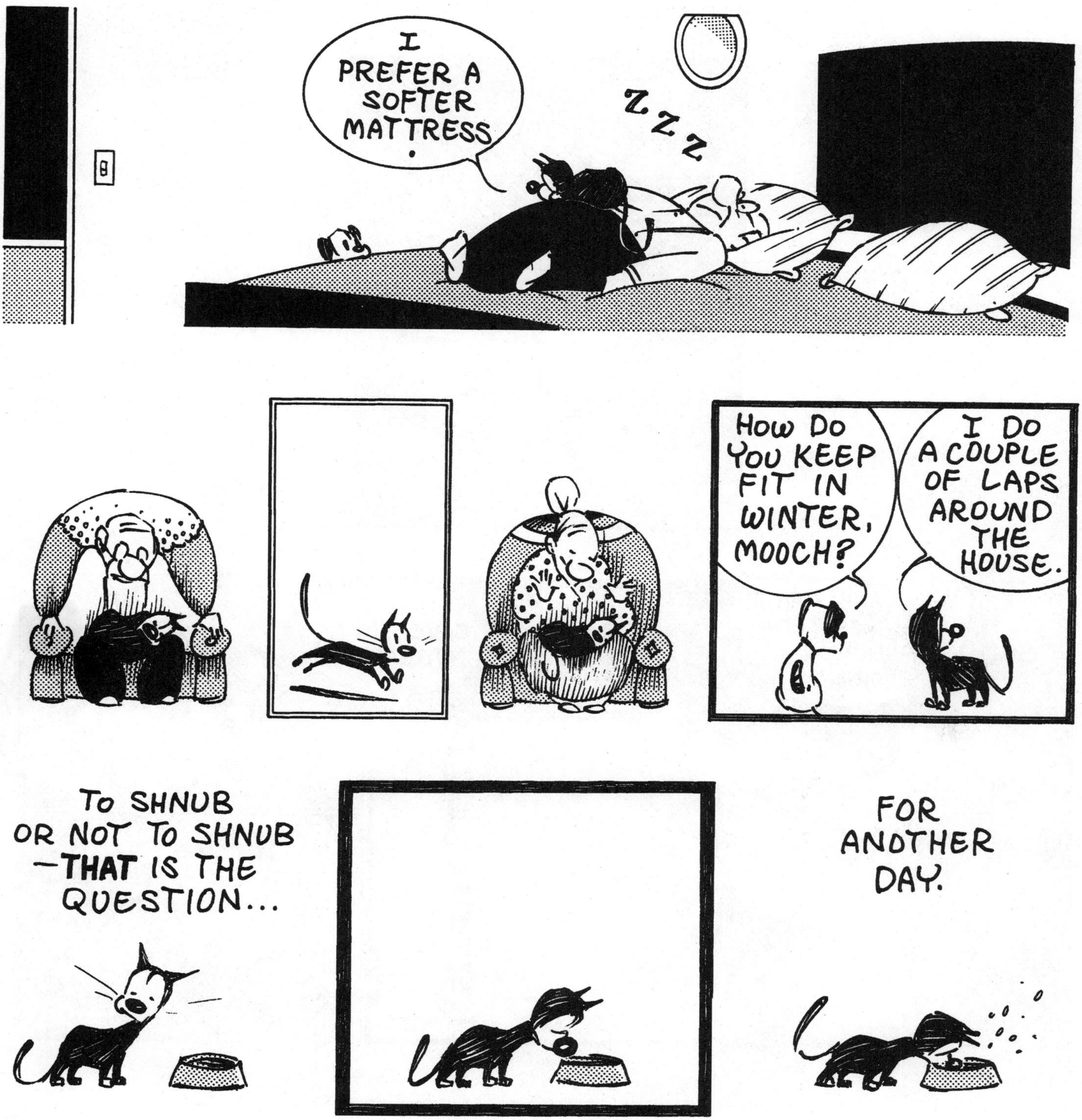
I PREFER A SOFTER MATTRESS.
Z Z Z
HOW DO YOU KEEP FIT IN WINTER, MOOCH?
I DO A COUPLE OF LAPS AROUND THE HOUSE.
TO SHNUB OR NOT TO SHNUB —THAT IS THE QUESTION...
FOR ANOTHER DAY.

MY SON, THE MUTT

SON, "EVERY MAN IS THE ARCHITECT OF HIS OWN FORTUNE."
" A NUT SAVED IS A NUT EARNED".
"A NUT IN THE HAND IS WORTH TWO IN THE BUSH."
" HOLD ON TIGHTLY — LET GO LIGHTLY."
BONK

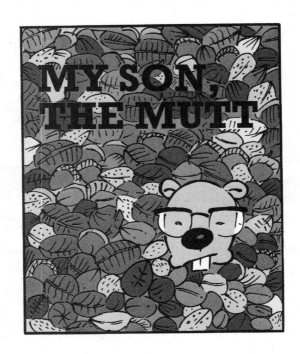

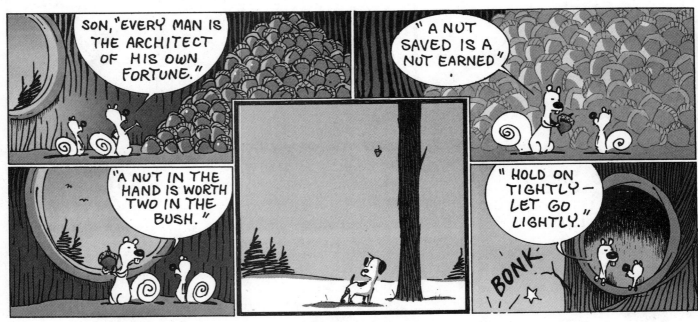

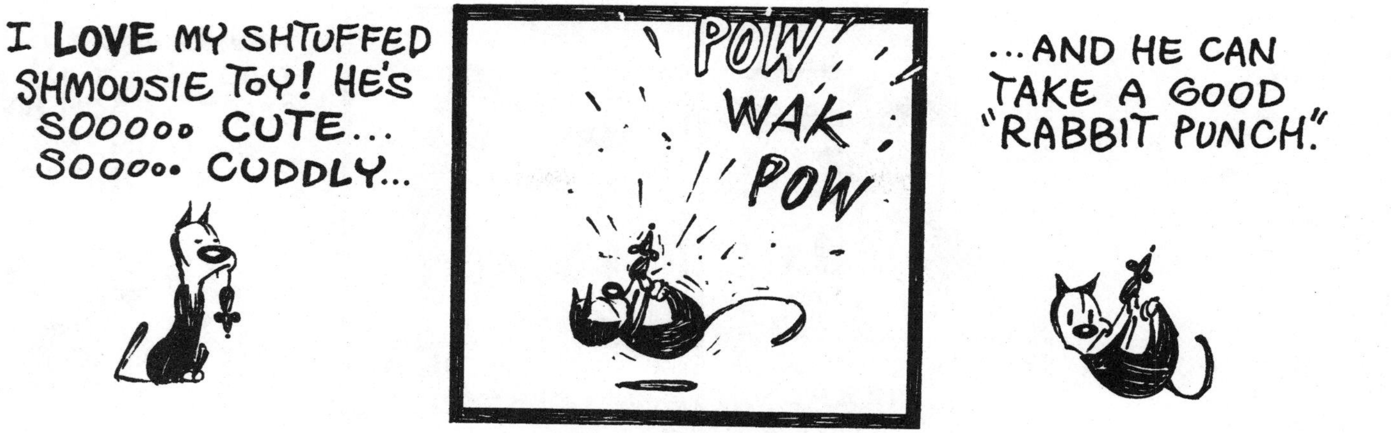
I LOVE MY SHTUFFED SHMOUSIE TOY! HE'S SOOOOO CUTE... SOOOOO CUDDLY...
POW
WAK
POW
...AND HE CAN TAKE A GOOD "RABBIT PUNCH."

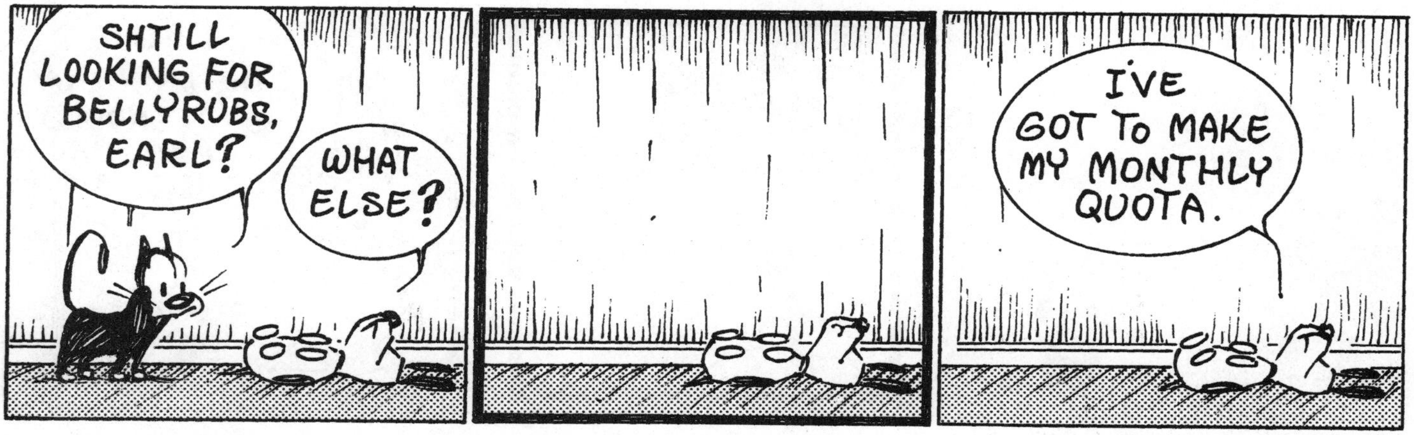
SHTILL LOOKING FOR BELLYRUBS, EARL?
WHAT ELSE?
I'VE GOT TO MAKE MY MONTHLY QUOTA.

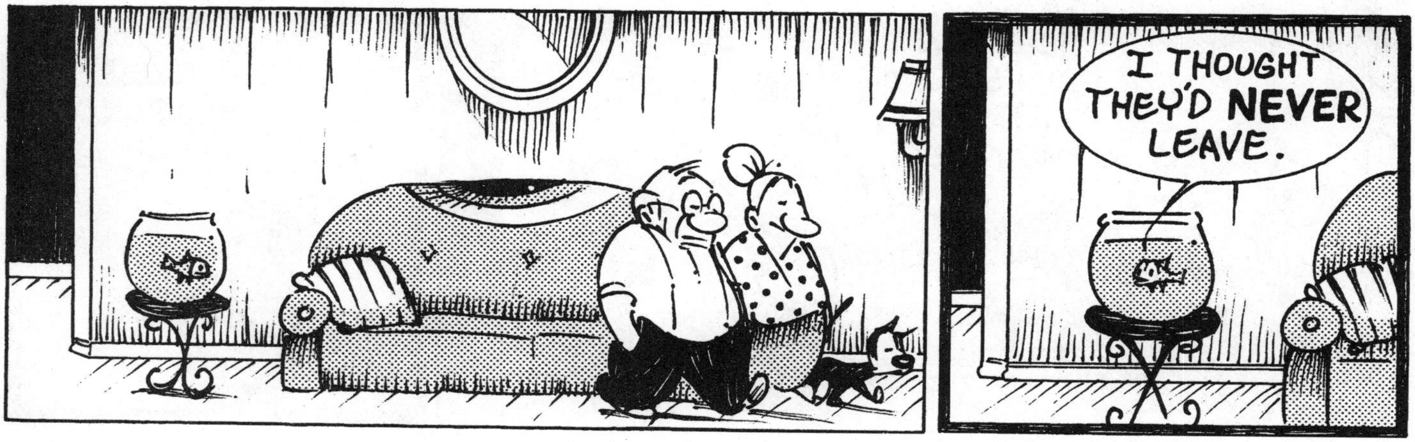
I THOUGHT THEY'D NEVER LEAVE.

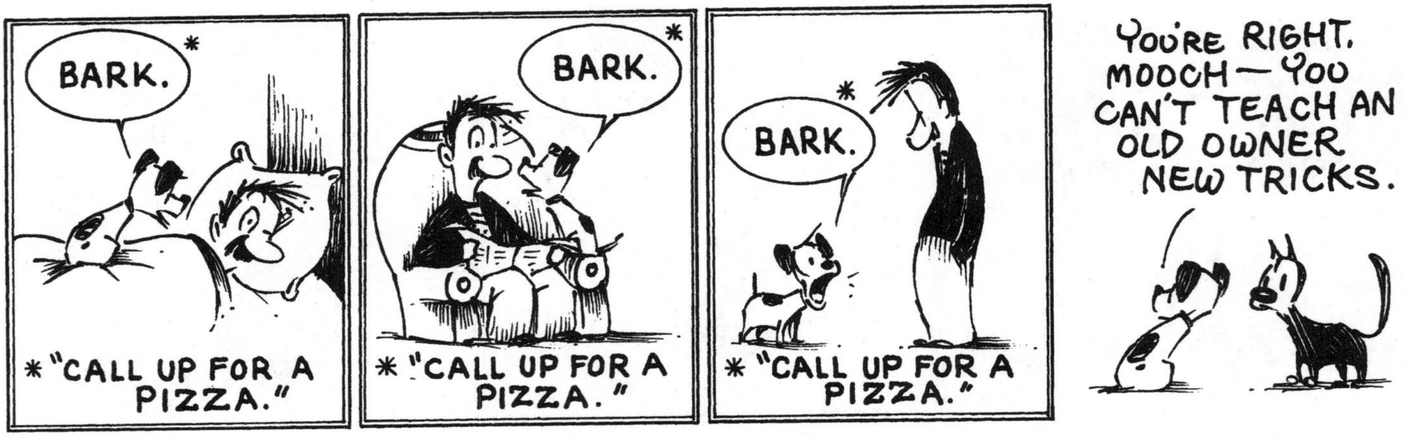
BARK.
* "CALL UP FOR A PIZZA."
BARK.
* "CALL UP FOR A PIZZA."
BARK.
* "CALL UP FOR A PIZZA."
YOU'RE RIGHT, MOOCH — YOU CAN'T TEACH AN OLD OWNER NEW TRICKS.

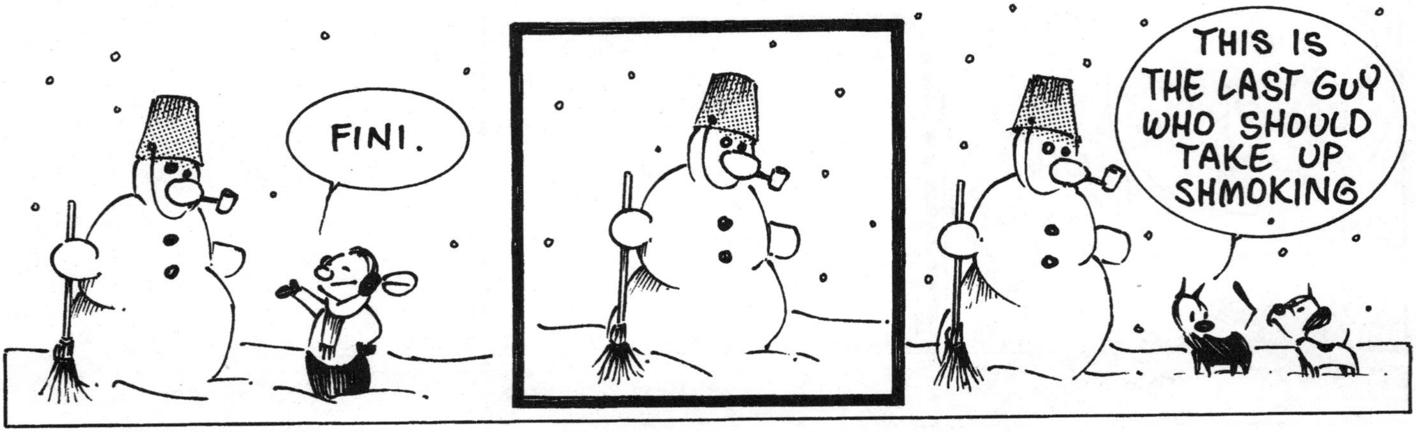
FINI.
THIS IS THE LAST GUY WHO SHOULD TAKE UP SHMOKING.

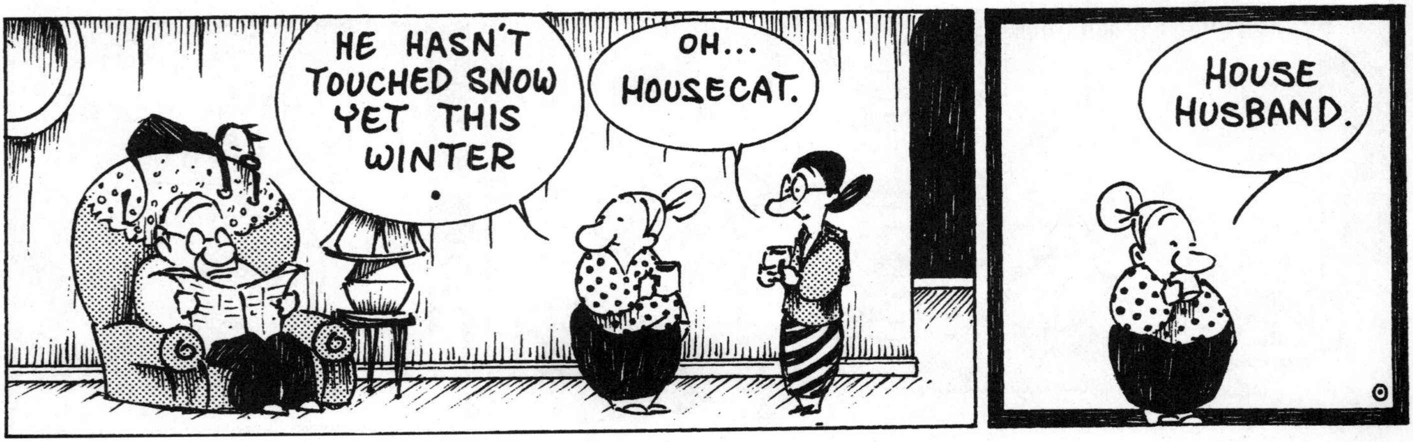
HE HASN'T TOUCHED SNOW YET THIS WINTER.
OH... HOUSECAT.
HOUSE HUSBAND.

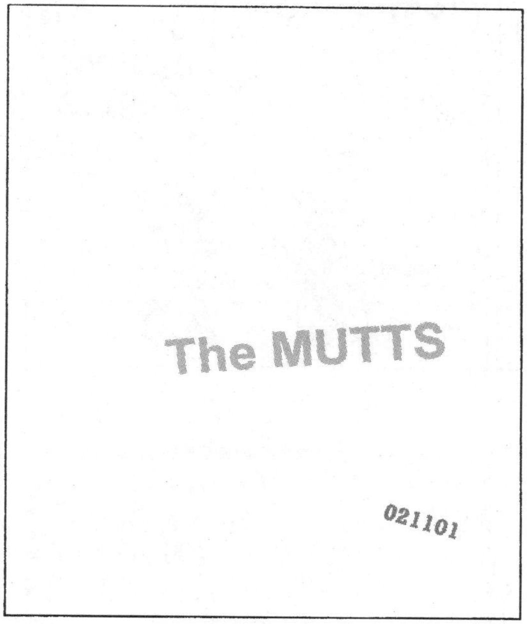
The MUTTS
021101

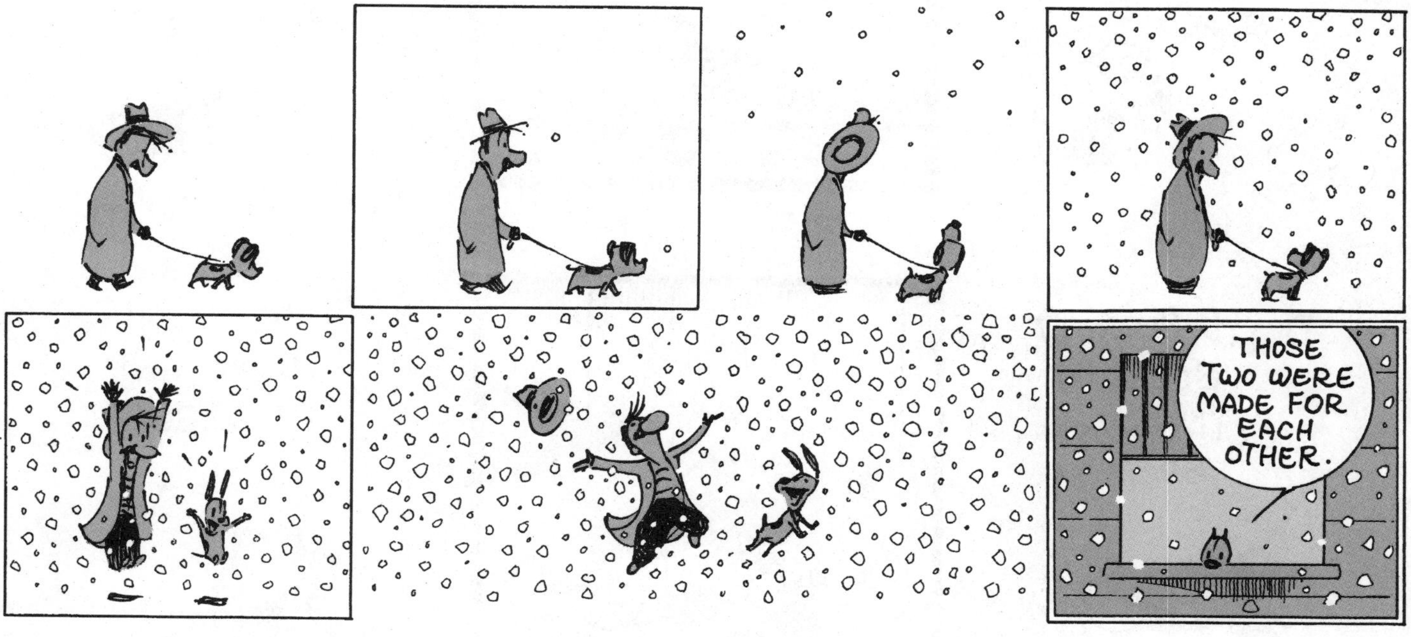
THOSE TWO WERE MADE FOR EACH OTHER.

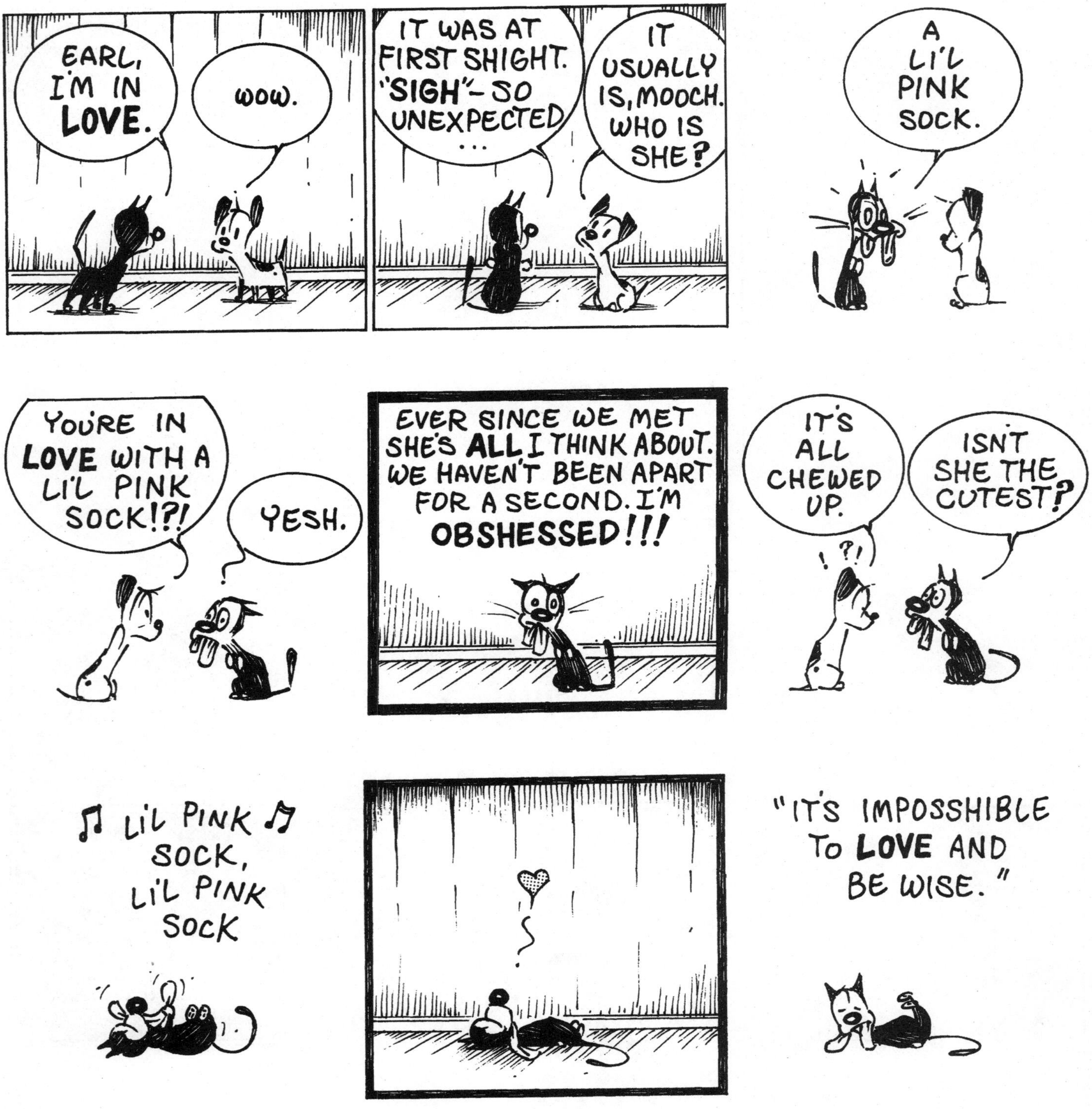
EARL, I'M IN **LOVE**.
WOW.
IT WAS AT FIRST SHIGHT. "**SIGH**"– SO UNEXPECTED ...
IT USUALLY IS, MOOCH. WHO IS SHE?
A LI'L PINK SOCK.
YOU'RE IN **LOVE** WITH A LI'L PINK SOCK!?!
YESH.
EVER SINCE WE MET SHE'S **ALL** I THINK ABOUT. WE HAVEN'T BEEN APART FOR A SECOND. I'M **OBSHESSED**!!!
IT'S ALL CHEWED UP.
! ?!
ISN'T SHE THE CUTEST?
♫ LI'L PINK ♫ SOCK, LI'L PINK SOCK
"IT'S IMPOSSHIBLE TO **LOVE** AND BE WISE."

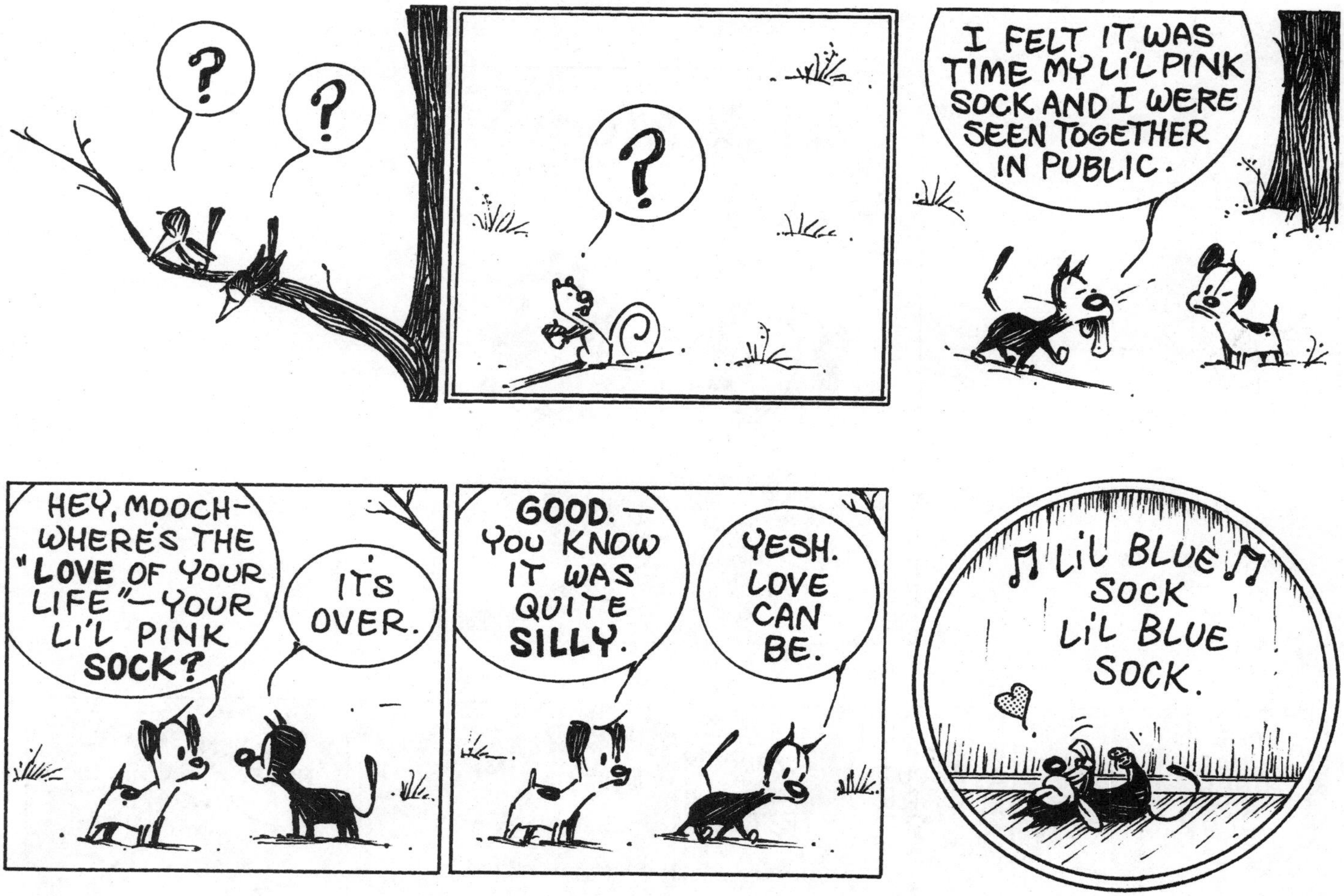
?
?
?
I FELT IT WAS TIME MY LI'L PINK SOCK AND I WERE SEEN TOGETHER IN PUBLIC.
HEY, MOOCH- WHERE'S THE "LOVE OF YOUR LIFE"-YOUR LI'L PINK SOCK?
IT'S OVER.
GOOD.- YOU KNOW IT WAS QUITE SILLY.
YESH. LOVE CAN BE.
♫ LI'L BLUE ♫ SOCK LI'L BLUE SOCK.

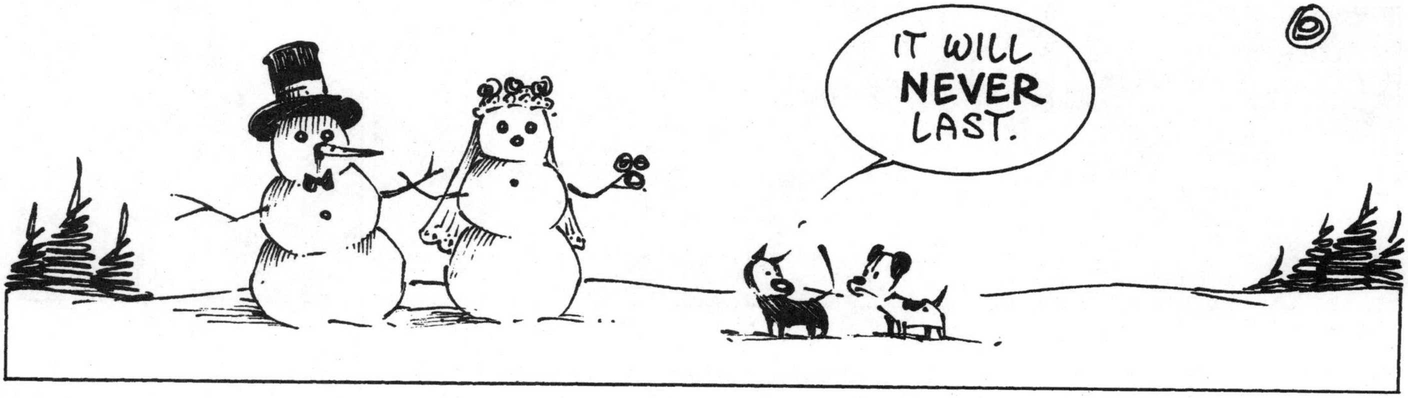
IT WILL NEVER LAST.

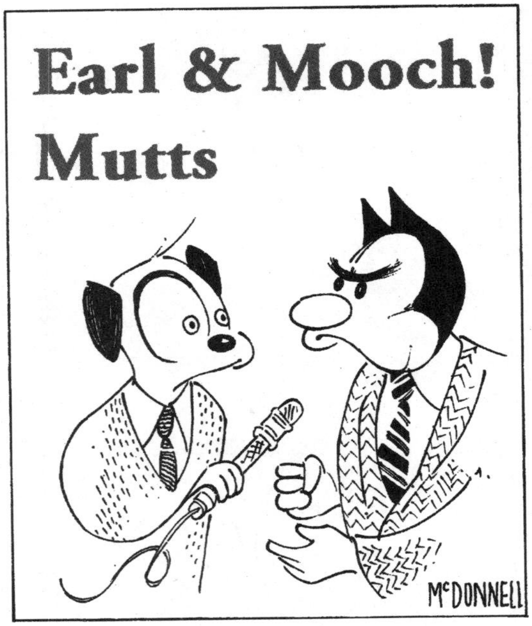
Earl & Mooch!
Mutts
McDONNELL

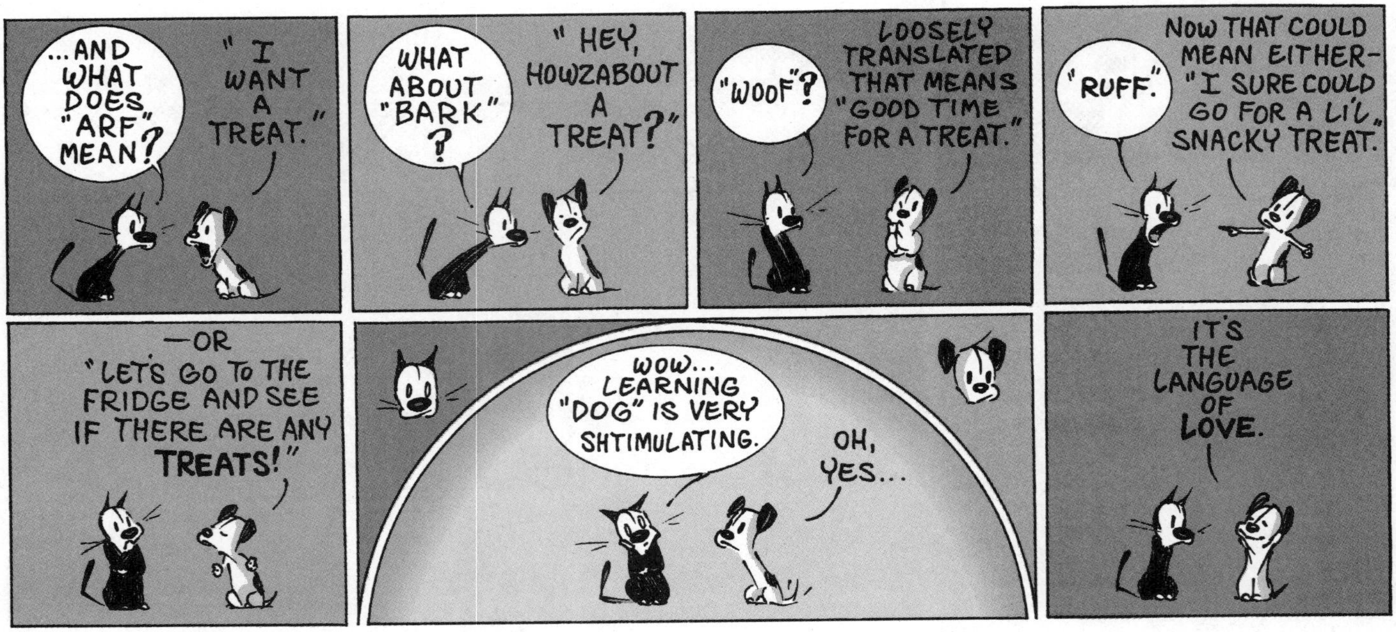
...AND WHAT DOES "ARF" MEAN?
"I WANT A TREAT."
WHAT ABOUT "BARK"?
"HEY, HOWZABOUT A TREAT?"
"WOOF"?
LOOSELY TRANSLATED THAT MEANS "GOOD TIME FOR A TREAT."
"RUFF."
NOW THAT COULD MEAN EITHER- "I SURE COULD GO FOR A LI'L SNACKY TREAT."
—OR "LET'S GO TO THE FRIDGE AND SEE IF THERE ARE ANY TREATS!"
WOW... LEARNING "DOG" IS VERY SHTIMULATING.
OH, YES...
IT'S THE LANGUAGE OF LOVE.

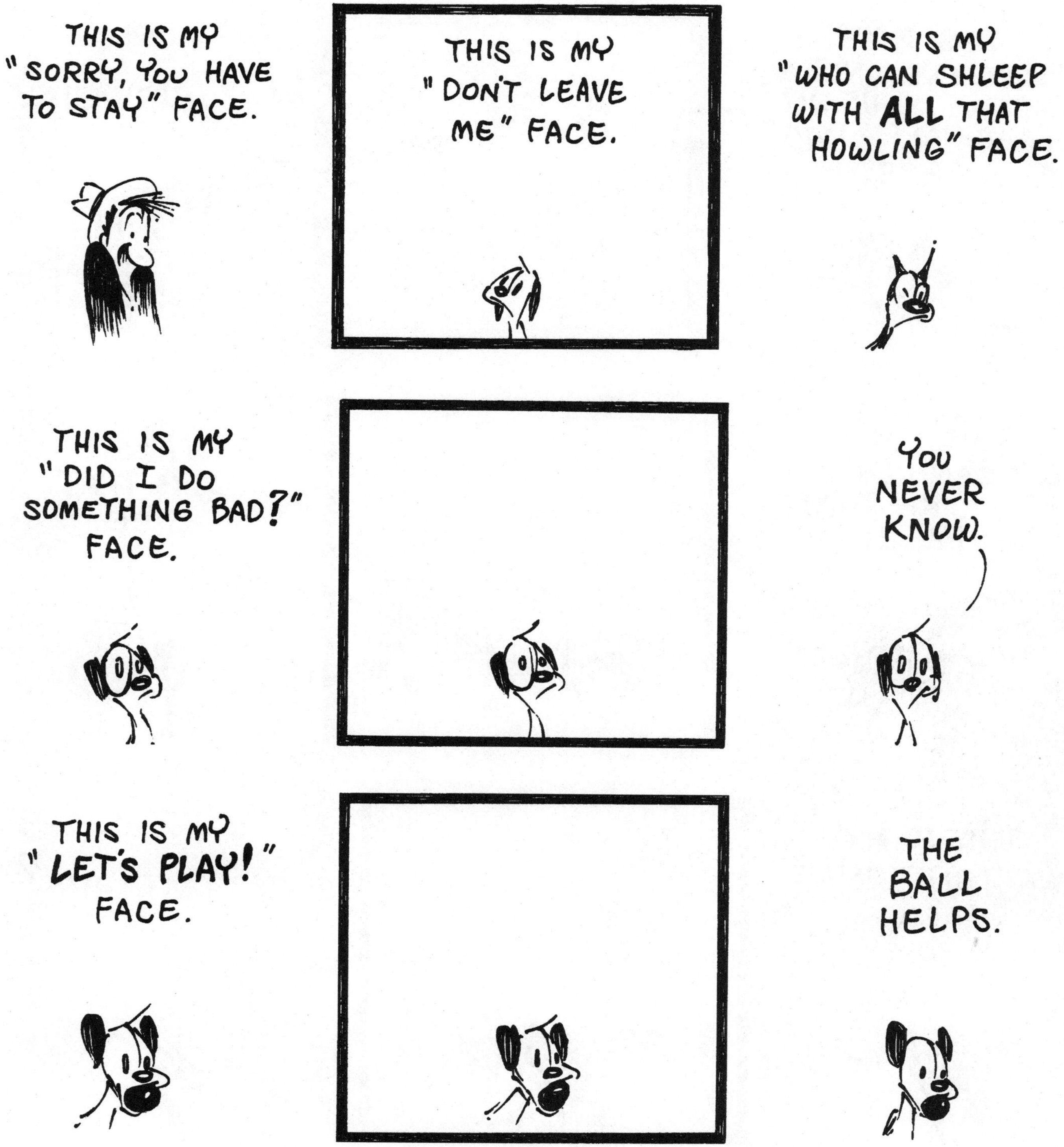
THIS IS MY "SORRY, YOU HAVE TO STAY" FACE.
THIS IS MY "DON'T LEAVE ME" FACE.
THIS IS MY "WHO CAN SHLEEP WITH ALL THAT HOWLING" FACE.
THIS IS MY "DID I DO SOMETHING BAD?" FACE.
YOU NEVER KNOW.
THIS IS MY "LET'S PLAY!" FACE.
THE BALL HELPS.

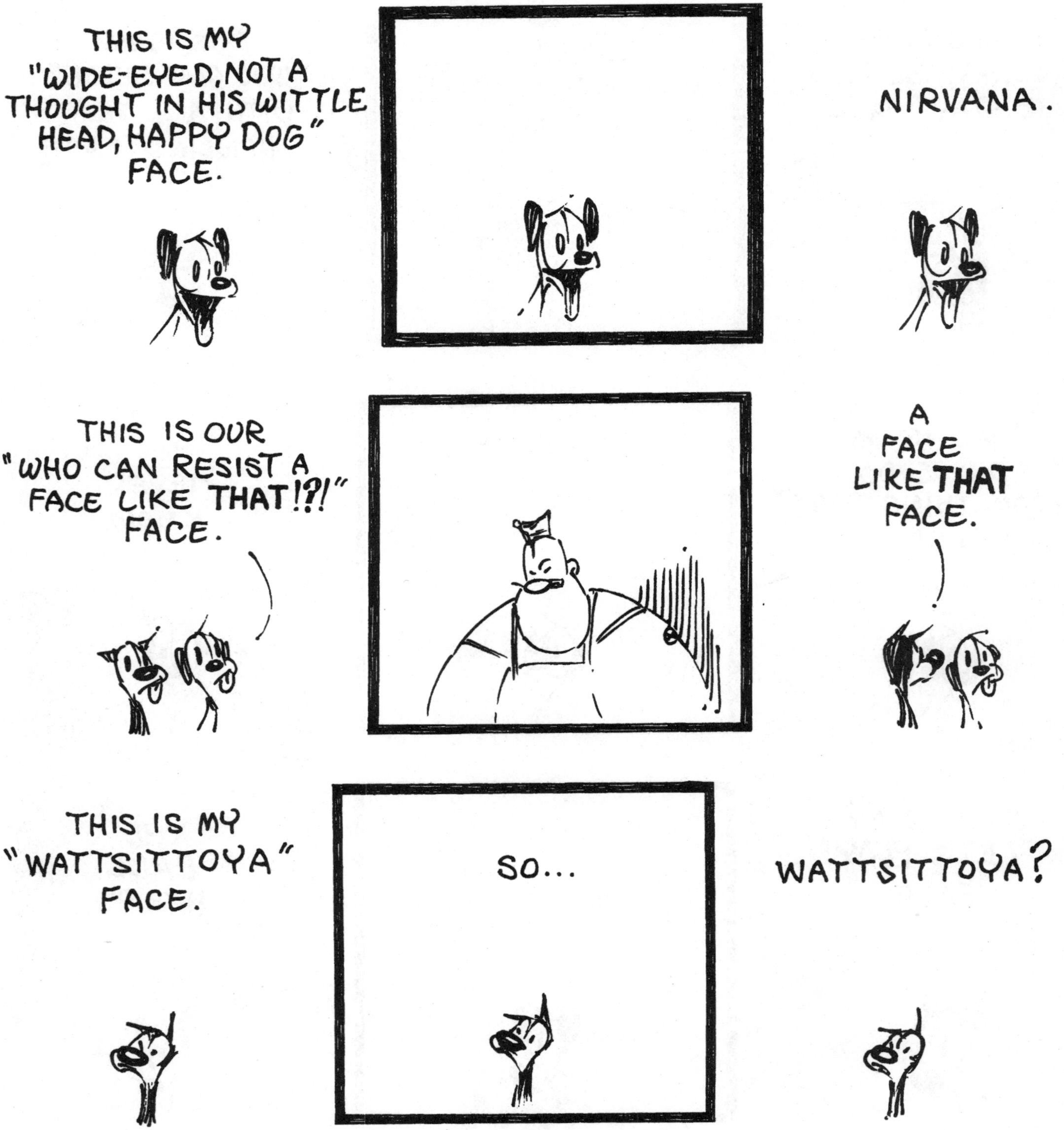
THIS IS MY "WIDE-EYED, NOT A THOUGHT IN HIS WITTLE HEAD, HAPPY DOG" FACE.
NIRVANA.
THIS IS OUR "WHO CAN RESIST A FACE LIKE THAT!?!" FACE.
A FACE LIKE THAT FACE.
THIS IS MY "WATTSITTOYA" FACE.
SO...
WATTSITTOYA?

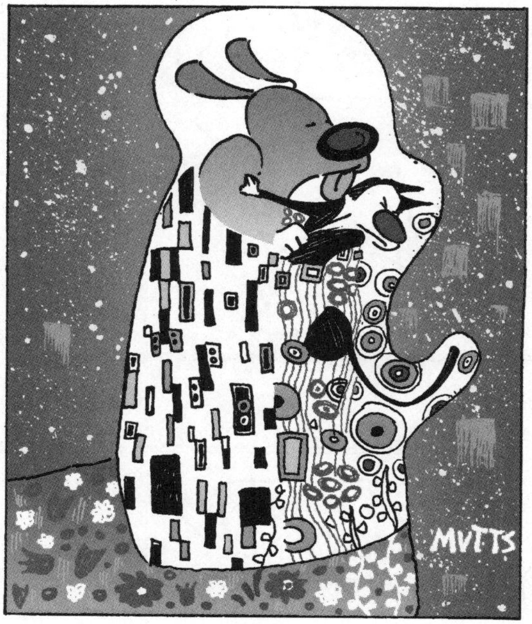
MUTTS

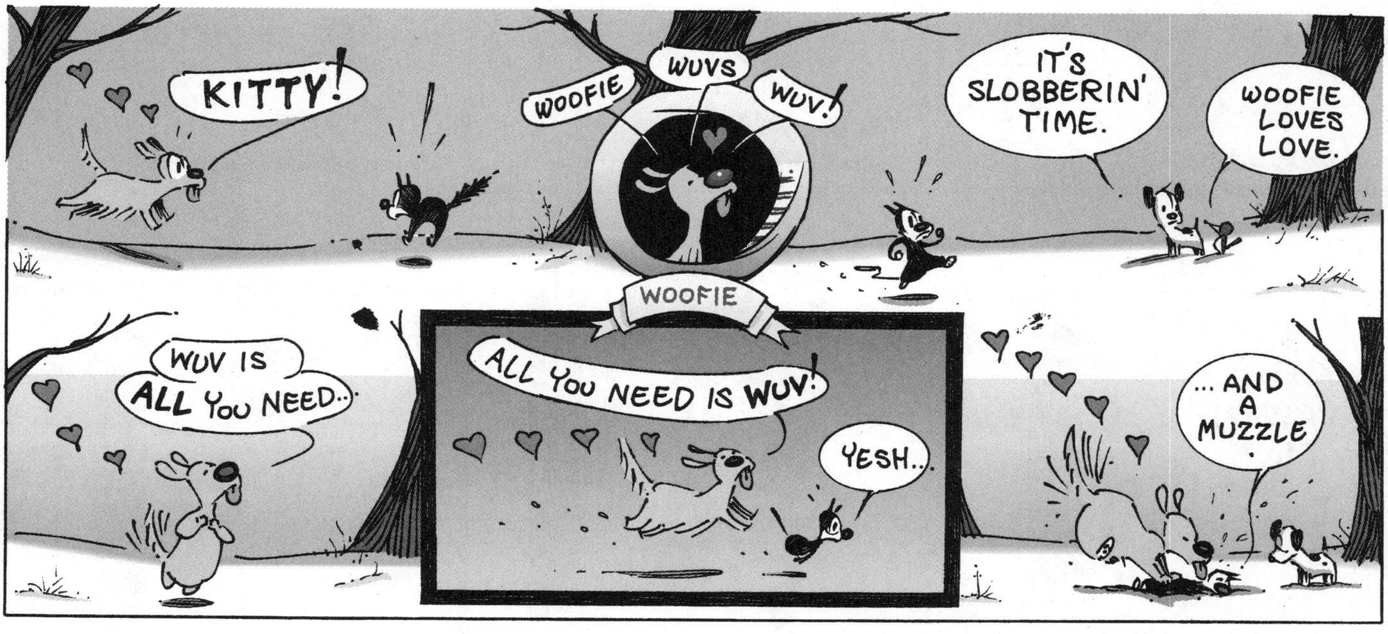
KITTY!
WOOFIE
WUVS
WUV!
WOOFIE
IT'S SLOBBERIN' TIME.
WOOFIE LOVES LOVE.
WUV IS ALL YOU NEED..
ALL YOU NEED IS WUV!
YESH..
... AND A MUZZLE.

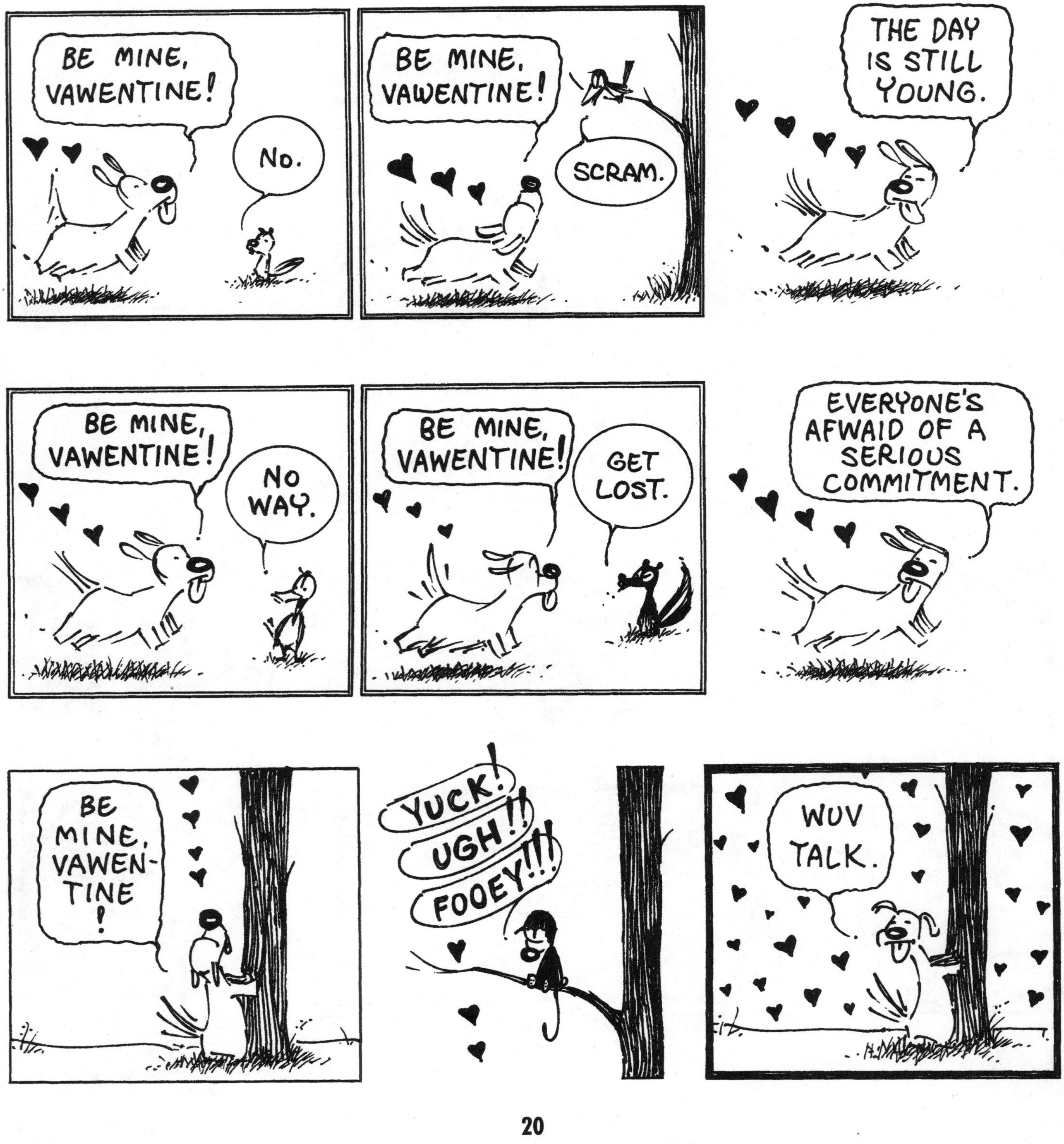
BE MINE, VAWENTINE!
No.
BE MINE, VAWENTINE!
SCRAM.
THE DAY IS STILL YOUNG.
BE MINE, VAWENTINE!
NO WAY.
BE MINE, VAWENTINE!
GET LOST.
EVERYONE'S AFWAID OF A SERIOUS COMMITMENT.
BE MINE, VAWEN-TINE!
YUCK!
UGH!!
FOOEY!!!
WUV TALK.

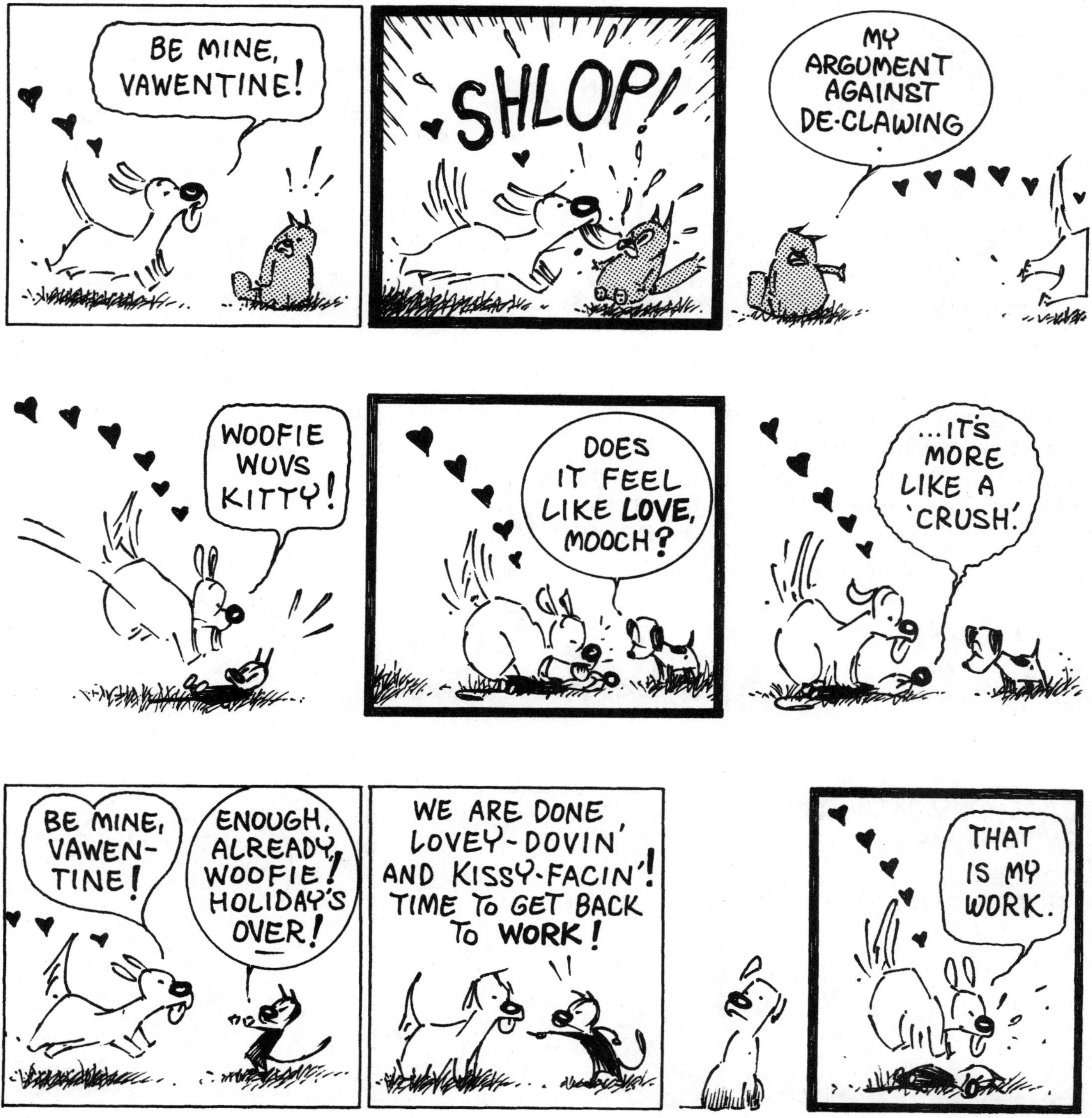
BE MINE, VAWENTINE!
SHLOP!
MY ARGUMENT AGAINST DE-CLAWING
WOOFIE WUVS KITTY!
DOES IT FEEL LIKE **LOVE**, MOOCH?
...IT'S MORE LIKE A 'CRUSH.'
BE MINE, VAWEN-TINE!
ENOUGH, ALREADY, WOOFIE! HOLIDAY'S OVER!
WE ARE DONE LOVEY-DOVIN' AND KISSY-FACIN'! TIME TO GET BACK TO **WORK**!
THAT IS MY WORK.

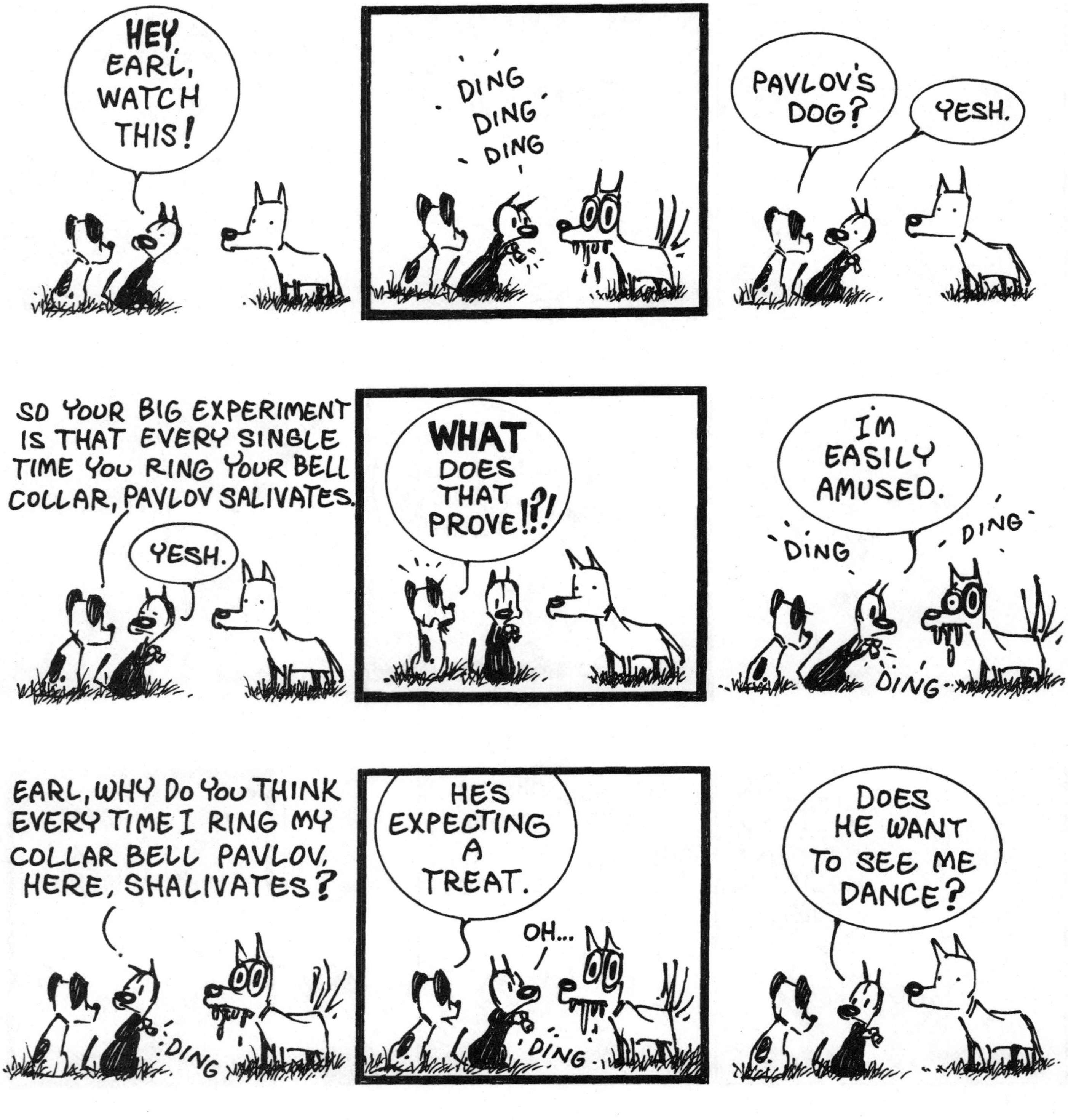
HEY, EARL, WATCH THIS!
DING DING DING
PAVLOV'S DOG?
YESH.
SO YOUR BIG EXPERIMENT IS THAT EVERY SINGLE TIME YOU RING YOUR BELL COLLAR, PAVLOV SALIVATES.
YESH.
WHAT DOES THAT PROVE!?!
I'M EASILY AMUSED.
DING
DING
DING
EARL, WHY DO YOU THINK EVERY TIME I RING MY COLLAR BELL PAVLOV, HERE, SHALIVATES?
DING
HE'S EXPECTING A TREAT.
OH...
DING
DOES HE WANT TO SEE ME DANCE?

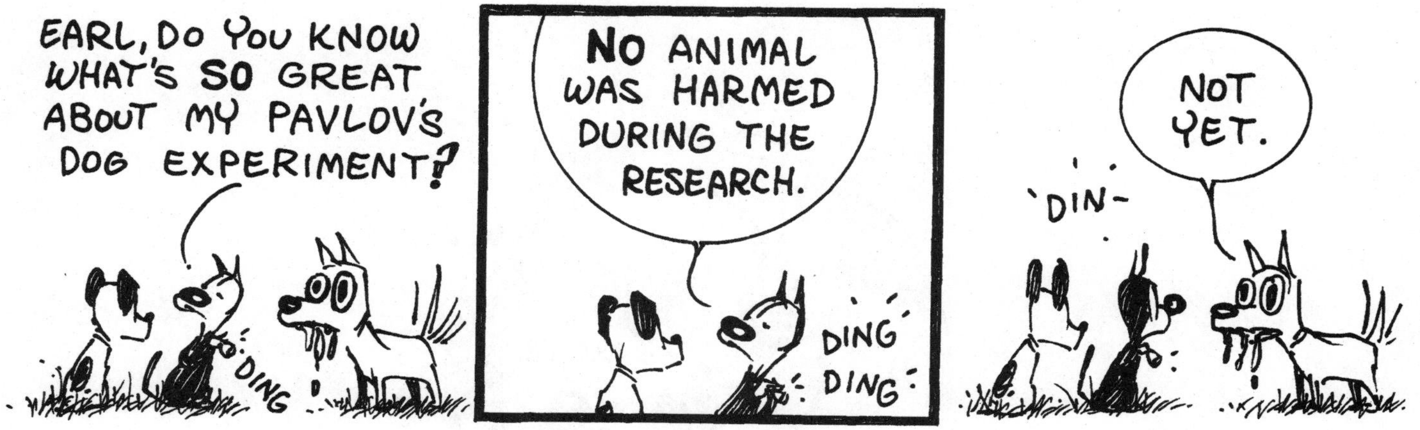
EARL, DO YOU KNOW WHAT'S SO GREAT ABOUT MY PAVLOV'S DOG EXPERIMENT?
DING
NO ANIMAL WAS HARMED DURING THE RESEARCH.
DING DING
DIN-
NOT YET.

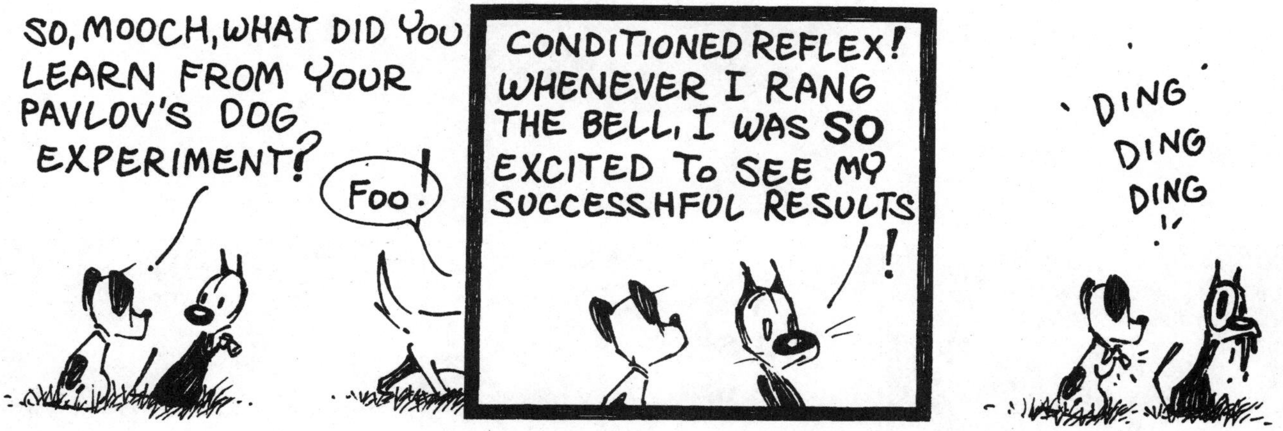
SO, MOOCH, WHAT DID YOU LEARN FROM YOUR PAVLOV'S DOG EXPERIMENT?
FOO!
CONDITIONED REFLEX! WHENEVER I RANG THE BELL, I WAS SO EXCITED TO SEE MY SUCCESSHFUL RESULTS!
DING DING DING

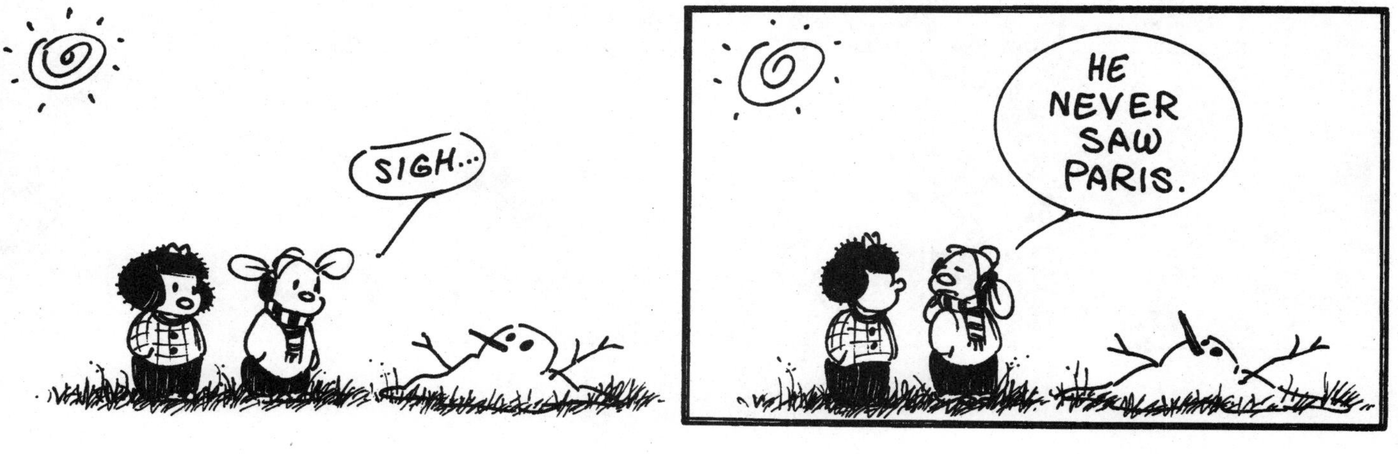
SIGH...
HE NEVER SAW PARIS.

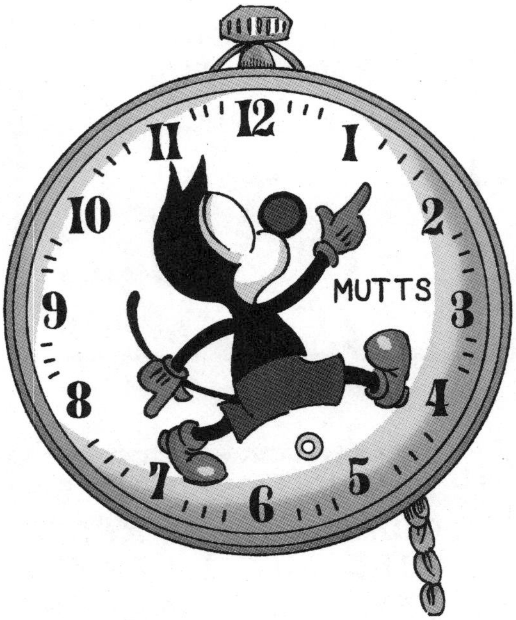
12
1
2
3
4
5
6
7
8
9
10
11
MUTTS

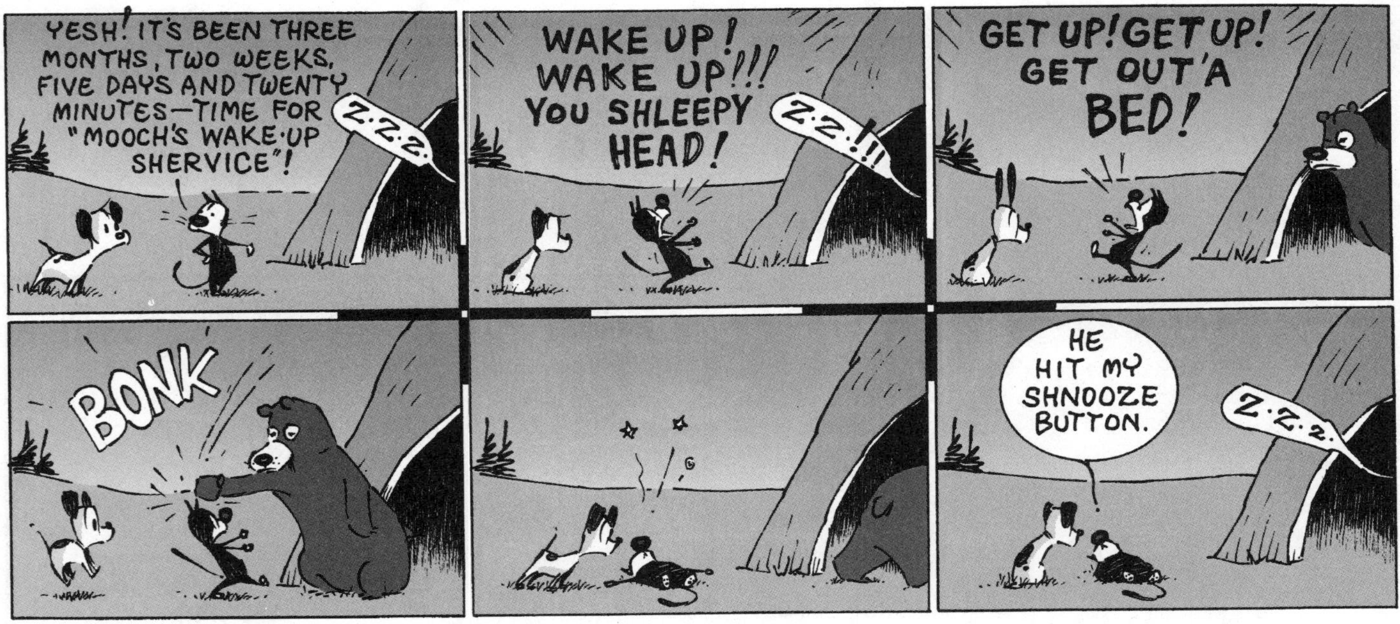
YESH! IT'S BEEN THREE MONTHS, TWO WEEKS, FIVE DAYS AND TWENTY MINUTES—TIME FOR "MOOCH'S WAKE-UP SHERVICE"!
Z·Z·Z·
WAKE UP! WAKE UP!!! YOU SHLEEPY HEAD!
Z·Z·!!!
GET UP! GET UP! GET OUT'A BED!
BONK
HE HIT MY SHNOOZE BUTTON.
Z·Z·z

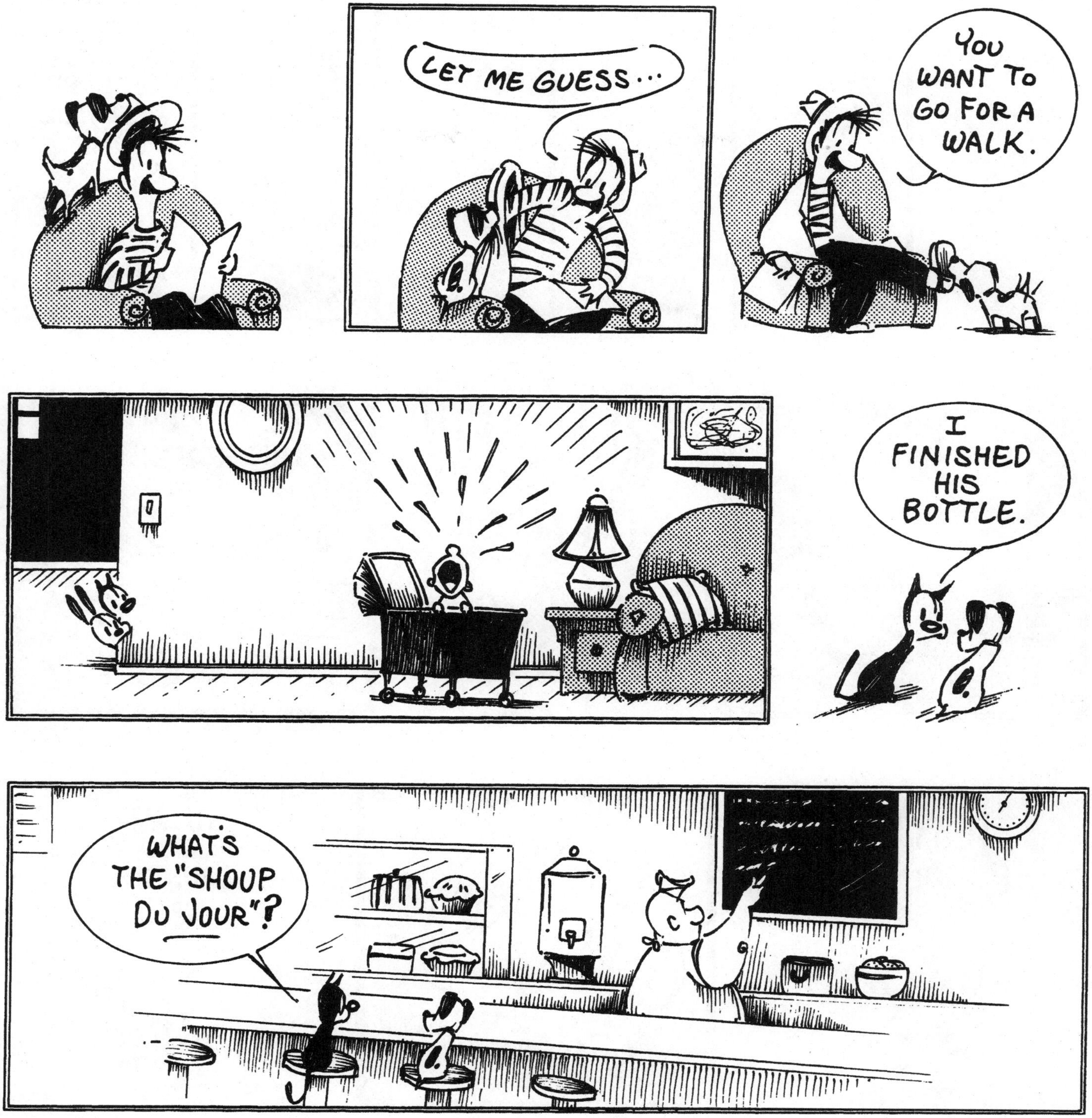
LET ME GUESS...
YOU WANT TO GO FOR A WALK.
I FINISHED HIS BOTTLE.
WHAT'S THE "SHOUP DU JOUR"?

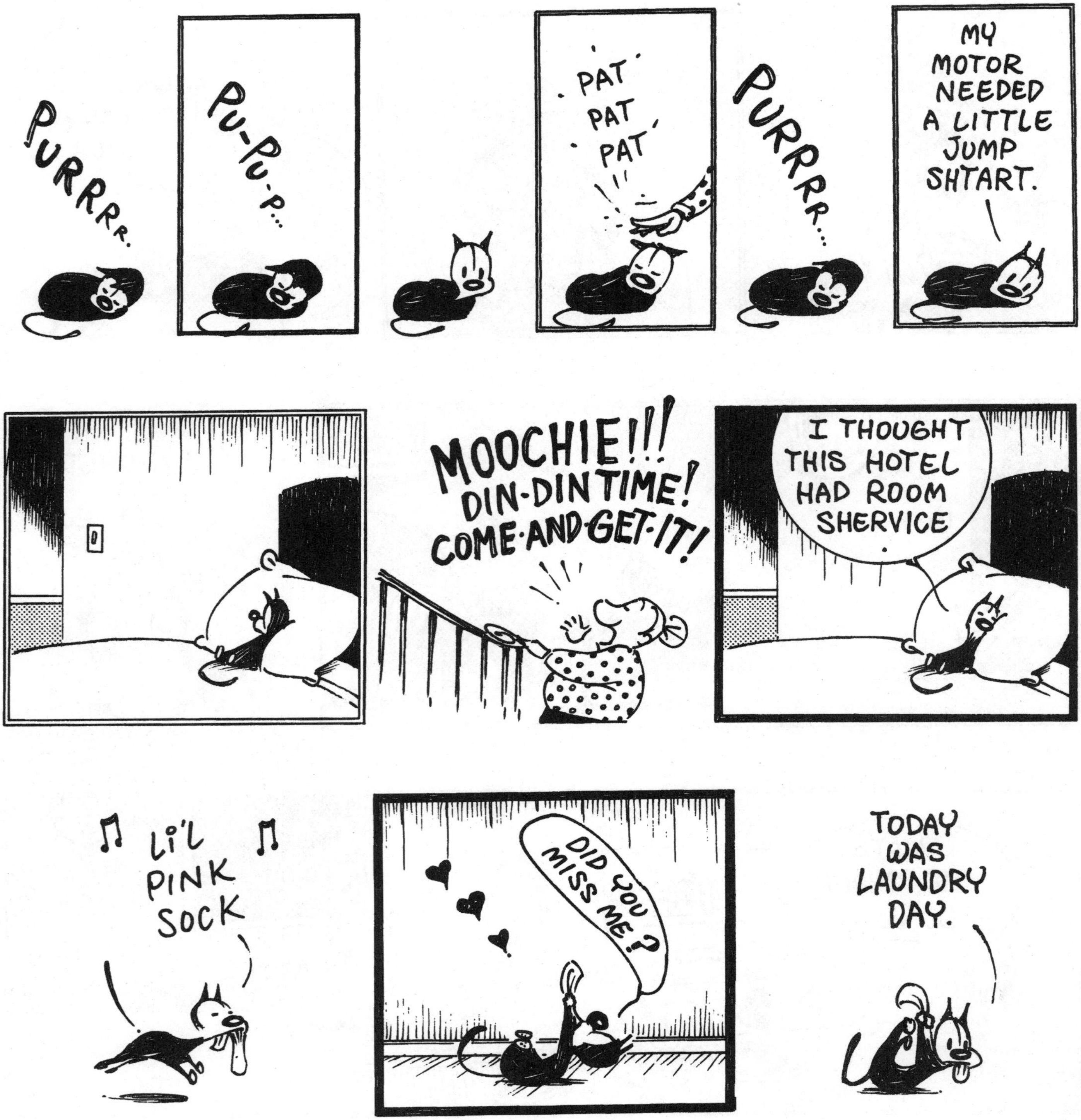
PURRRRR.
PU-PU-P...
PAT PAT PAT
PURRRR...
MY MOTOR NEEDED A LITTLE JUMP SHTART.
MOOCHIE!!! DIN·DIN TIME! COME·AND·GET·IT!
I THOUGHT THIS HOTEL HAD ROOM SHERVICE.
LI'L PINK SOCK
DID YOU MISS ME?
TODAY WAS LAUNDRY DAY.

MUTTS.
by PATRICK Mc Donnell

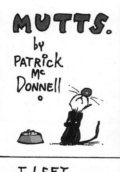

MOOCH, ARE YOU EATING THIS?

NO— I'M SHNUBBING IT.

AA ARGH, EARL!!! WHAT ARE YOU DOIN'? SHTOP!!!

I THOUGHT YOU DIDN'T WANT IT.

HOW CAN I SHNUB NUTHIN'—I HAVE TO SHNUB SHOMETHIN'!

I LEFT A LITTLE— SHNUB THAT!

THAT!?! THAT'S NOT EVEN WORTH SHNUBBIN'! IT'S UNSHNUBBABLE!

GOOD!

NICE EATING WITH YOU.

OOOOH, I THINK WE FINALLY FOUND SOMETHING "WE" LIKE!

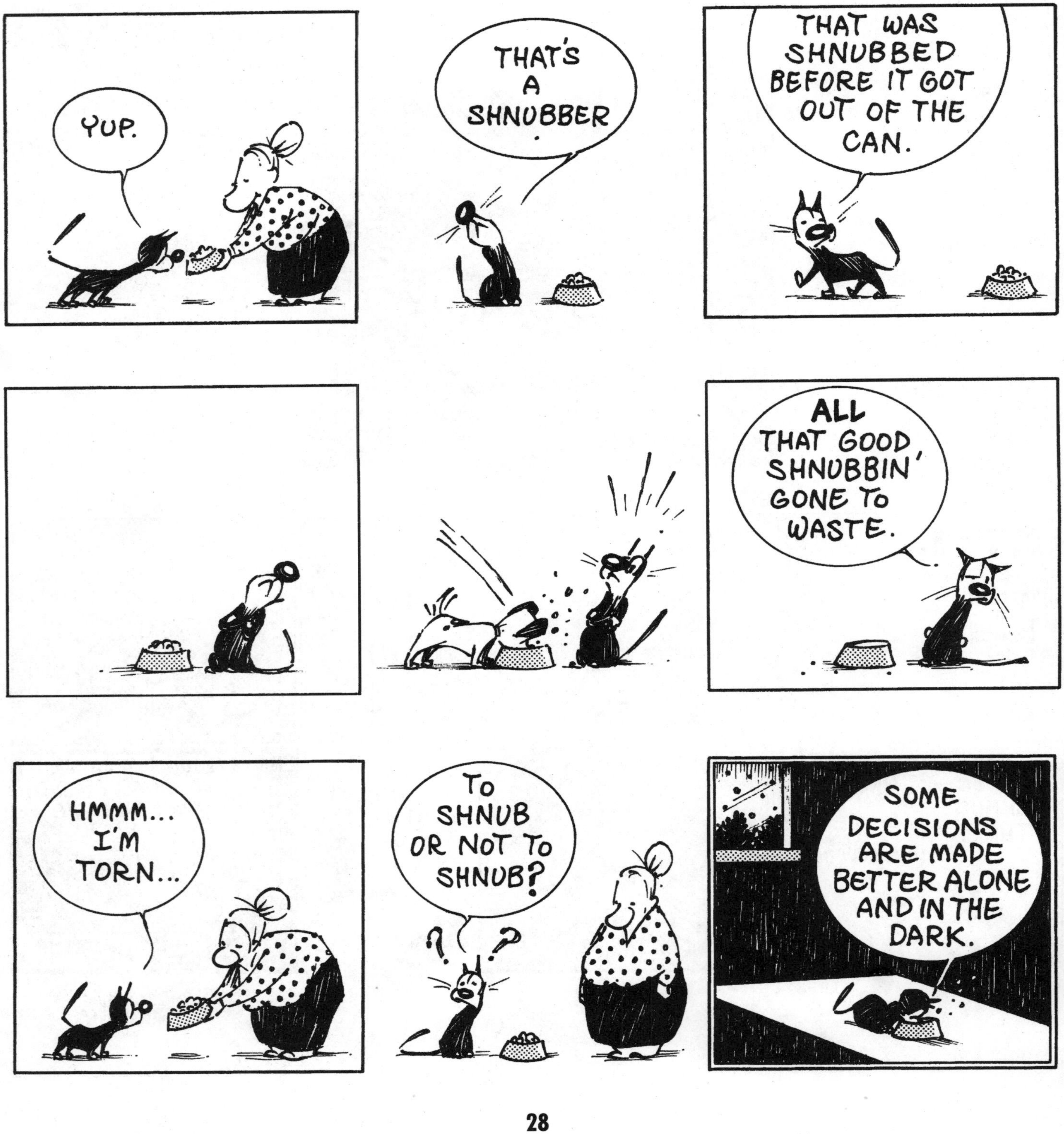
YUP.
THAT'S A SHNUBBER.
THAT WAS SHNUBBED BEFORE IT GOT OUT OF THE CAN.
ALL THAT GOOD, SHNUBBIN' GONE TO WASTE.
HMMM... I'M TORN...
TO SHNUB OR NOT TO SHNUB?
SOME DECISIONS ARE MADE BETTER ALONE AND IN THE DARK.

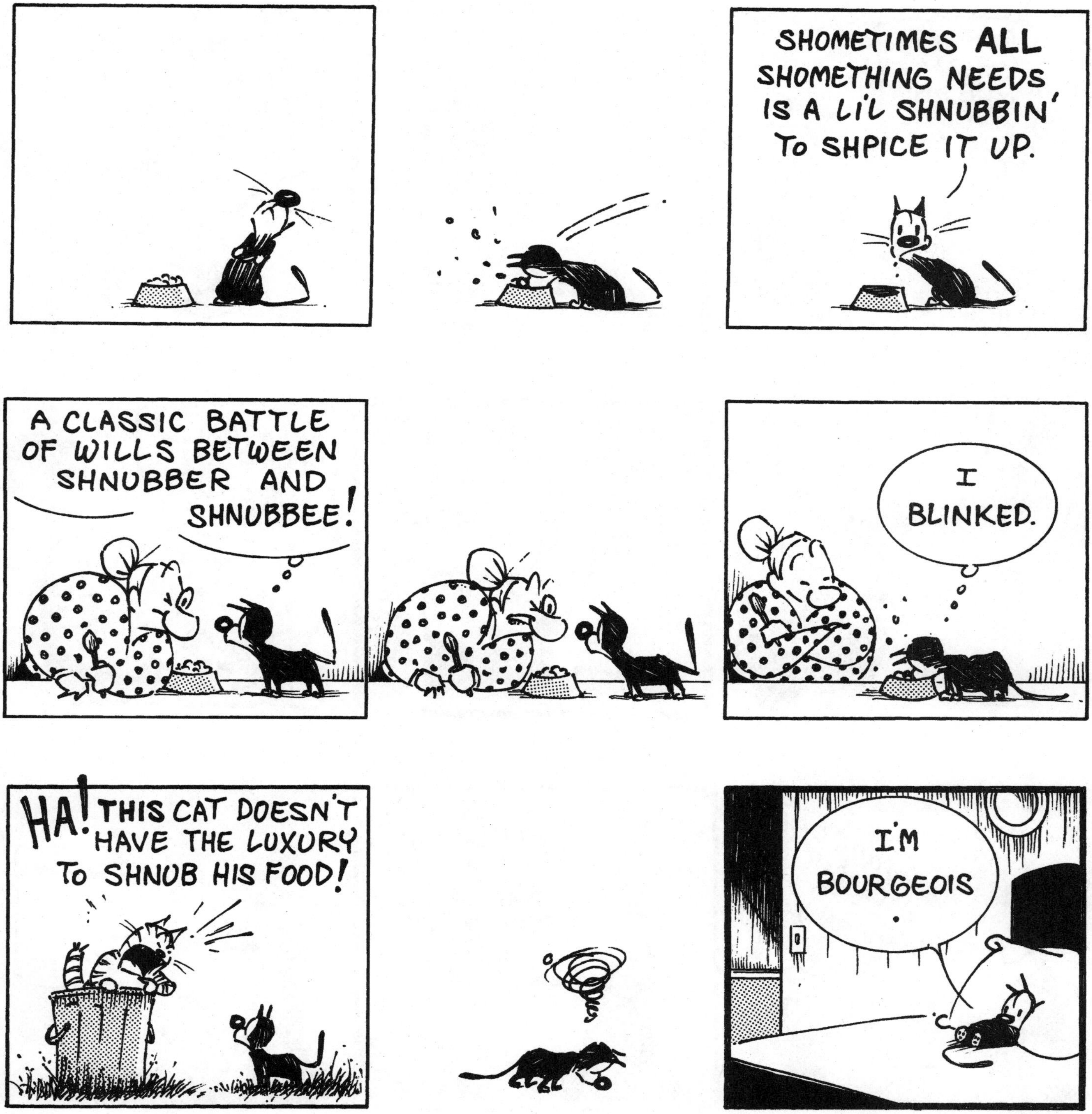
SHOMETIMES ALL SHOMETHING NEEDS IS A LI'L SHNUBBIN' TO SHPICE IT UP.
A CLASSIC BATTLE OF WILLS BETWEEN SHNUBBER AND SHNUBBEE!
I BLINKED.
HA! THIS CAT DOESN'T HAVE THE LUXURY TO SHNUB HIS FOOD!
I'M BOURGEOIS.

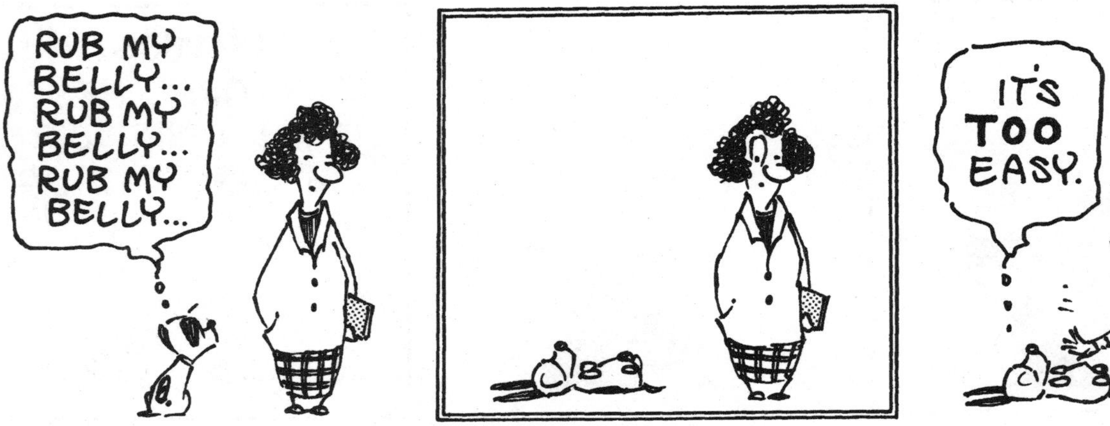
RUB MY BELLY... RUB MY BELLY... RUB MY BELLY...
IT'S **TOO** EASY.

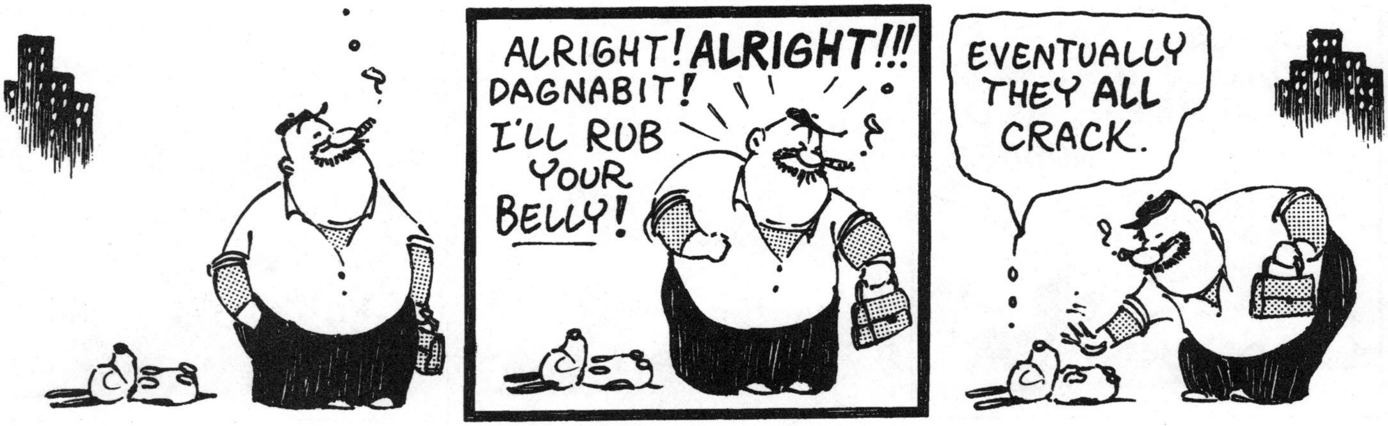
ALRIGHT! **ALRIGHT!!!** DAGNABIT! I'LL RUB YOUR BELLY!
EVENTUALLY THEY **ALL** CRACK.

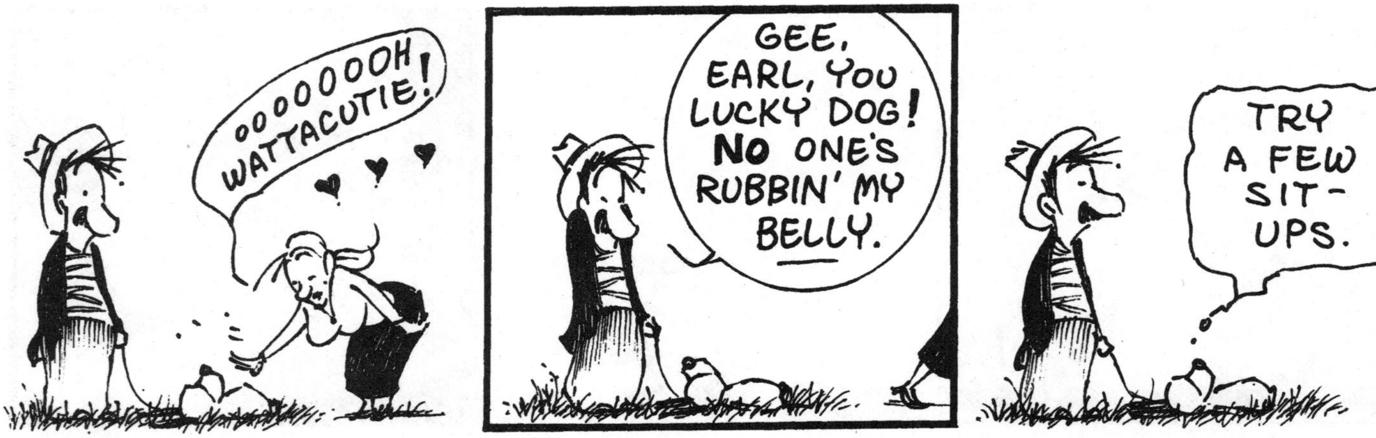
OOOOOOOOH WATTACUTIE!
GEE, EARL, YOU LUCKY DOG! **NO** ONE'S RUBBIN' MY BELLY.
TRY A FEW SIT-UPS.

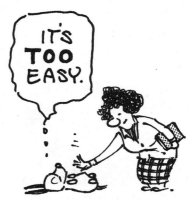

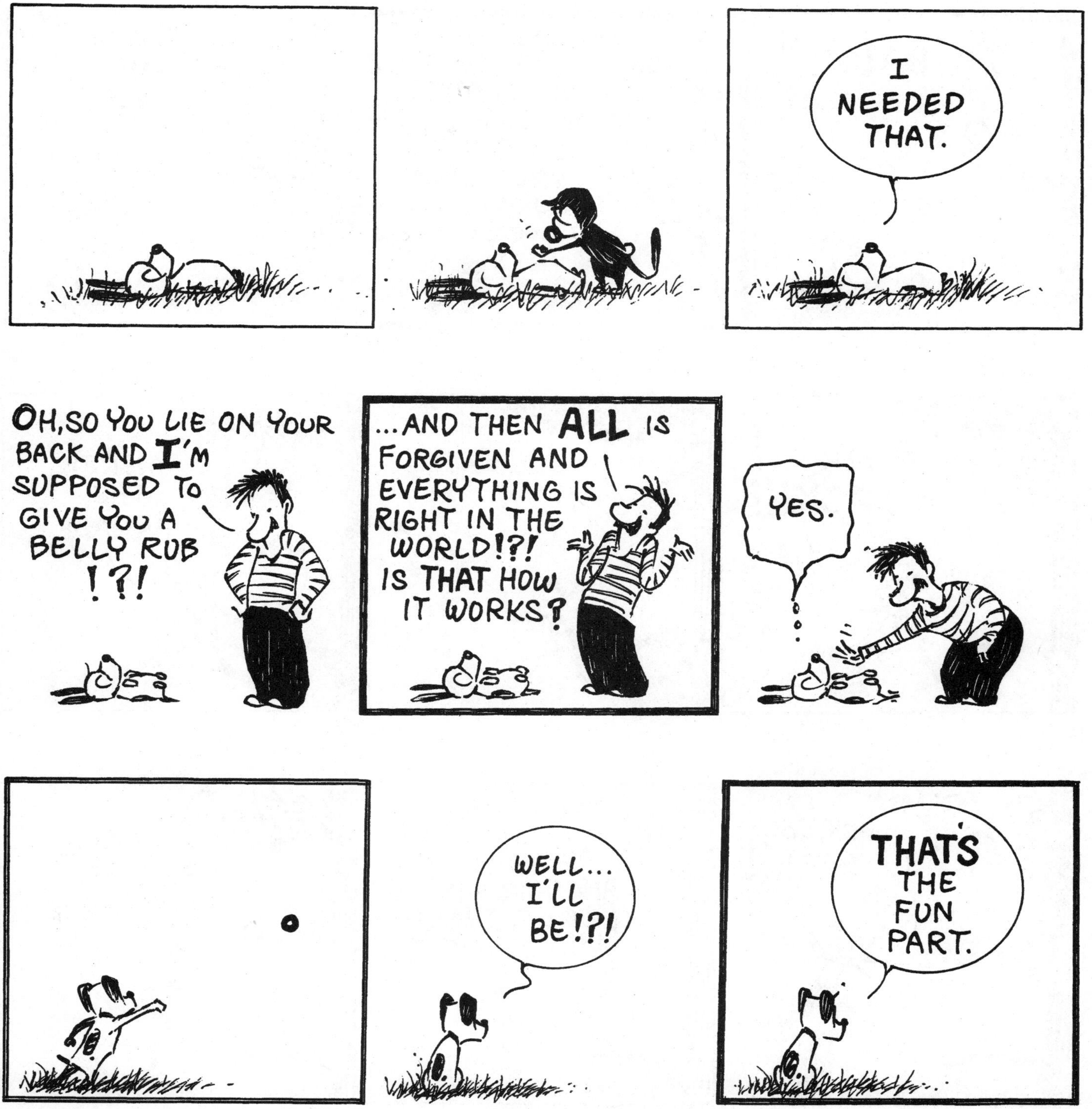
I NEEDED THAT.
OH, SO YOU LIE ON YOUR BACK AND I'M SUPPOSED TO GIVE YOU A BELLY RUB !?!
...AND THEN ALL IS FORGIVEN AND EVERYTHING IS RIGHT IN THE WORLD!?! IS THAT HOW IT WORKS?
YES.
WELL... I'LL BE!?!
THAT'S THE FUN PART.

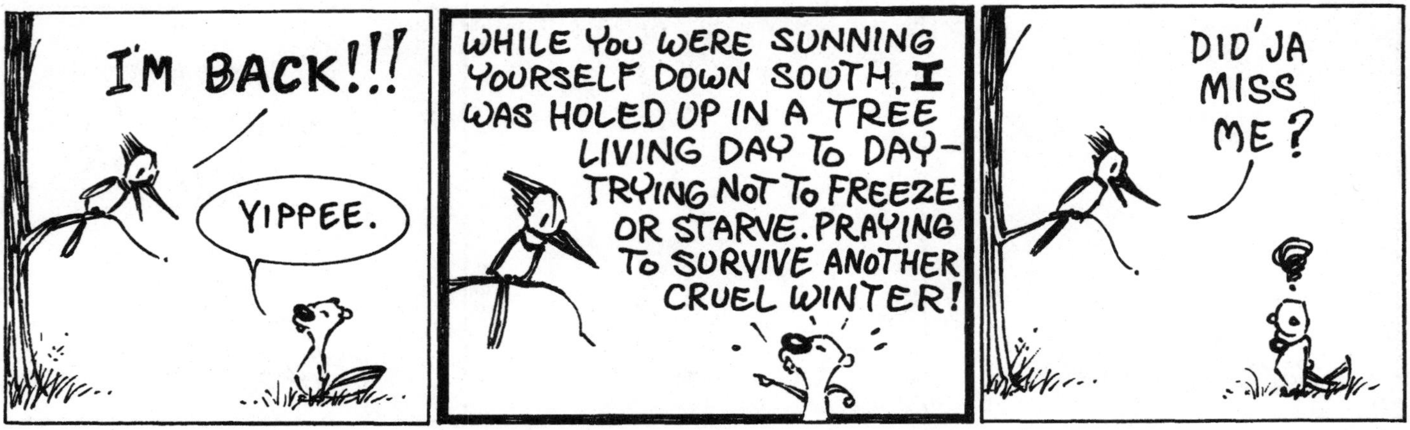
I'M BACK!!!
YIPPEE.
WHILE YOU WERE SUNNING YOURSELF DOWN SOUTH, I WAS HOLED UP IN A TREE LIVING DAY TO DAY– TRYING NOT TO FREEZE OR STARVE. PRAYING TO SURVIVE ANOTHER CRUEL WINTER!
DID'JA MISS ME?

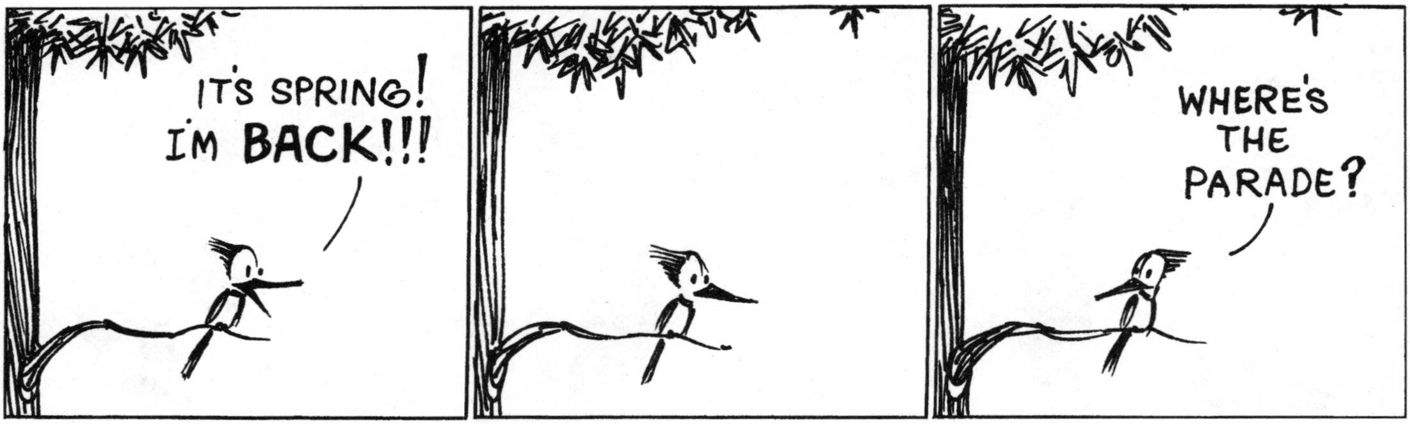
IT'S SPRING! I'M BACK!!!
WHERE'S THE PARADE?

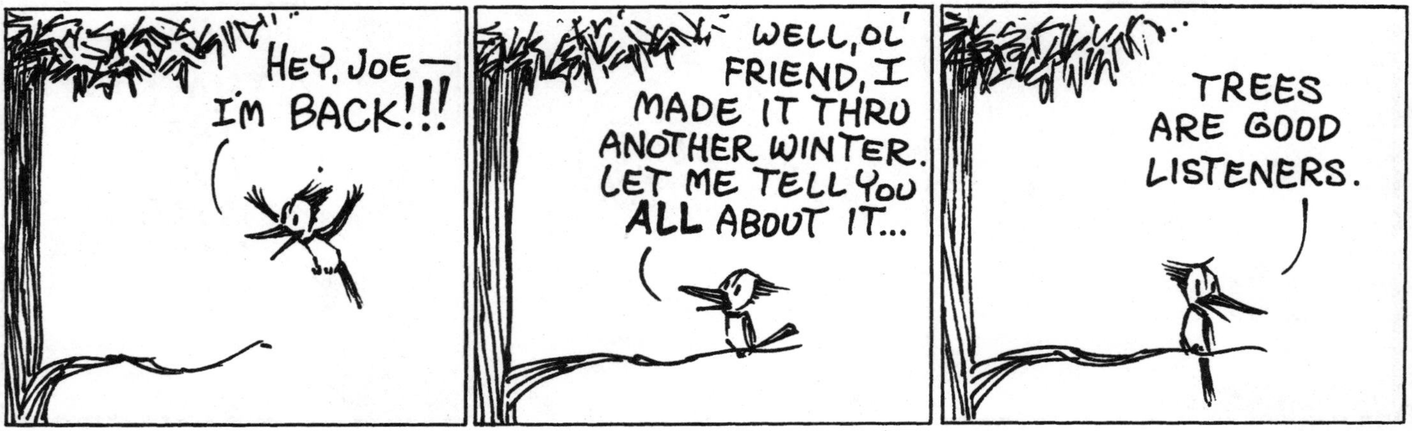
HEY, JOE– I'M BACK!!!
WELL, OL' FRIEND, I MADE IT THRU ANOTHER WINTER. LET ME TELL YOU ALL ABOUT IT...
TREES ARE GOOD LISTENERS.

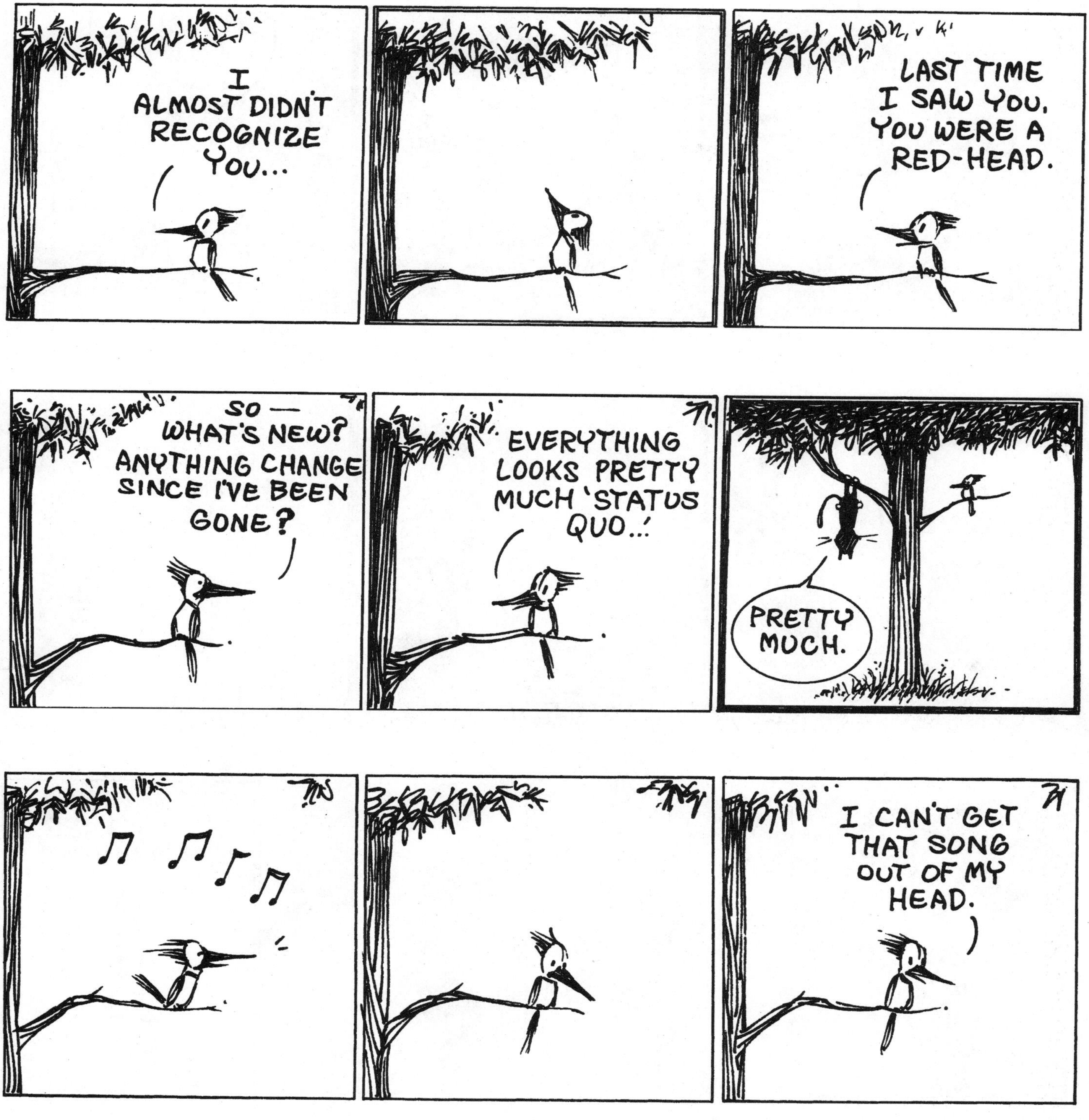
I ALMOST DIDN'T RECOGNIZE YOU...
LAST TIME I SAW YOU, YOU WERE A RED-HEAD.
SO — WHAT'S NEW? ANYTHING CHANGE SINCE I'VE BEEN GONE?
EVERYTHING LOOKS PRETTY MUCH 'STATUS QUO..!
PRETTY MUCH.
I CAN'T GET THAT SONG OUT OF MY HEAD.

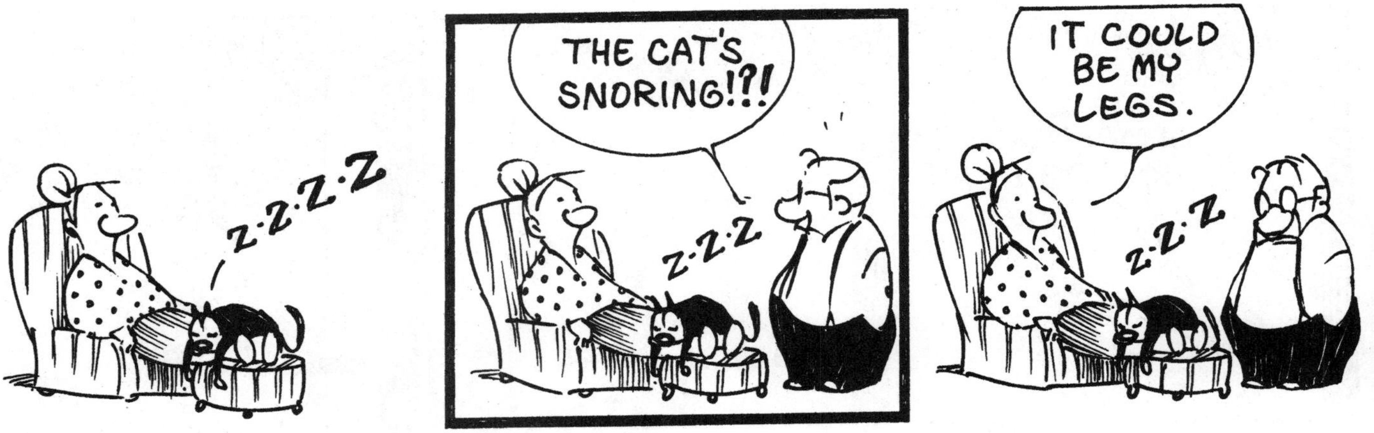

Z·Z·Z·Z
THE CAT'S SNORING!?!
Z·Z·Z
IT COULD BE MY LEGS.
Z·Z·Z

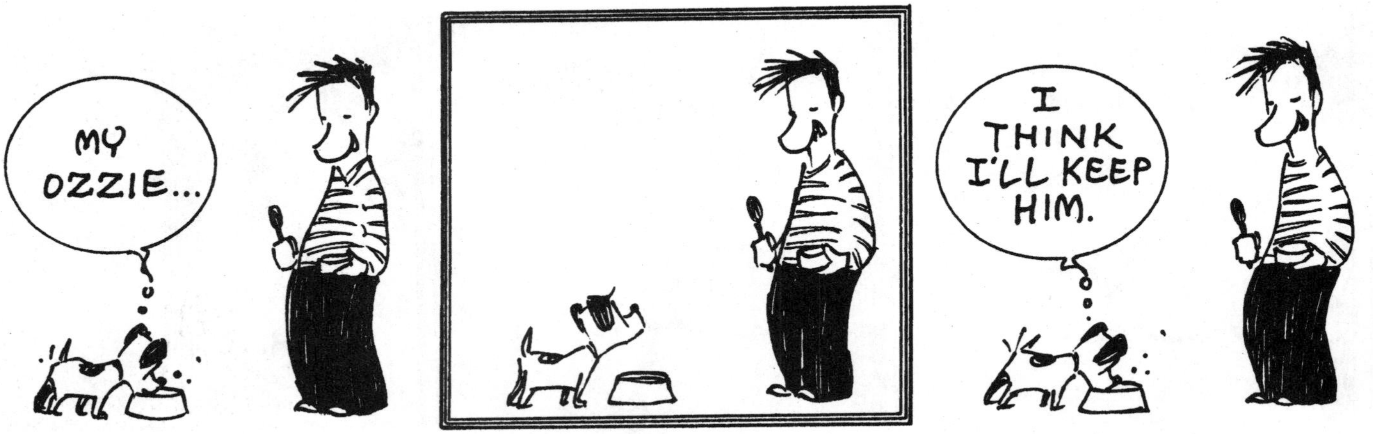

MY OZZIE...
I THINK I'LL KEEP HIM.

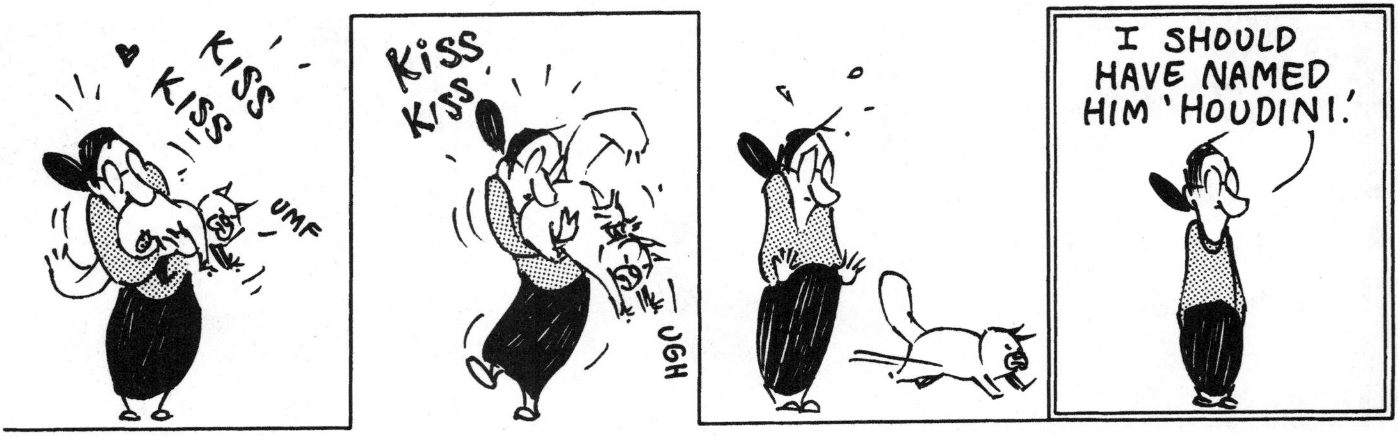

KISS KISS
UMF
KISS KISS
UGH
I SHOULD HAVE NAMED HIM 'HOUDINI.'

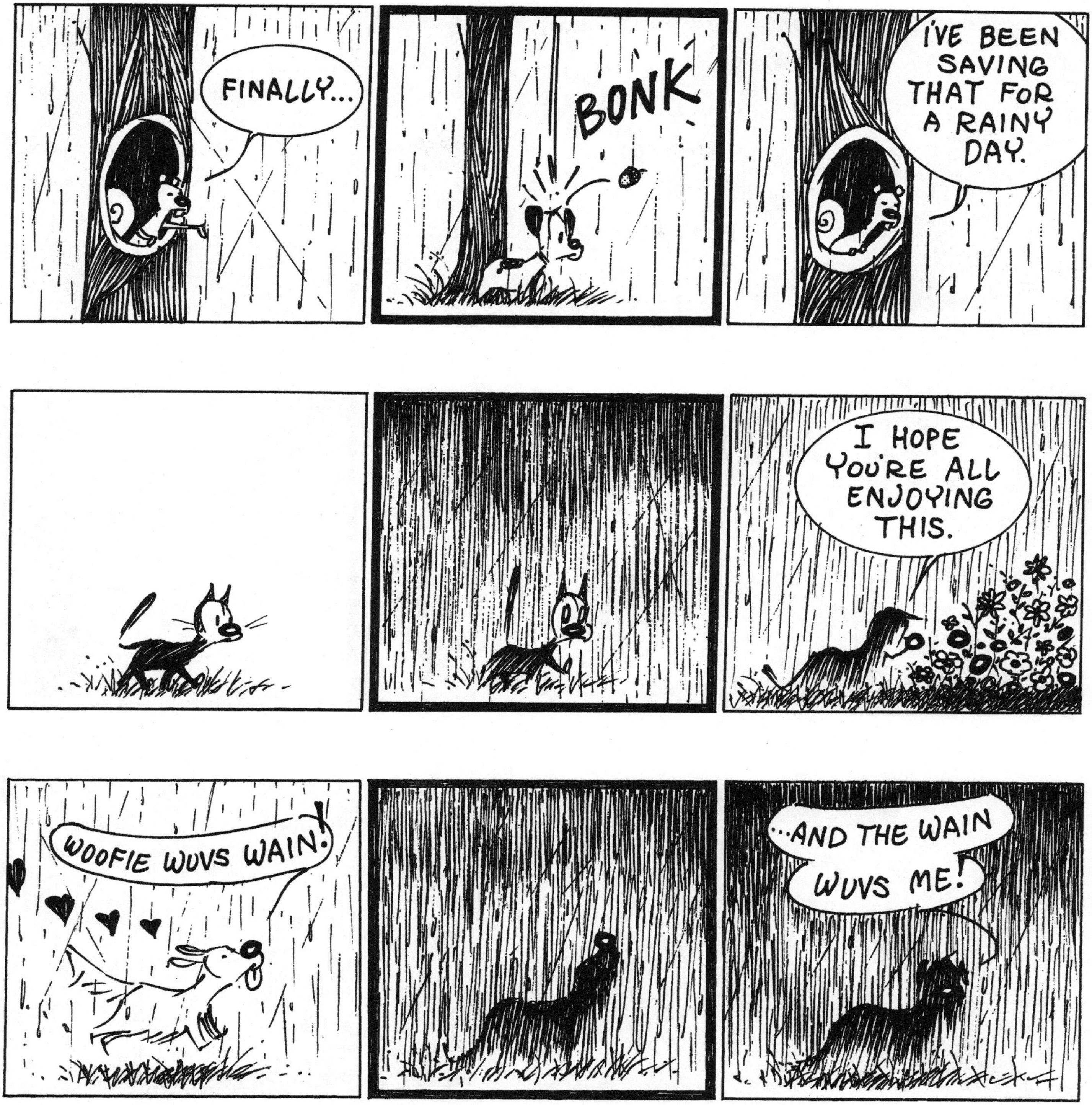

FINALLY...
BONK
I'VE BEEN SAVING THAT FOR A RAINY DAY.
I HOPE YOU'RE ALL ENJOYING THIS.
WOOFIE WUVS WAIN!
...AND THE WAIN WUVS ME!

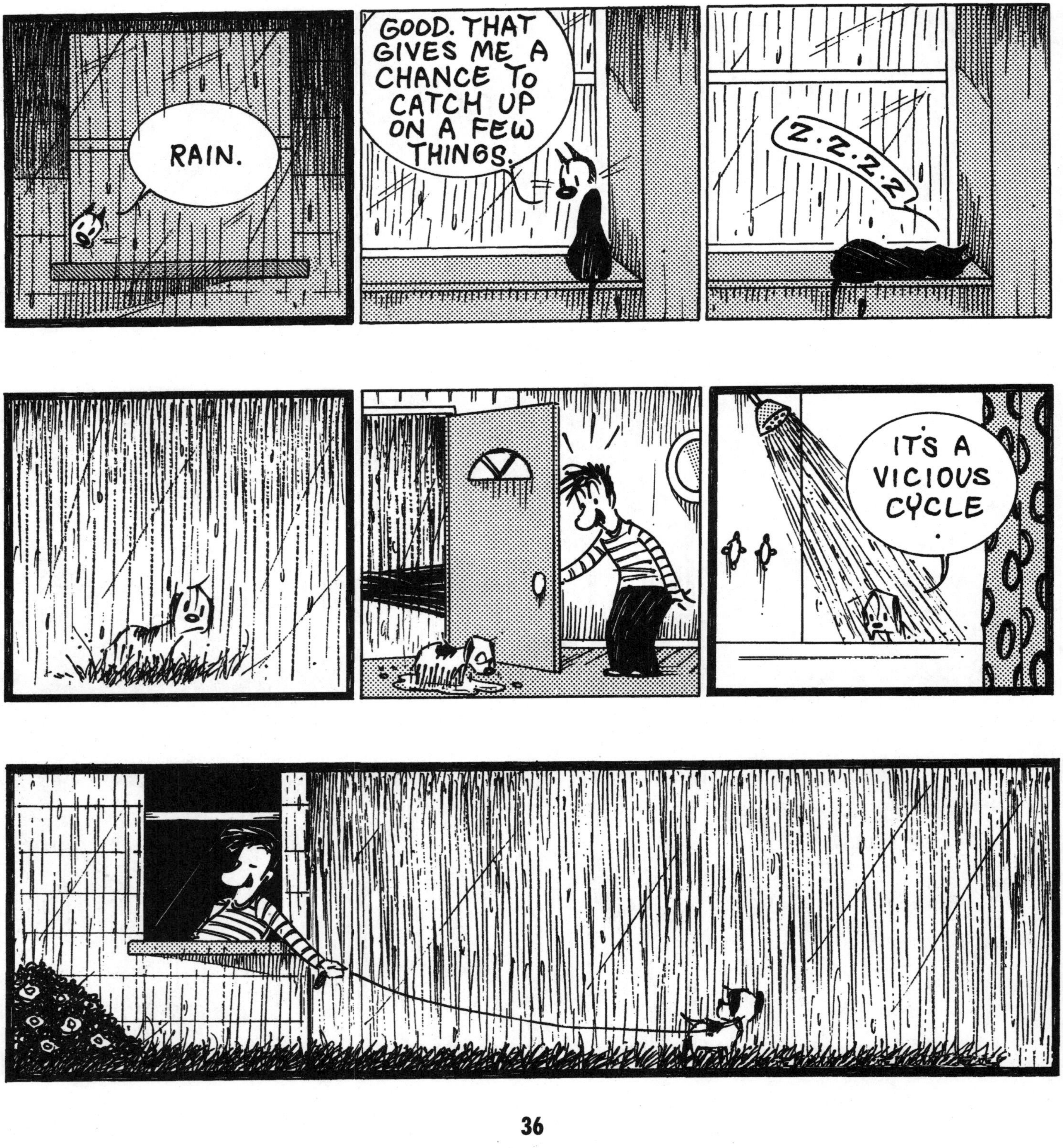
RAIN.
GOOD. THAT GIVES ME A CHANCE TO CATCH UP ON A FEW THINGS.
Z.Z.Z.Z
IT'S A VICIOUS CYCLE.

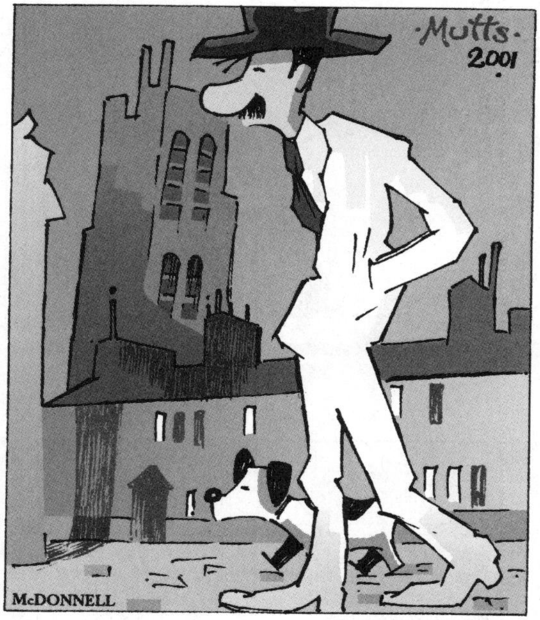
·Mutts·
2001
McDONNELL

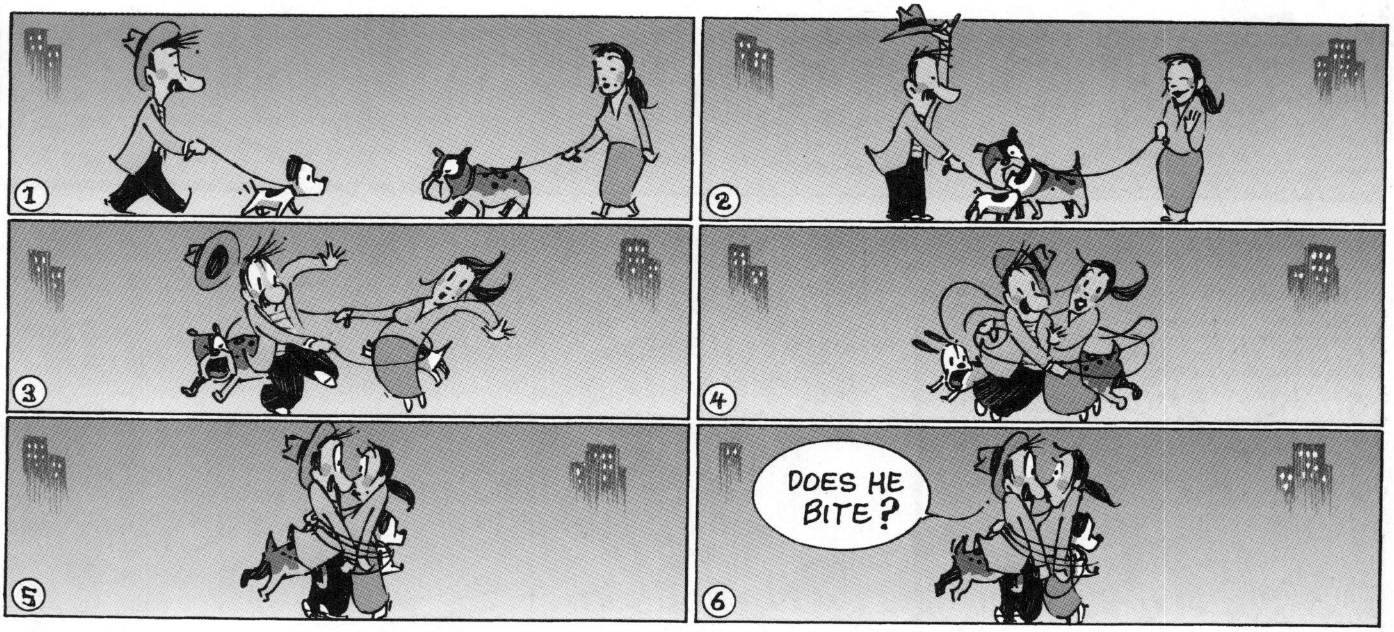
DOES HE BITE?

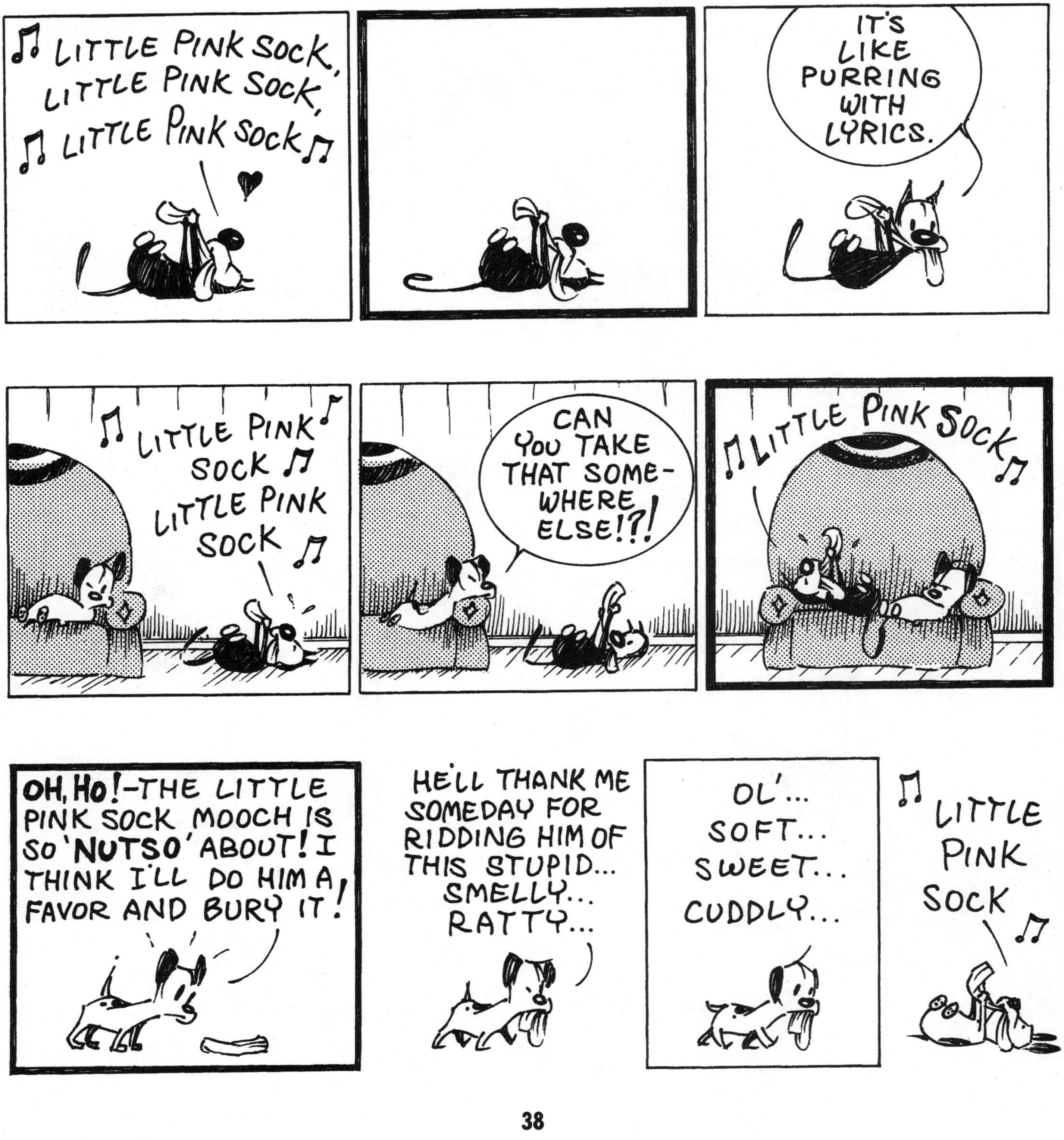
LITTLE PINK SOCK, LITTLE PINK SOCK, LITTLE PINK SOCK
IT'S LIKE PURRING WITH LYRICS.
LITTLE PINK SOCK LITTLE PINK SOCK
CAN YOU TAKE THAT SOMEWHERE ELSE!?!
LITTLE PINK SOCK
OH, HO!–THE LITTLE PINK SOCK MOOCH IS SO 'NUTSO' ABOUT! I THINK I'LL DO HIM A FAVOR AND BURY IT!
HE'LL THANK ME SOMEDAY FOR RIDDING HIM OF THIS STUPID... SMELLY... RATTY...
OL'... SOFT... SWEET... CUDDLY...
LITTLE PINK SOCK

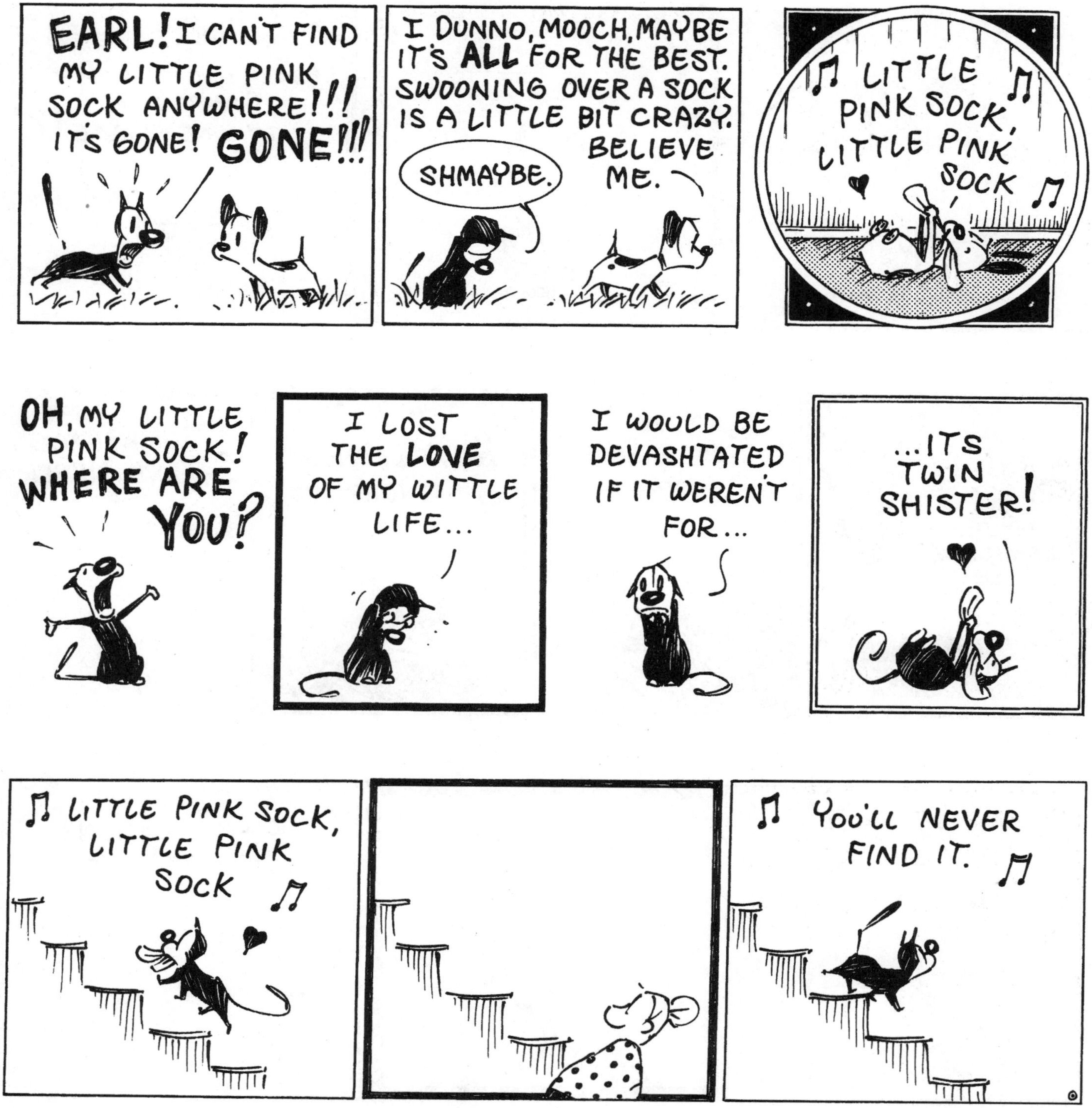
EARL! I CAN'T FIND MY LITTLE PINK SOCK ANYWHERE!!! IT'S GONE! GONE!!!
I DUNNO, MOOCH, MAYBE IT'S ALL FOR THE BEST. SWOONING OVER A SOCK IS A LITTLE BIT CRAZY.
SHMAYBE.
BELIEVE ME.
♫ LITTLE PINK SOCK, LITTLE PINK SOCK ♫
OH, MY LITTLE PINK SOCK! WHERE ARE YOU?
I LOST THE LOVE OF MY WITTLE LIFE...
I WOULD BE DEVASHTATED IF IT WEREN'T FOR...
...ITS TWIN SHISTER!
♫ LITTLE PINK SOCK, LITTLE PINK SOCK ♫
♫ YOU'LL NEVER FIND IT. ♫

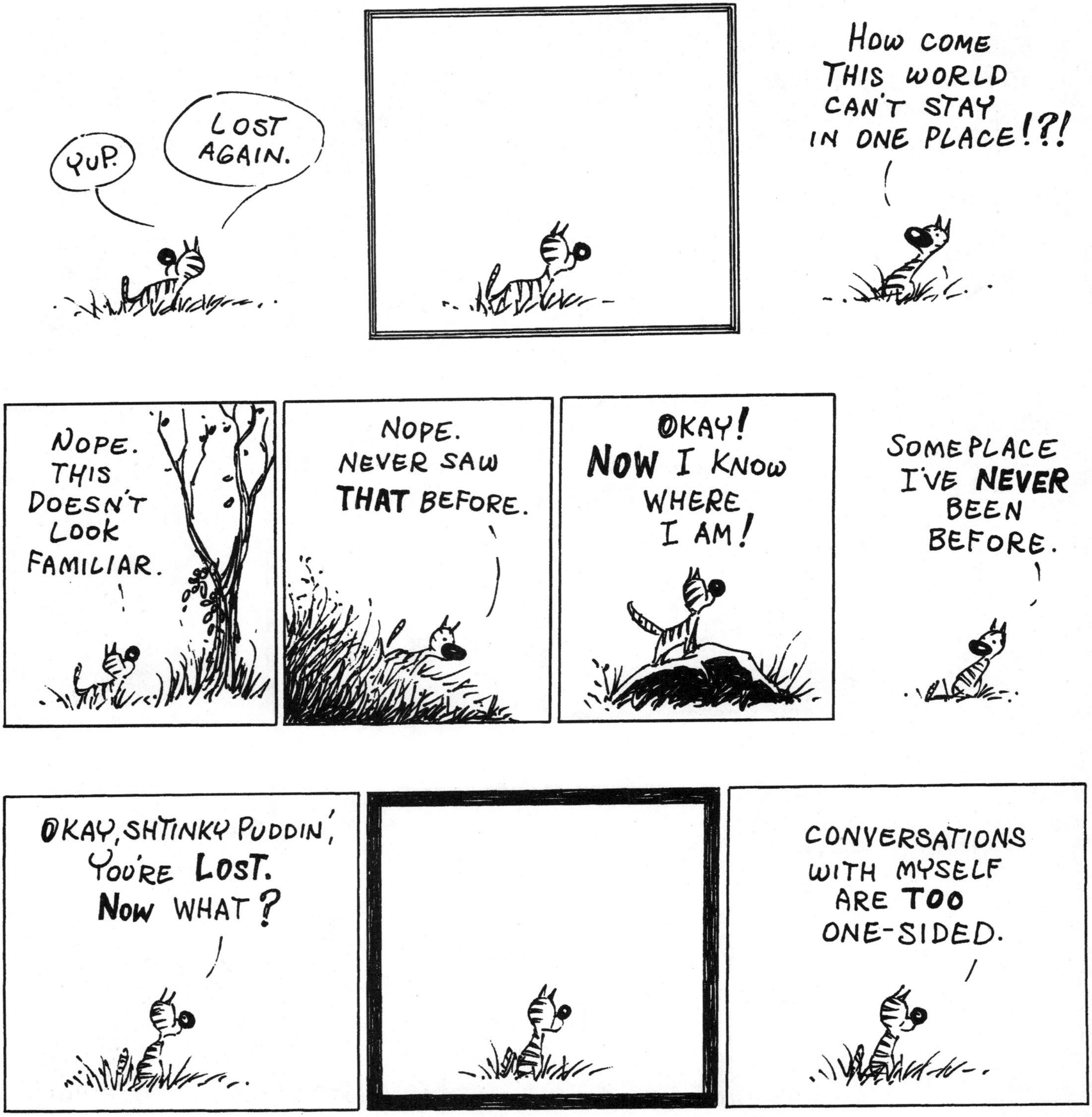

LOST AGAIN.
YUP.
HOW COME THIS WORLD CAN'T STAY IN ONE PLACE!?!
NOPE. THIS DOESN'T LOOK FAMILIAR.
NOPE. NEVER SAW THAT BEFORE.
OKAY! NOW I KNOW WHERE I AM!
SOMEPLACE I'VE NEVER BEEN BEFORE.
OKAY, SHTINKY PUDDIN', YOU'RE LOST. NOW WHAT?
CONVERSATIONS WITH MYSELF ARE TOO ONE-SIDED.

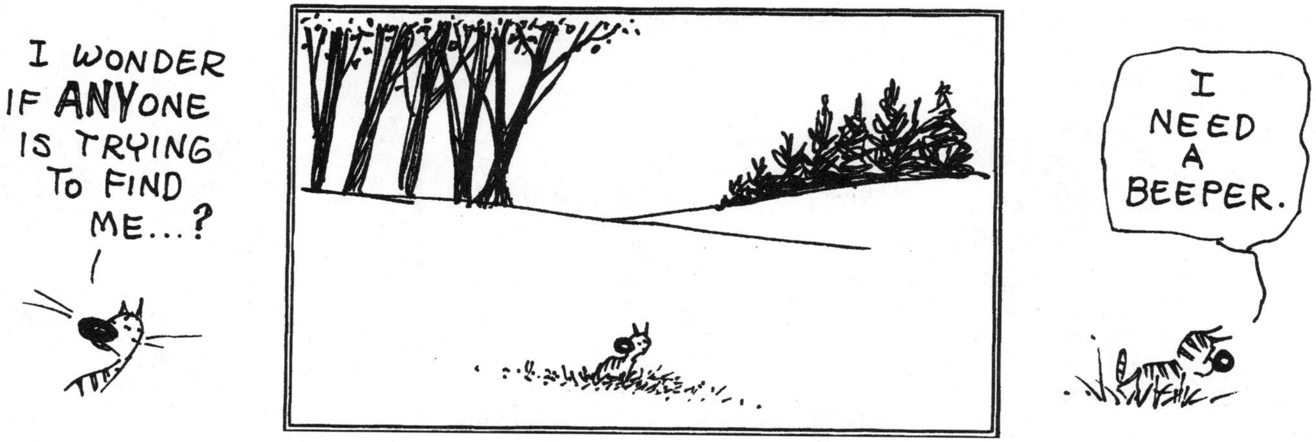
I WONDER IF ANYONE IS TRYING TO FIND ME...?
I NEED A BEEPER.

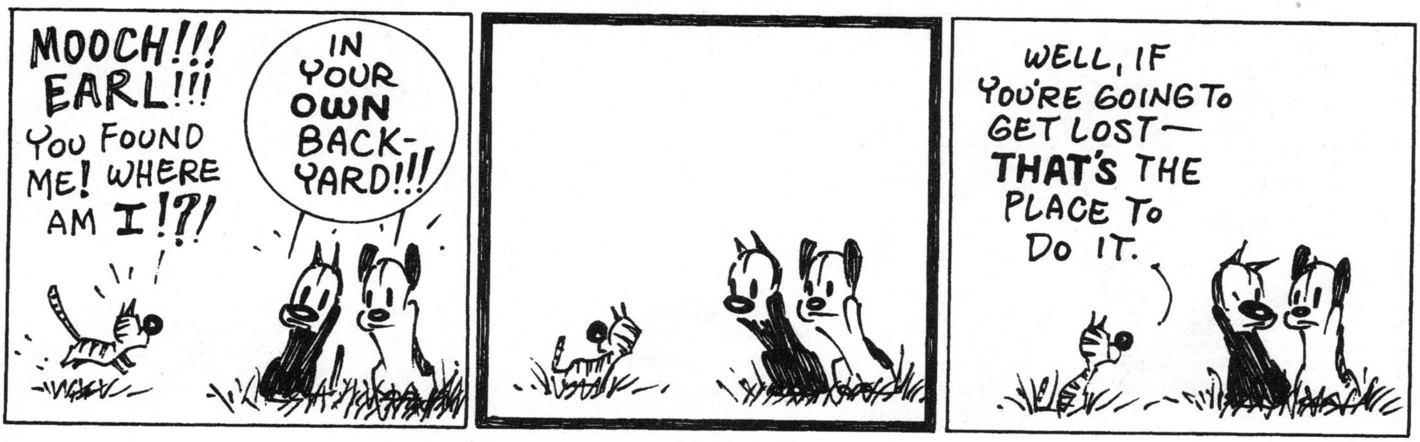
MOOCH!!! EARL!!! YOU FOUND ME! WHERE AM I!?!
IN YOUR OWN BACK-YARD!!!
WELL, IF YOU'RE GOING TO GET LOST— THAT'S THE PLACE TO DO IT.

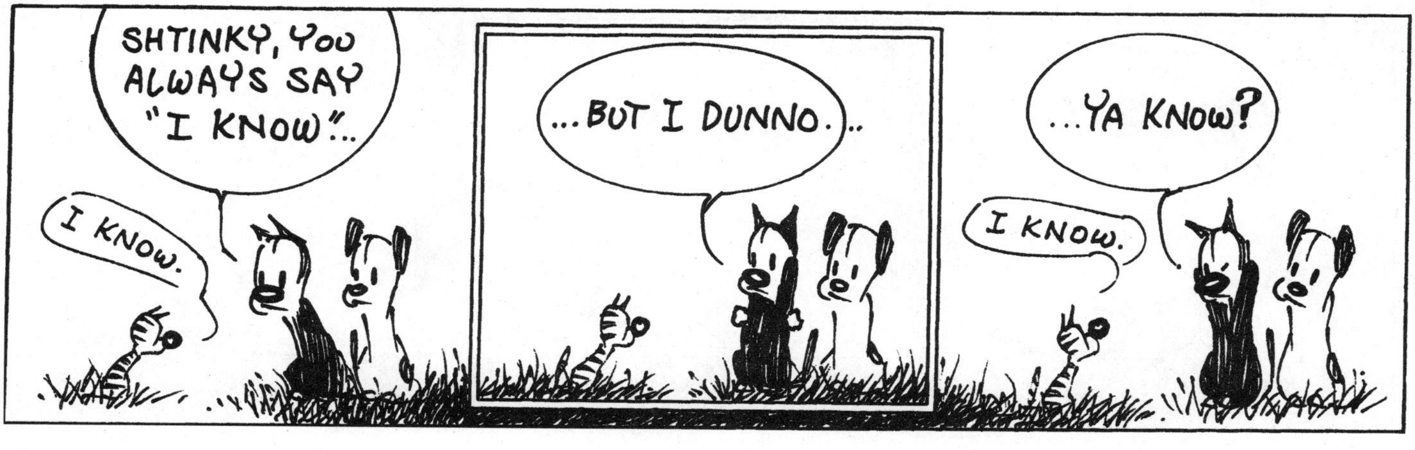
I KNOW.
SHTINKY, YOU ALWAYS SAY "I KNOW"...
...BUT I DUNNO...
I KNOW.
...YA KNOW?

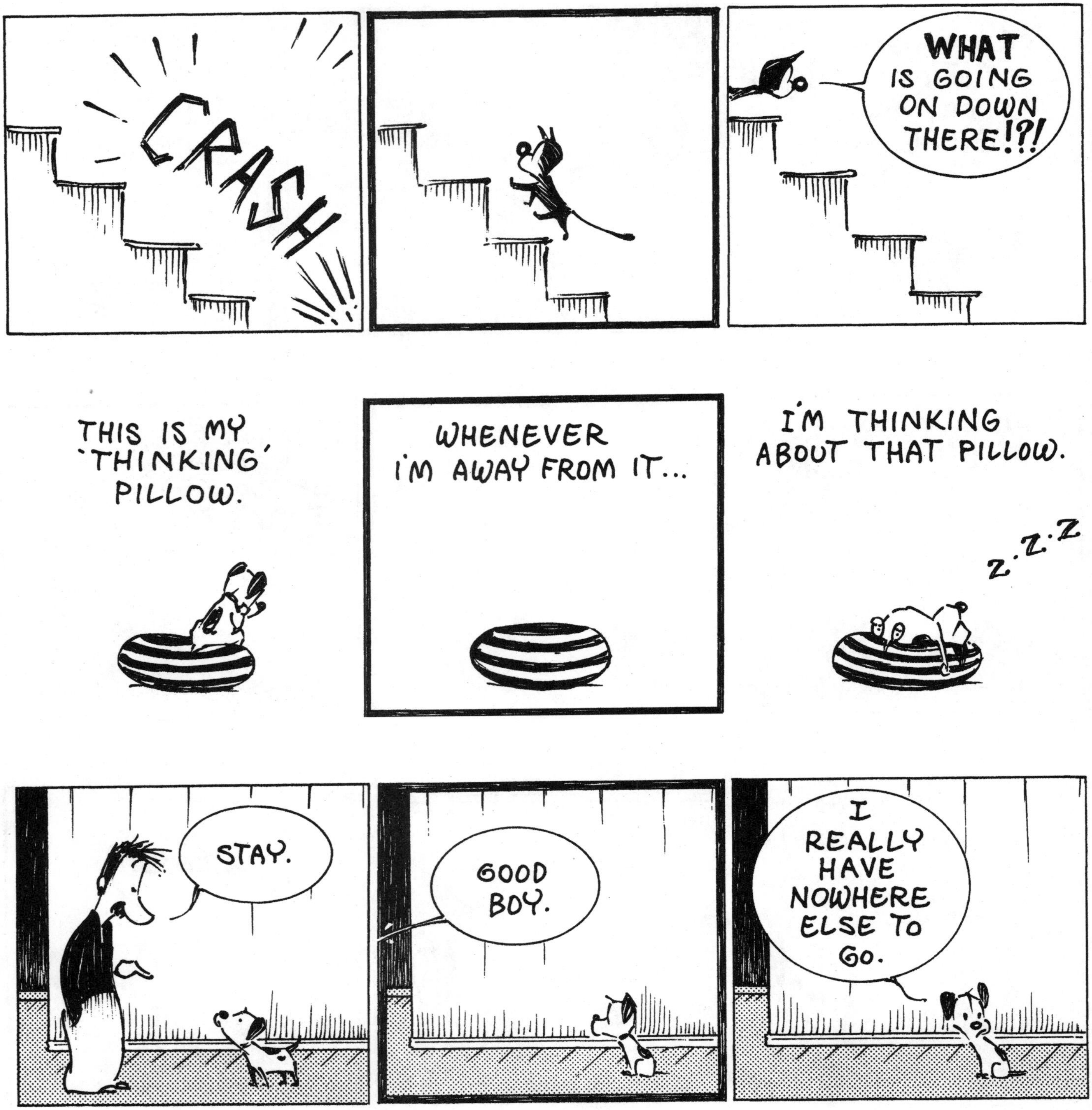
CRASH
WHAT IS GOING ON DOWN THERE!?!
THIS IS MY 'THINKING' PILLOW.
WHENEVER I'M AWAY FROM IT...
I'M THINKING ABOUT THAT PILLOW.
Z.Z.Z
STAY.
GOOD BOY.
I REALLY HAVE NOWHERE ELSE TO GO.

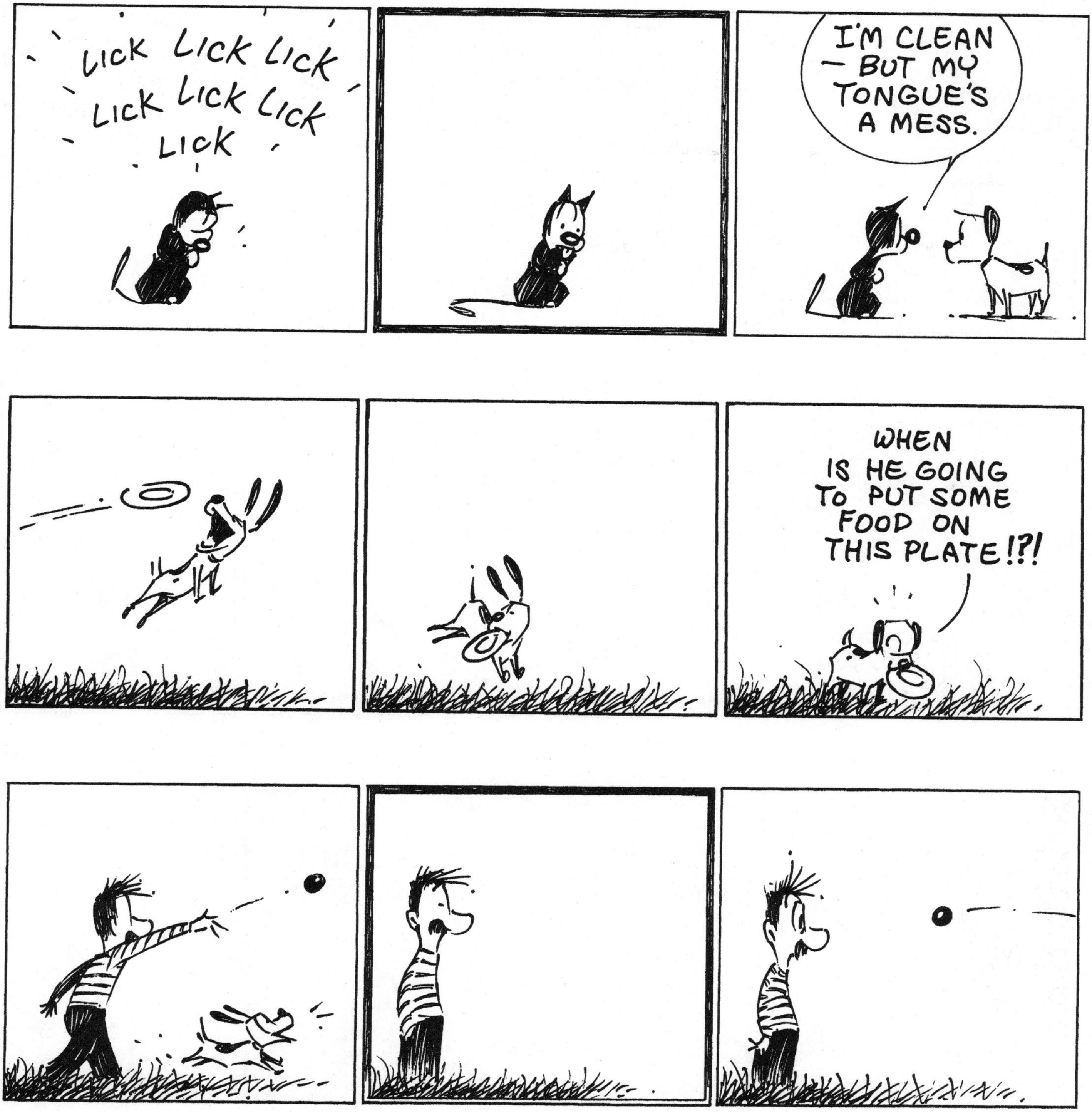
LICK LICK LICK
LICK LICK LICK
LICK
I'M CLEAN — BUT MY TONGUE'S A MESS.
WHEN IS HE GOING TO PUT SOME FOOD ON THIS PLATE!?!

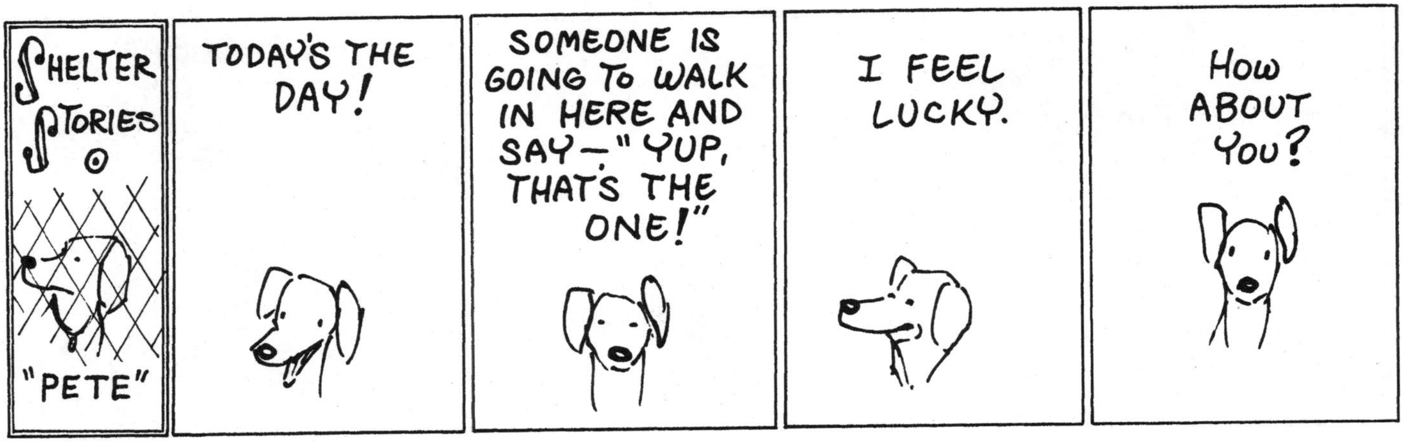
SHELTER STORIES
"PETE"
TODAY'S THE DAY!
SOMEONE IS GOING TO WALK IN HERE AND SAY— "YUP, THAT'S THE ONE!"
I FEEL LUCKY.
HOW ABOUT YOU?

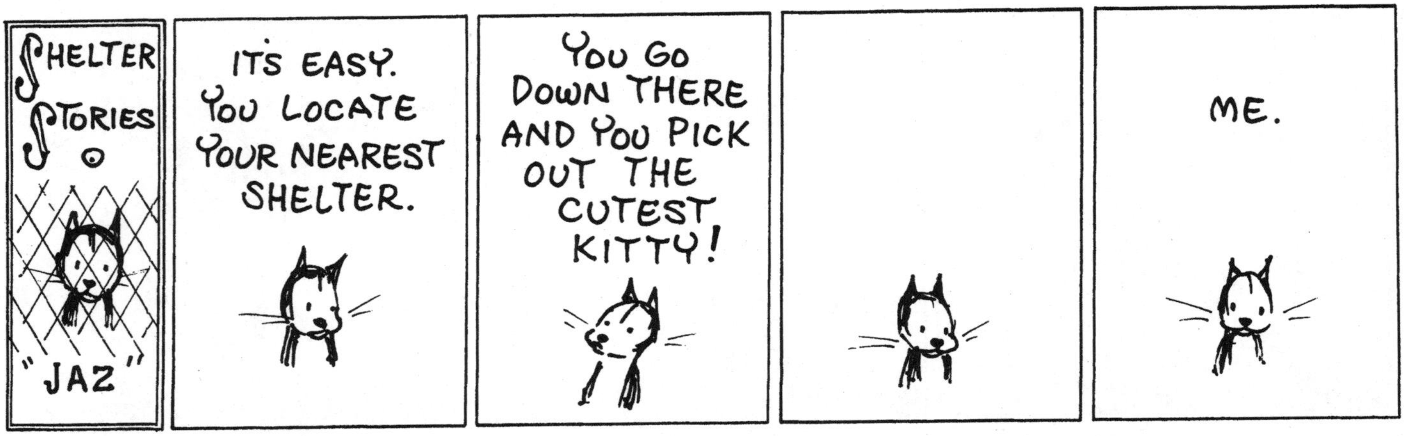
SHELTER STORIES
"JAZ"
IT'S EASY. YOU LOCATE YOUR NEAREST SHELTER.
YOU GO DOWN THERE AND YOU PICK OUT THE CUTEST KITTY!
ME.

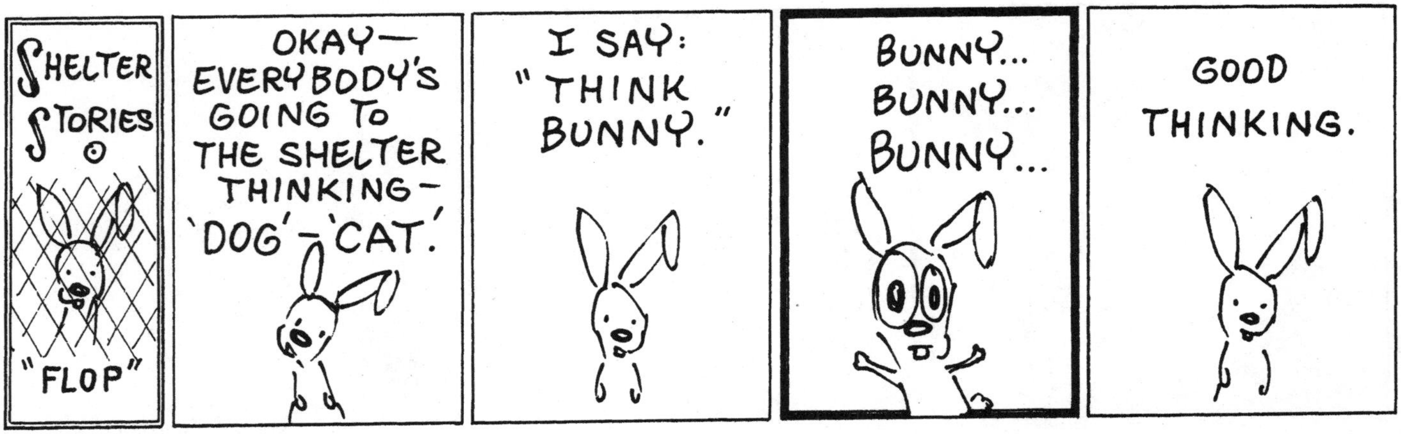
SHELTER STORIES
"FLOP"
OKAY— EVERYBODY'S GOING TO THE SHELTER THINKING— 'DOG'— 'CAT.'
I SAY: "THINK BUNNY."
BUNNY... BUNNY... BUNNY...
GOOD THINKING.

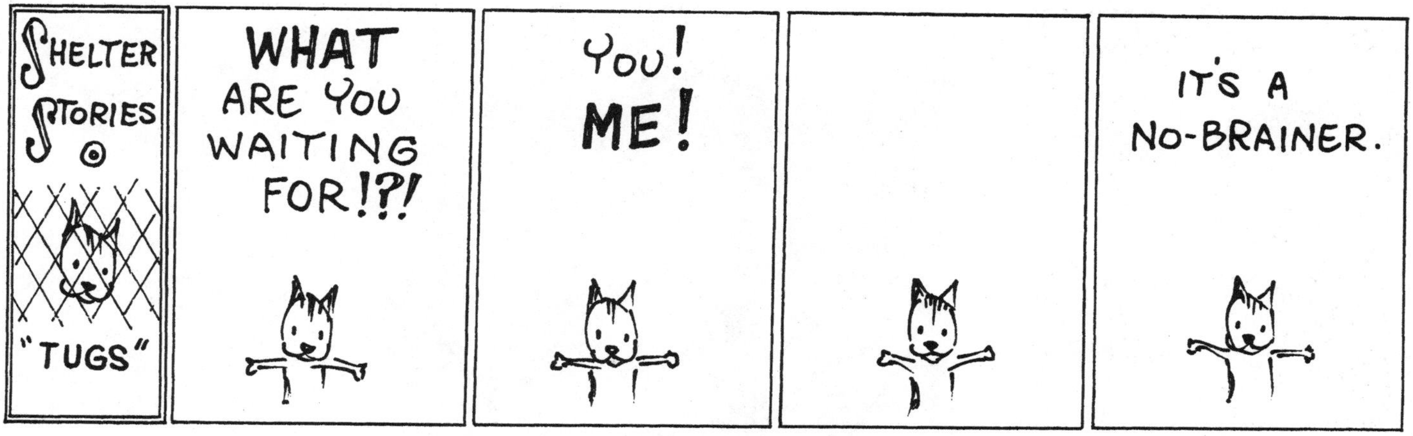
SHELTER STORIES
"TUGS"
WHAT ARE YOU WAITING FOR!?!
YOU! ME!
IT'S A NO-BRAINER.

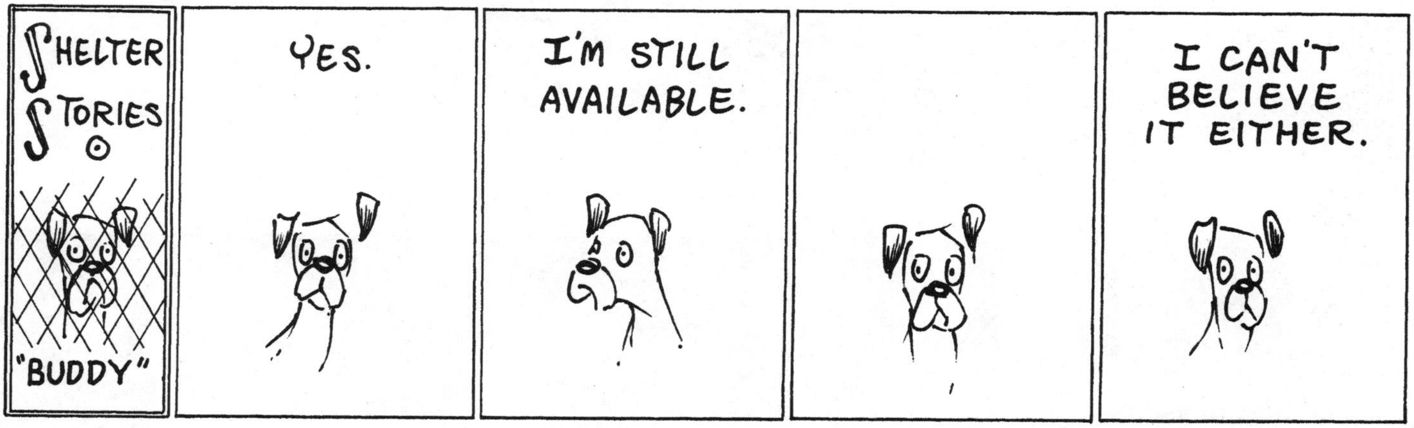
SHELTER STORIES
"BUDDY"
YES.
I'M STILL AVAILABLE.
I CAN'T BELIEVE IT EITHER.

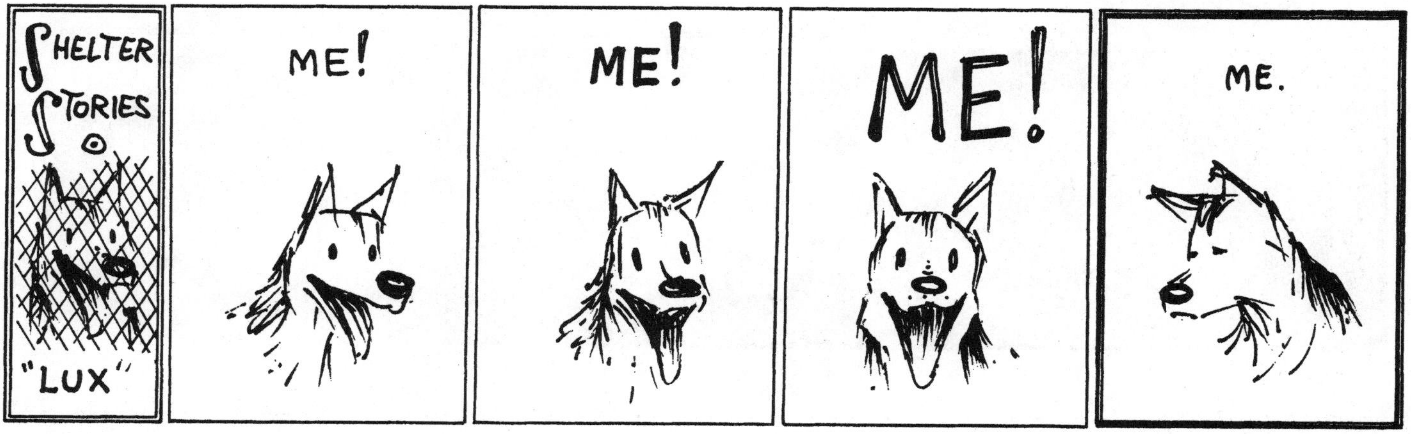
SHELTER STORIES
"LUX"
ME!
ME!
ME!
ME.

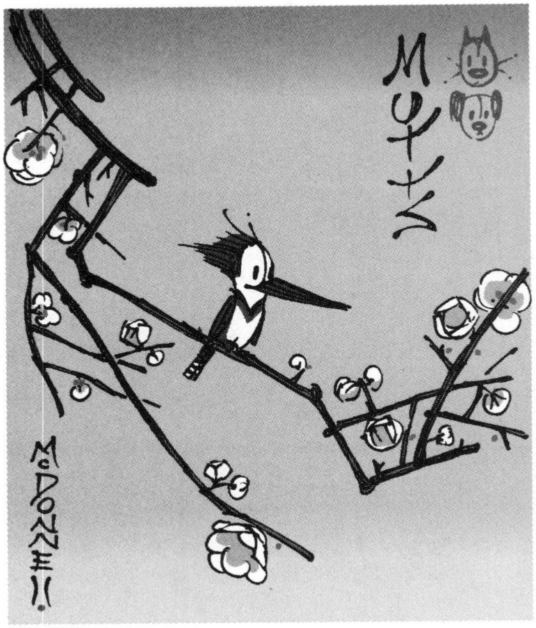
MUTTS
McDONNELL

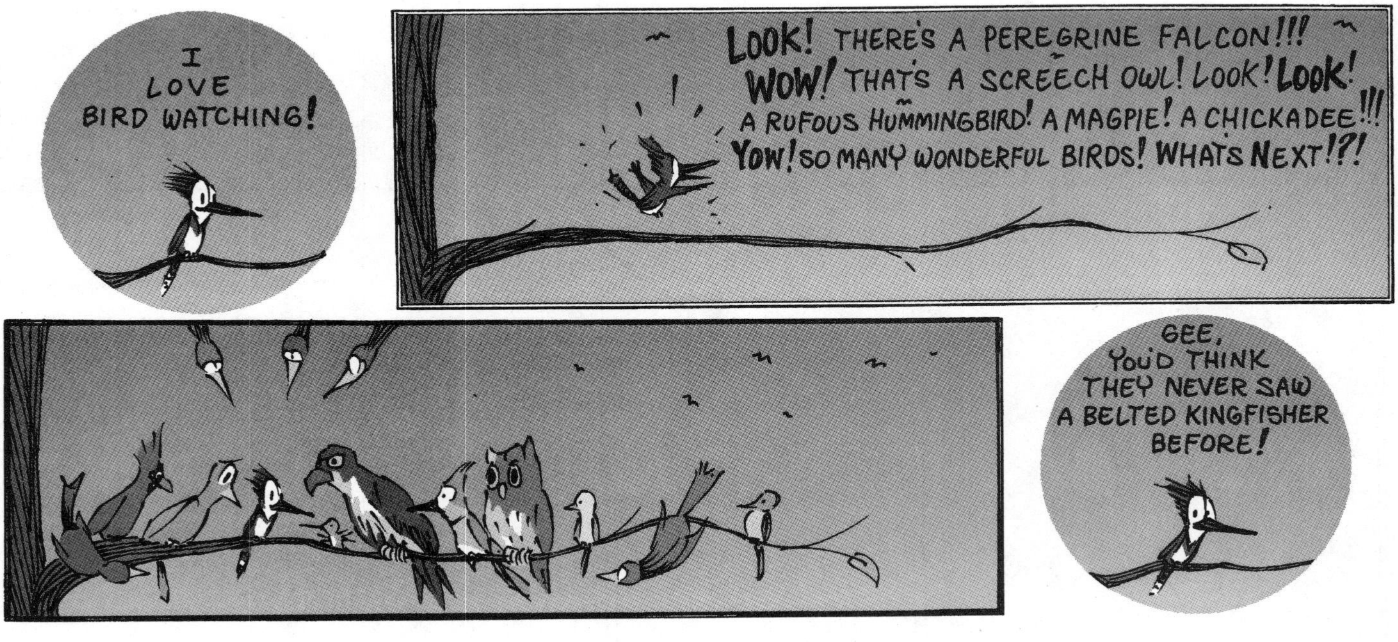
I LOVE BIRD WATCHING!
LOOK! THERE'S A PEREGRINE FALCON!!! WOW! THAT'S A SCREECH OWL! LOOK! LOOK! A RUFOUS HUMMINGBIRD! A MAGPIE! A CHICKADEE!!! YOW! SO MANY WONDERFUL BIRDS! WHAT'S NEXT!?!
GEE, YOU'D THINK THEY NEVER SAW A BELTED KINGFISHER BEFORE!

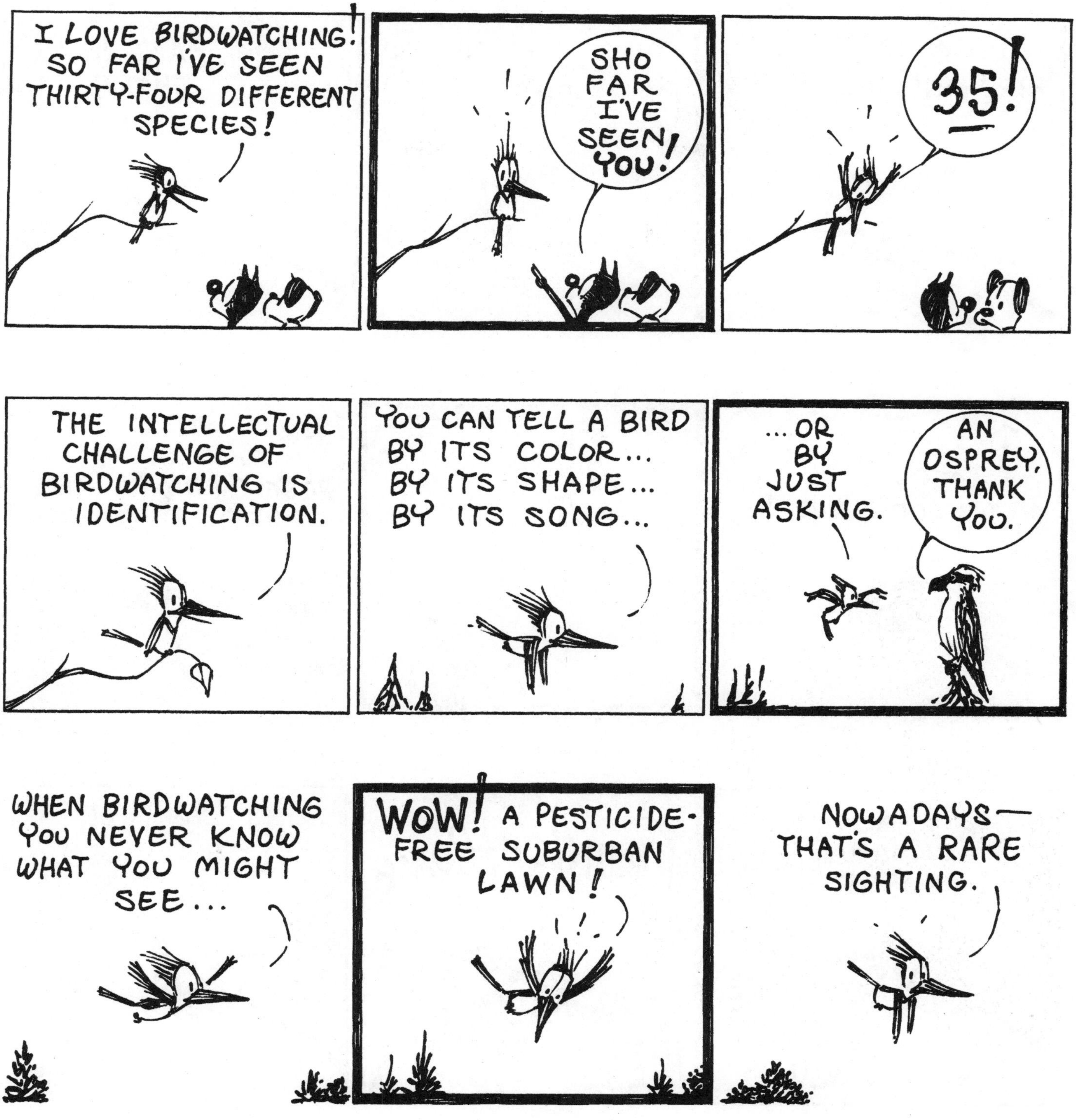
I LOVE BIRDWATCHING! SO FAR I'VE SEEN THIRTY-FOUR DIFFERENT SPECIES!
SHO FAR I'VE SEEN YOU!
35!
THE INTELLECTUAL CHALLENGE OF BIRDWATCHING IS IDENTIFICATION.
YOU CAN TELL A BIRD BY ITS COLOR... BY ITS SHAPE... BY ITS SONG...
...OR BY JUST ASKING.
AN OSPREY, THANK YOU.
WHEN BIRDWATCHING YOU NEVER KNOW WHAT YOU MIGHT SEE...
WOW! A PESTICIDE-FREE SUBURBAN LAWN!
NOWADAYS— THAT'S A RARE SIGHTING.

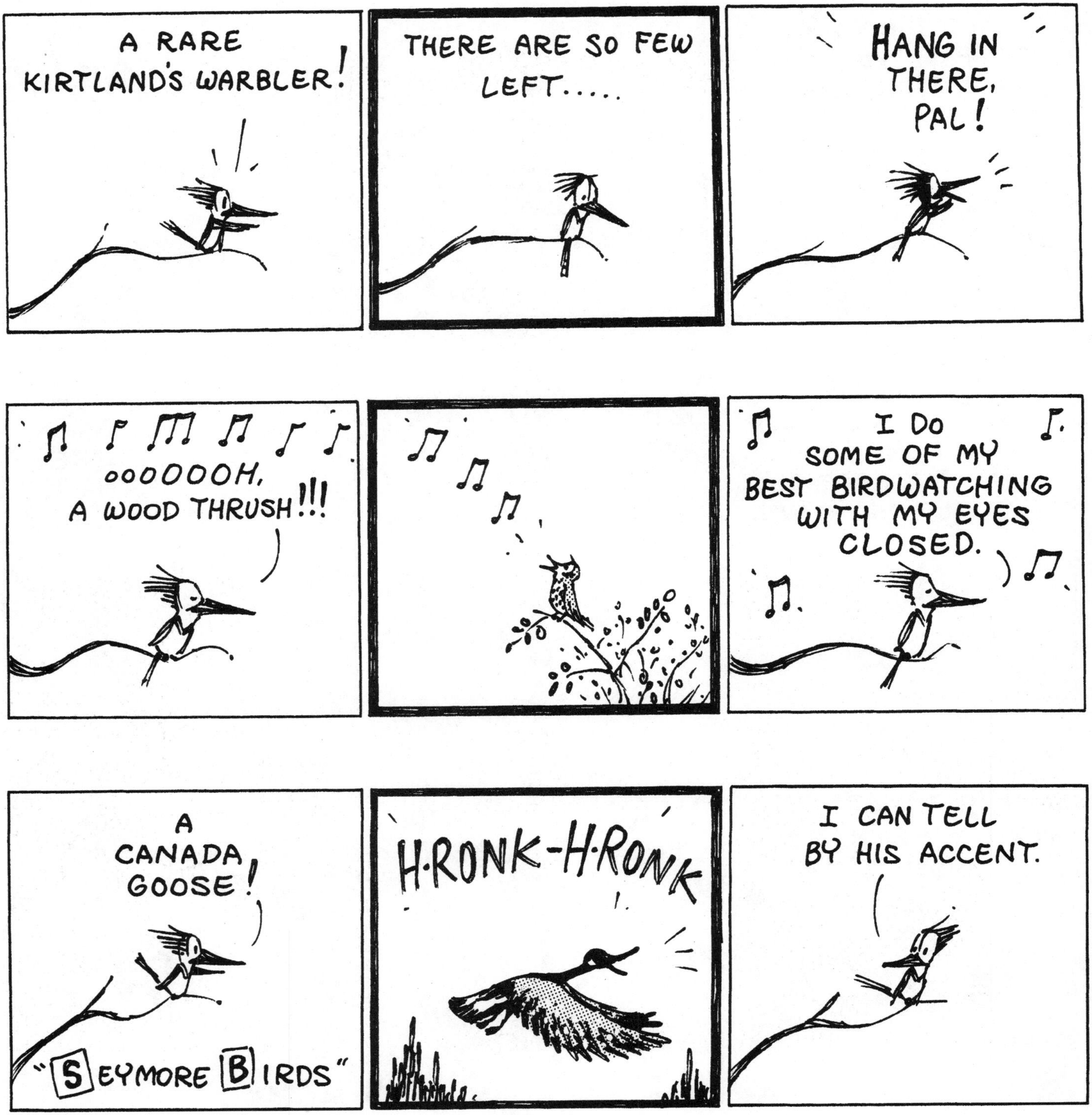
A RARE KIRTLAND'S WARBLER!
THERE ARE SO FEW LEFT.....
HANG IN THERE, PAL!
oooOOOH, A WOOD THRUSH!!!
I DO SOME OF MY BEST BIRDWATCHING WITH MY EYES CLOSED.
A CANADA GOOSE!
"SEYMORE BIRDS"
H·RONK-H·RONK
I CAN TELL BY HIS ACCENT.

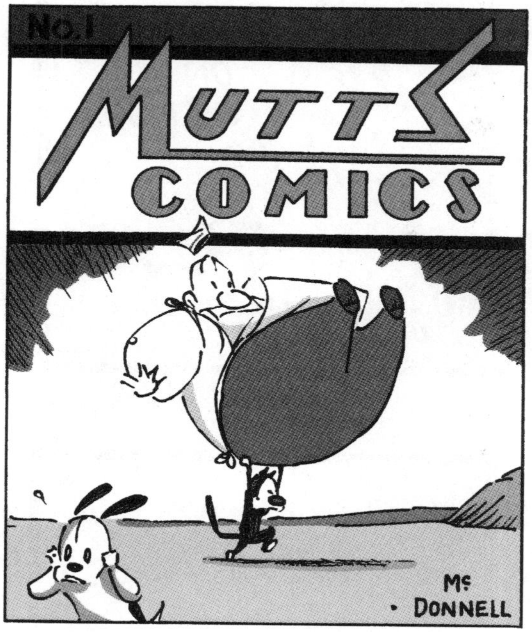
No. 1
MUTTS
COMICS
MC DONNELL

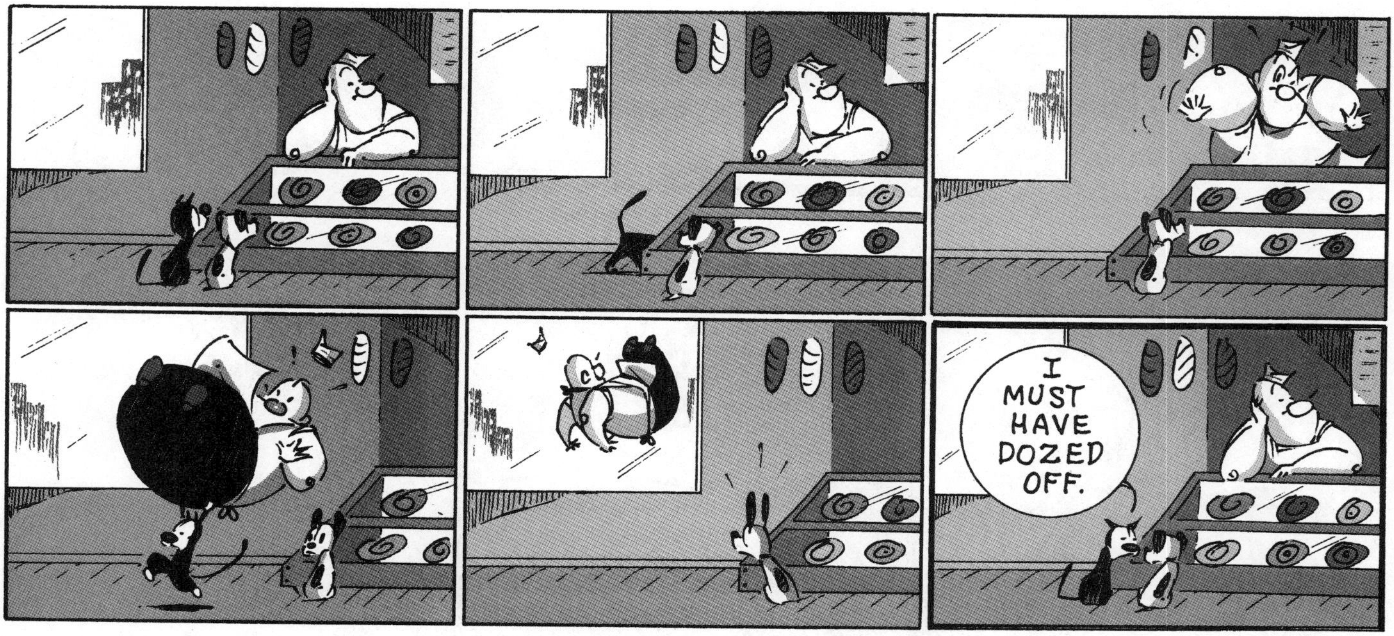
I MUST HAVE DOZED OFF.

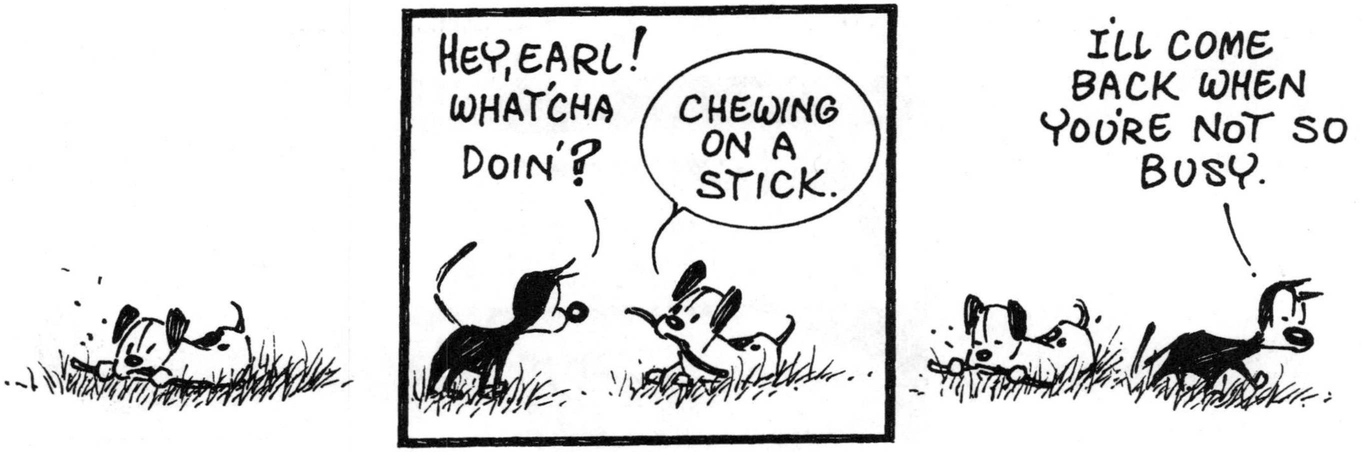
HEY, EARL! WHAT'CHA DOIN'?
CHEWING ON A STICK.
I'LL COME BACK WHEN YOU'RE NOT SO BUSY.

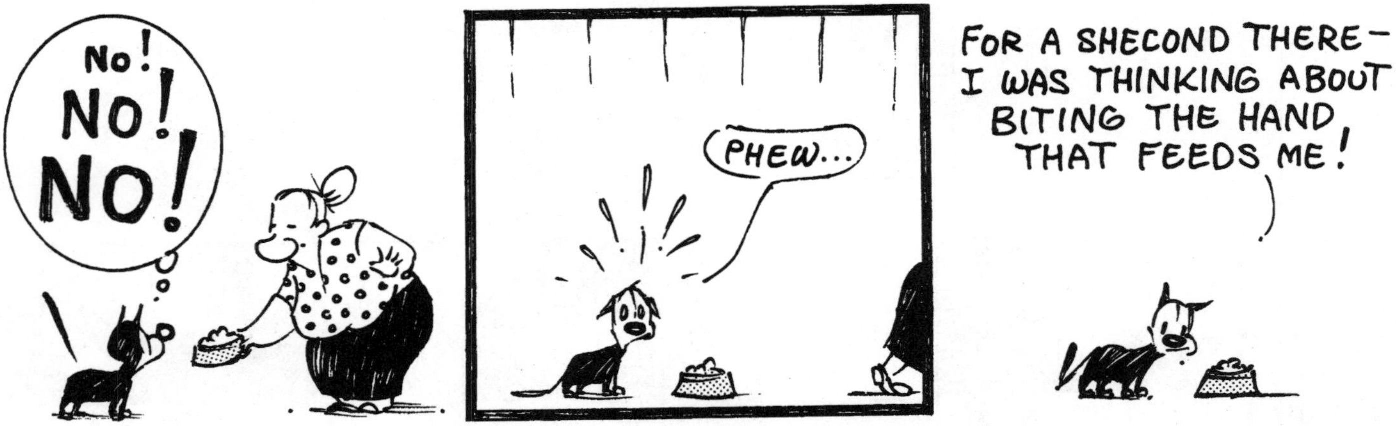
No! NO! NO!
PHEW...
FOR A SHECOND THERE— I WAS THINKING ABOUT BITING THE HAND THAT FEEDS ME!

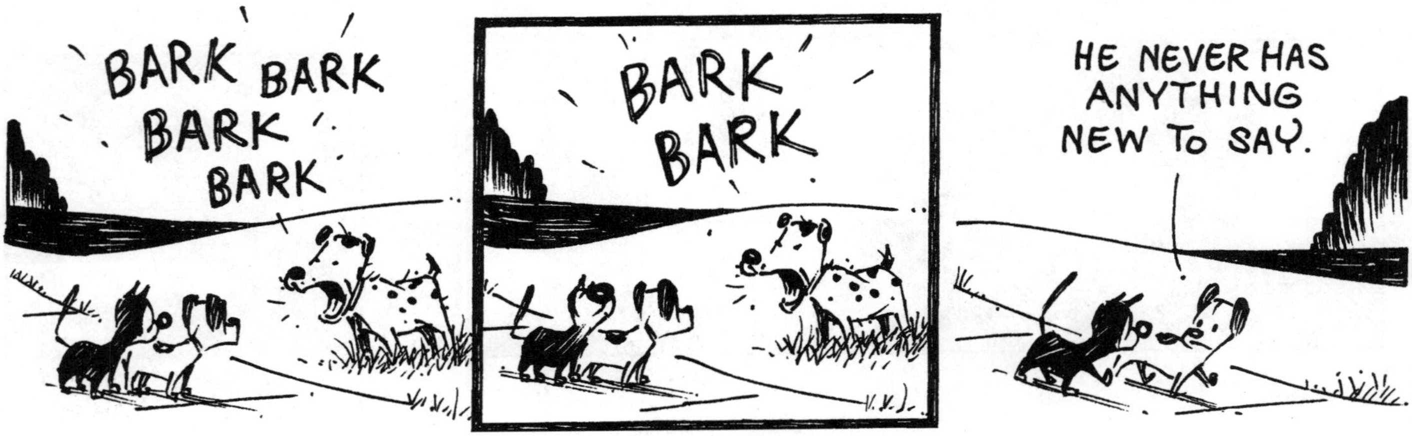
BARK BARK BARK BARK
BARK BARK
HE NEVER HAS ANYTHING NEW TO SAY.

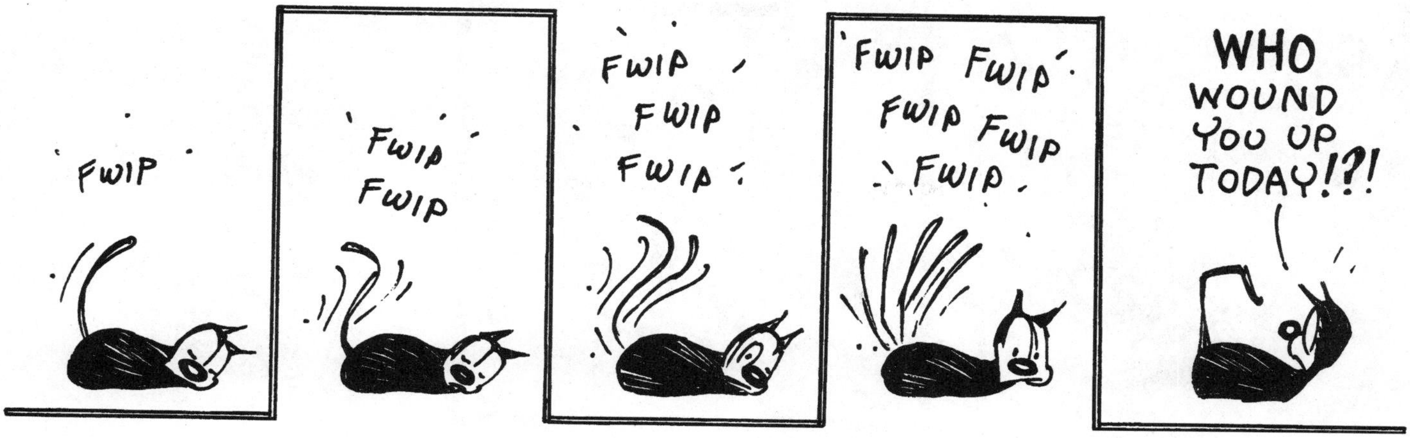
FWIP
FWIP FWIP
FWIP FWIP FWIP
FWIP FWIP FWIP FWIP FWIP
WHO WOUND YOU UP TODAY!?!

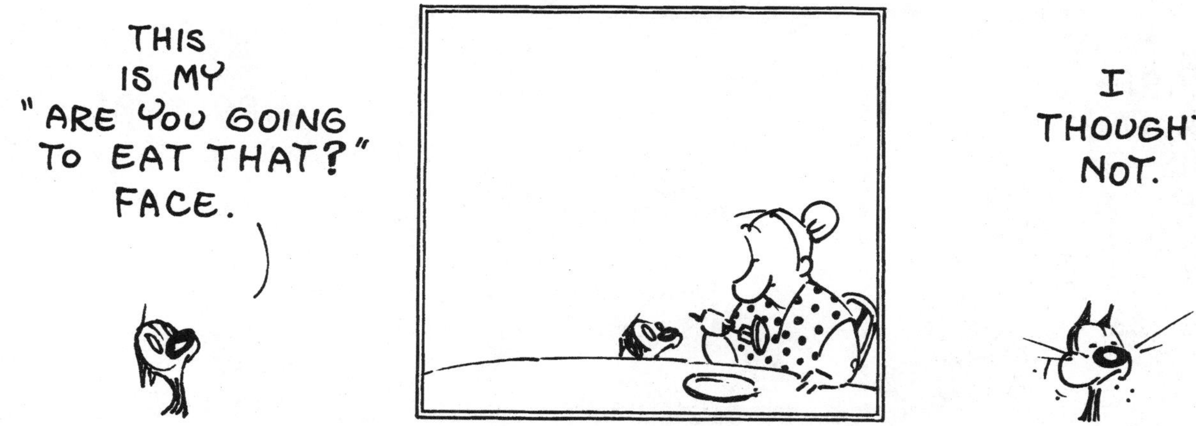
THIS IS MY "ARE YOU GOING TO EAT THAT?" FACE.
I THOUGHT NOT.

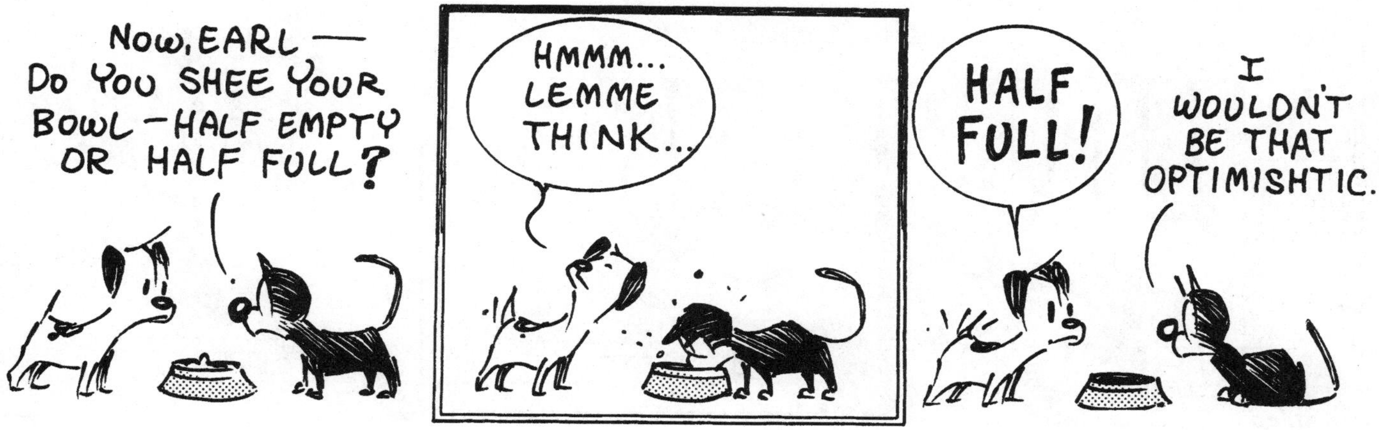
NOW, EARL — DO YOU SHEE YOUR BOWL — HALF EMPTY OR HALF FULL?
HMMM... LEMME THINK...
HALF FULL!
I WOULDN'T BE THAT OPTIMISHTIC.

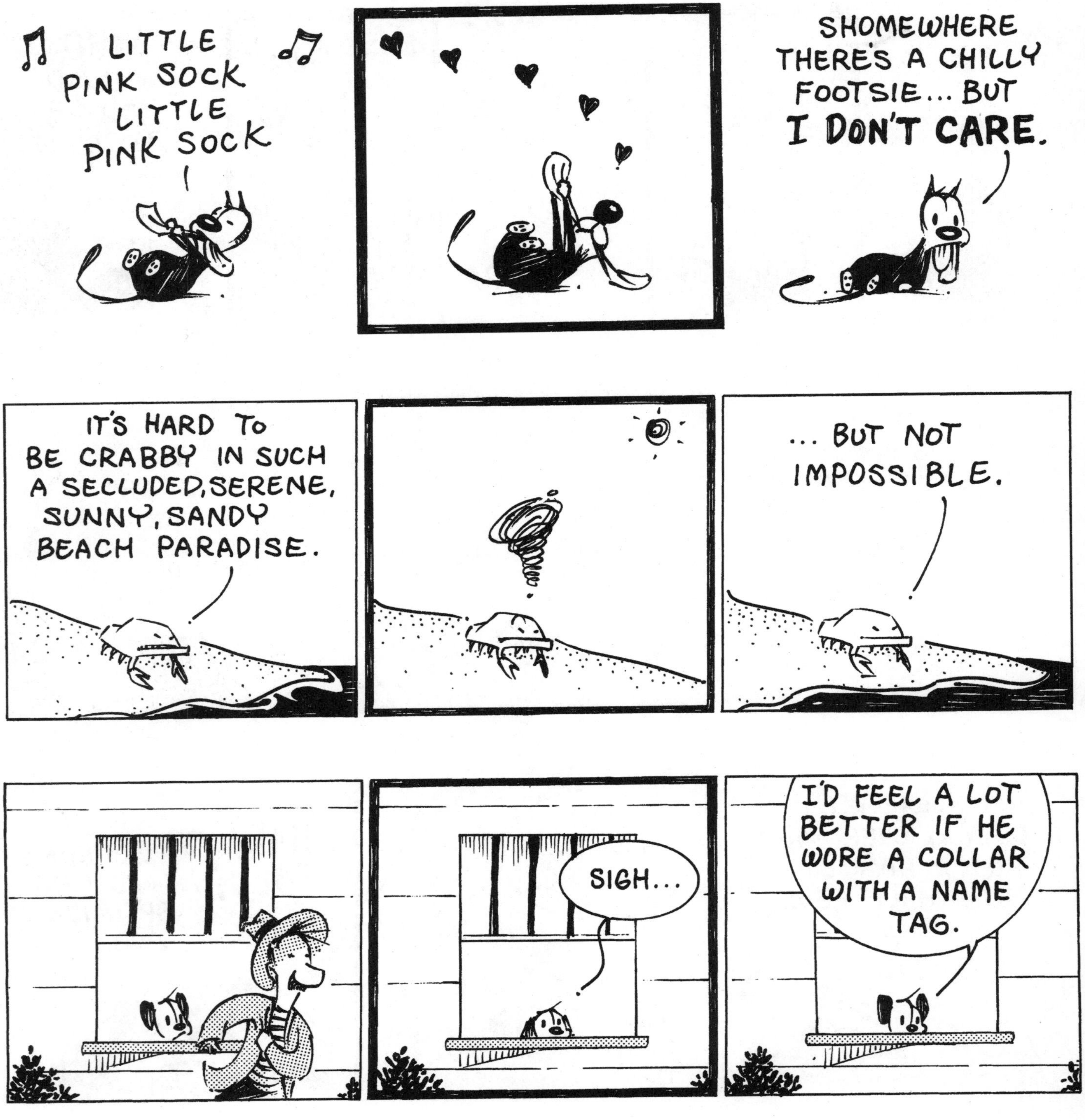
LITTLE PINK SOCK LITTLE PINK SOCK
SHOMEWHERE THERE'S A CHILLY FOOTSIE... BUT **I DON'T CARE.**
IT'S HARD TO BE CRABBY IN SUCH A SECLUDED, SERENE, SUNNY, SANDY BEACH PARADISE.
... BUT NOT IMPOSSIBLE.
SIGH...
I'D FEEL A LOT BETTER IF HE WORE A COLLAR WITH A NAME TAG.

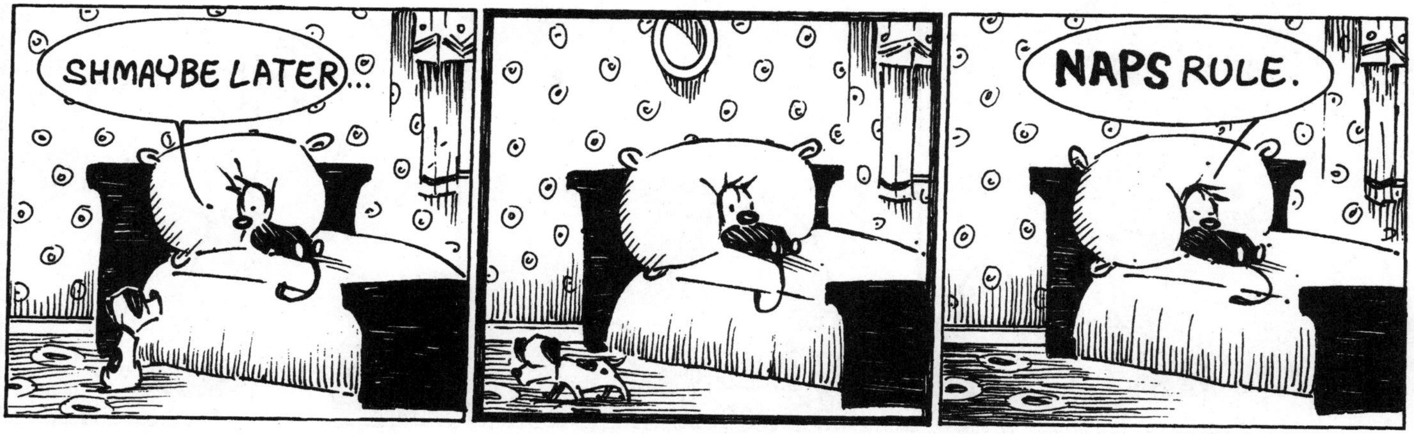
SHMAYBE LATER...
NAPS RULE.

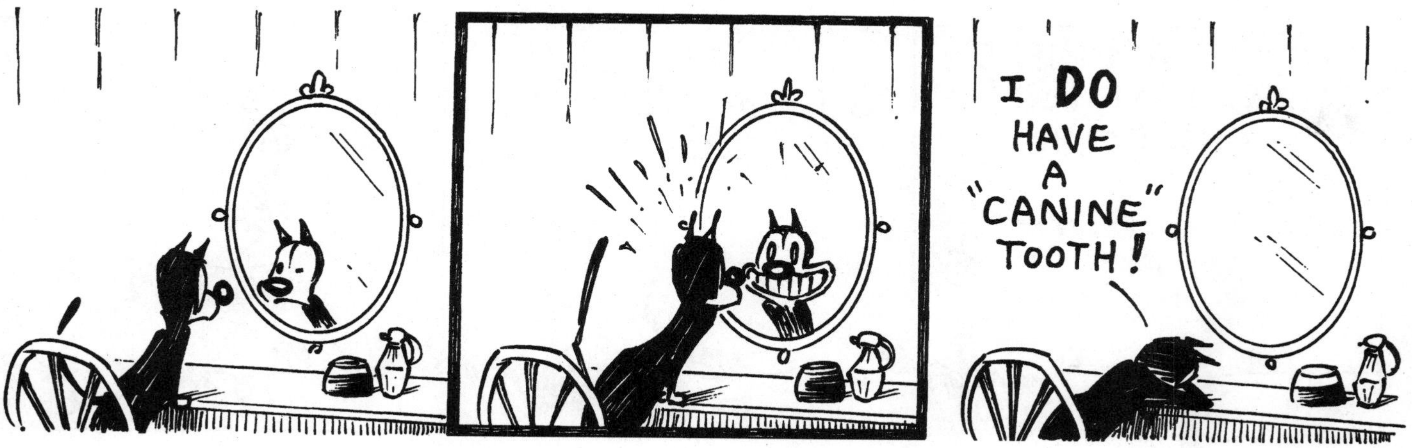
I DO HAVE A "CANINE" TOOTH!

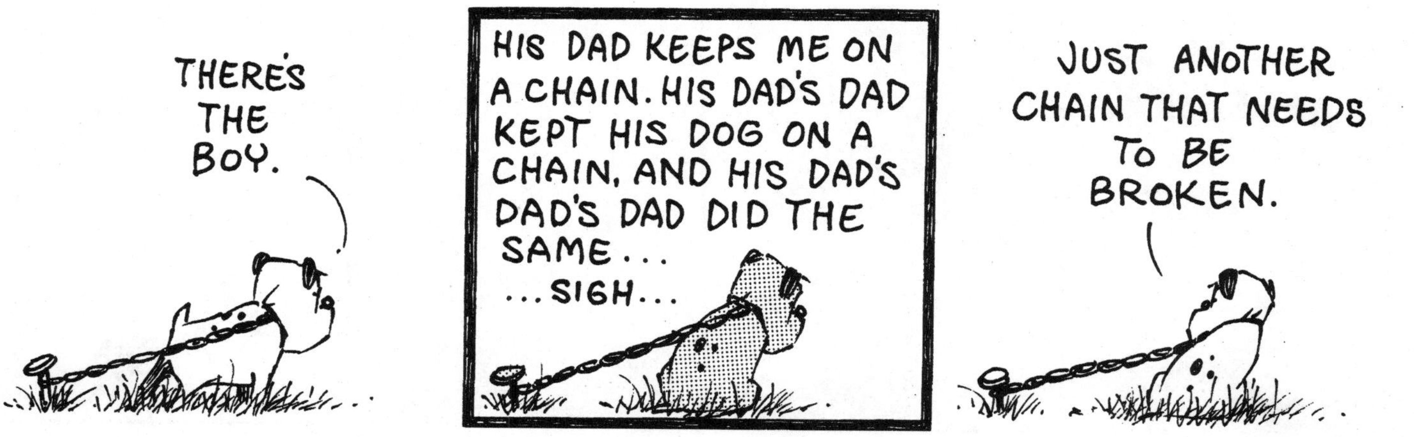
THERE'S THE BOY.
HIS DAD KEEPS ME ON A CHAIN. HIS DAD'S DAD KEPT HIS DOG ON A CHAIN, AND HIS DAD'S DAD'S DAD DID THE SAME... ...SIGH...
JUST ANOTHER CHAIN THAT NEEDS TO BE BROKEN.

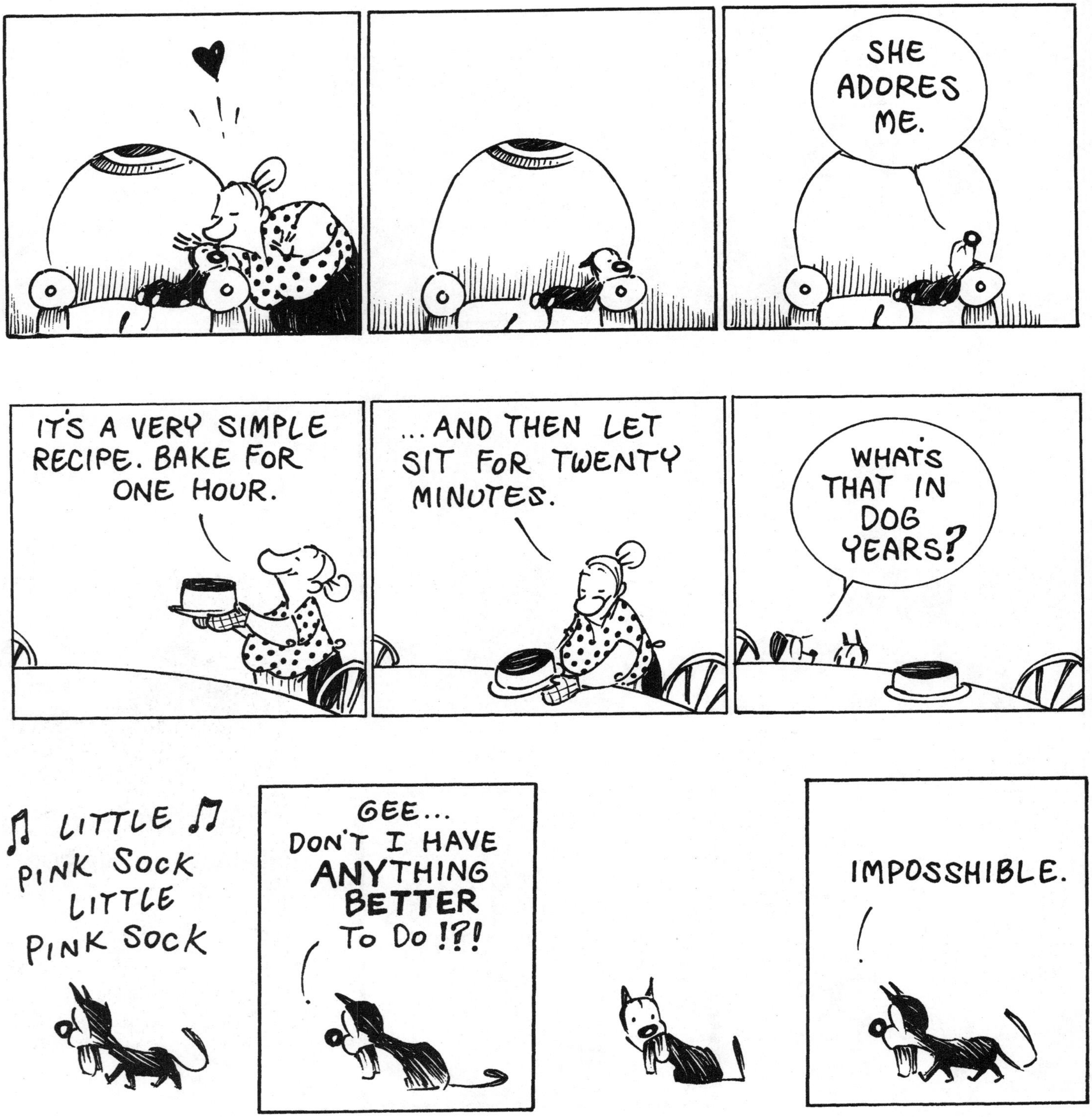
SHE ADORES ME.
IT'S A VERY SIMPLE RECIPE. BAKE FOR ONE HOUR.
...AND THEN LET SIT FOR TWENTY MINUTES.
WHAT'S THAT IN DOG YEARS?
♫ LITTLE ♫ PINK SOCK LITTLE PINK SOCK
GEE... DON'T I HAVE **ANYTHING BETTER** TO DO !?!
IMPOSSHIBLE.

MUTTS

NIGHT FEVER, NIGHT FEVER
LOVE TO LOVE YA, SHBABY
SHAKE, SHAKE, SHAKE-SHAKE YOUR SHBOOTY!
WIGGLE IT-JUST A WITTLE BIT
GET DOWN, GET DOWN!
WOOPS...
BONK
SHTAYIN' ALIVE— SHTAYIN' ALIVE

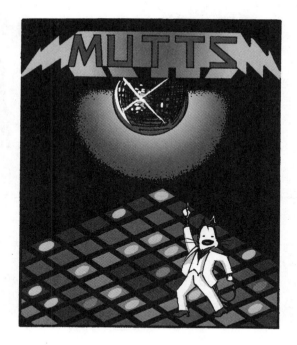

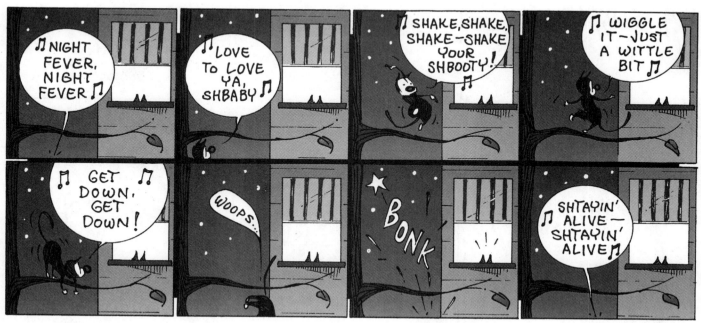

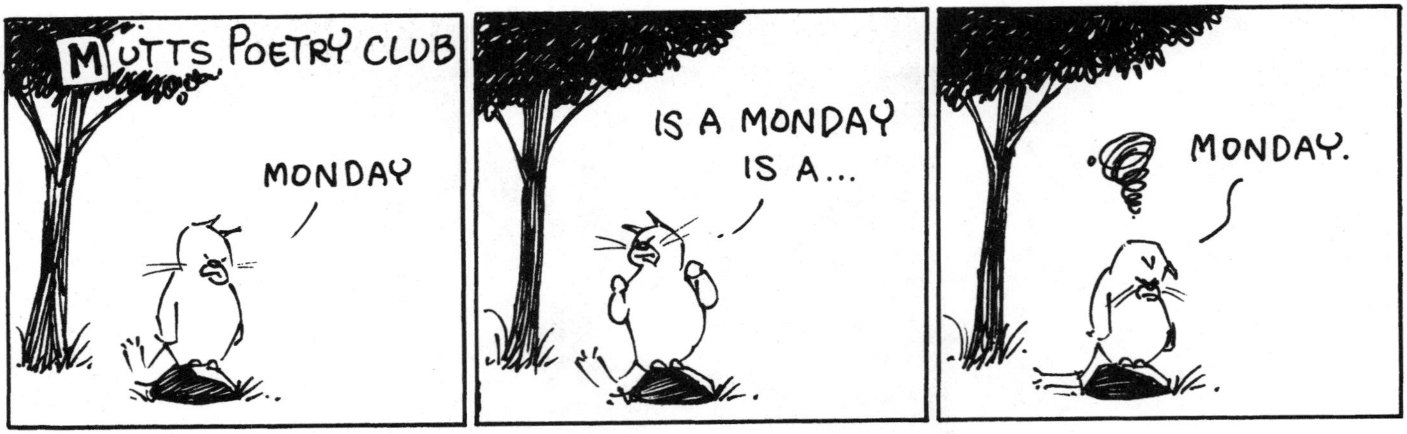
MUTTS POETRY CLUB
MONDAY
IS A MONDAY IS A...
MONDAY.

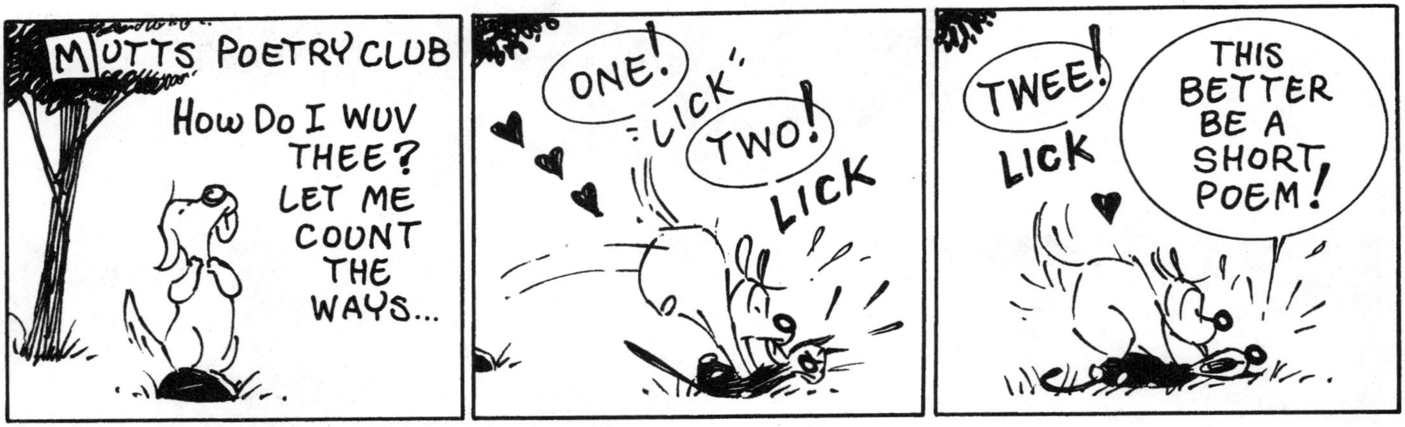
MUTTS POETRY CLUB
HOW DO I WUV THEE? LET ME COUNT THE WAYS...
ONE!
LICK
TWO!
LICK
TWEE!
LICK
THIS BETTER BE A SHORT POEM!

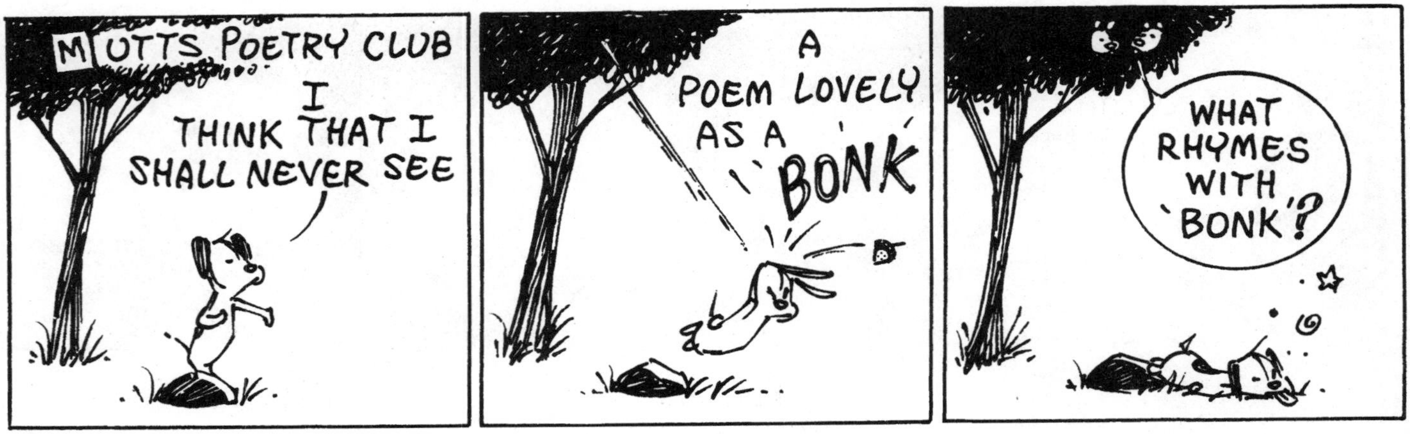
MUTTS POETRY CLUB
I THINK THAT I SHALL NEVER SEE
A POEM LOVELY AS A
BONK
WHAT RHYMES WITH 'BONK'?

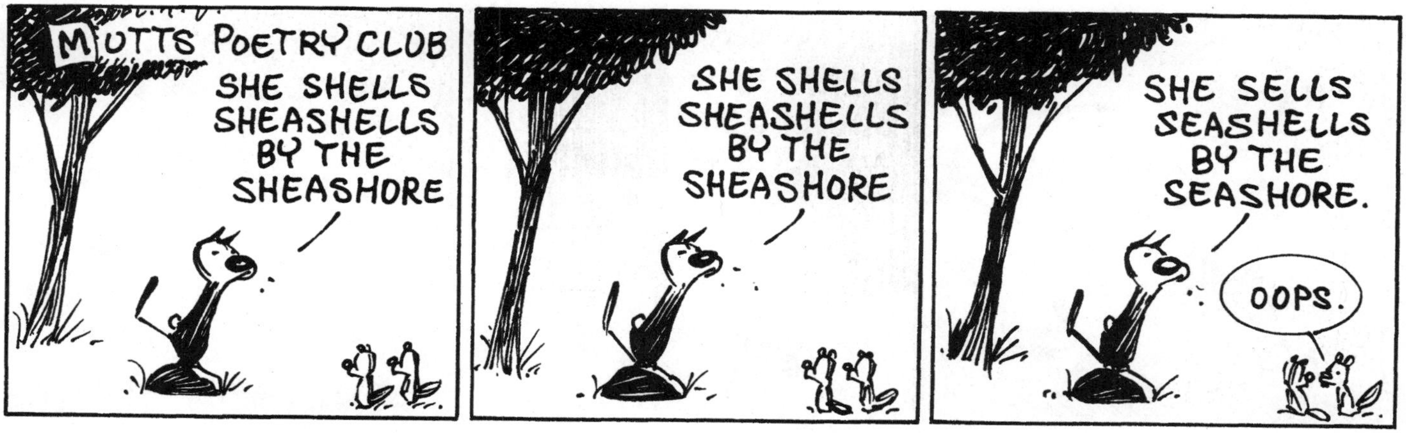
MUTTS POETRY CLUB
SHE SHELLS SHEASHELLS BY THE SHEASHORE
SHE SHELLS SHEASHELLS BY THE SHEASHORE
SHE SELLS SEASHELLS BY THE SEASHORE.
OOPS.

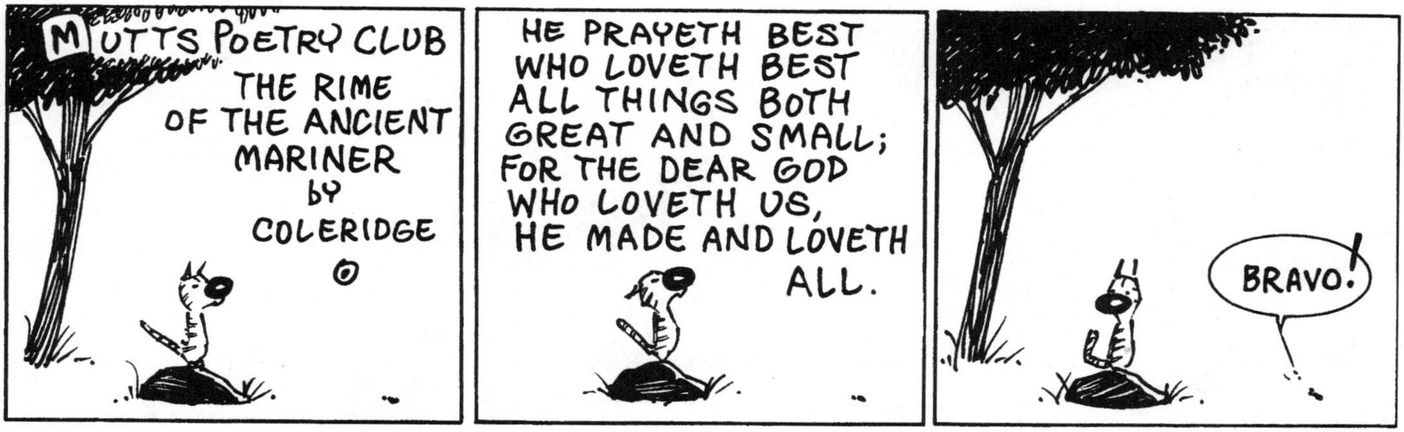
MUTTS POETRY CLUB
THE RIME OF THE ANCIENT MARINER by COLERIDGE
HE PRAYETH BEST WHO LOVETH BEST ALL THINGS BOTH GREAT AND SMALL; FOR THE DEAR GOD WHO LOVETH US, HE MADE AND LOVETH ALL.
BRAVO!

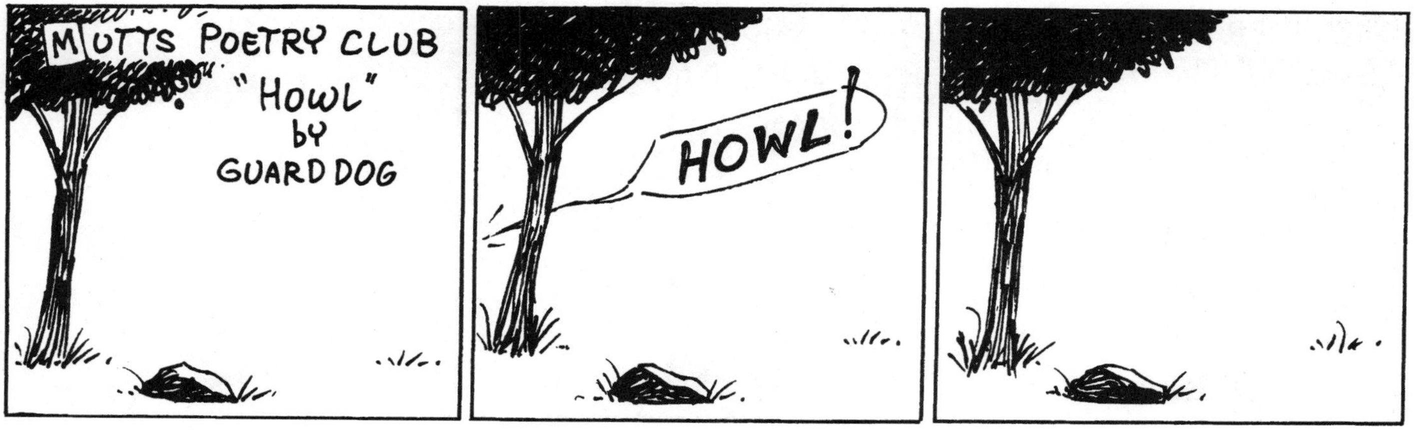
MUTTS POETRY CLUB
"HOWL" by GUARD DOG
HOWL!

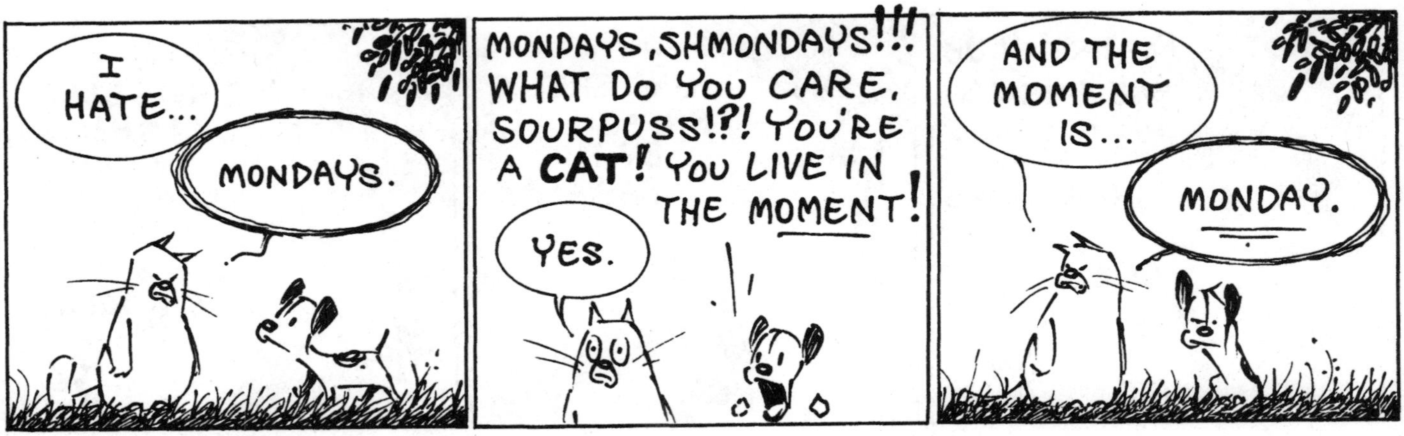
I HATE...
MONDAYS.
MONDAYS, SHMONDAYS!!! WHAT DO YOU CARE, SOURPUSS!?! YOU'RE A CAT! YOU LIVE IN THE MOMENT!
YES.
AND THE MOMENT IS...
MONDAY.

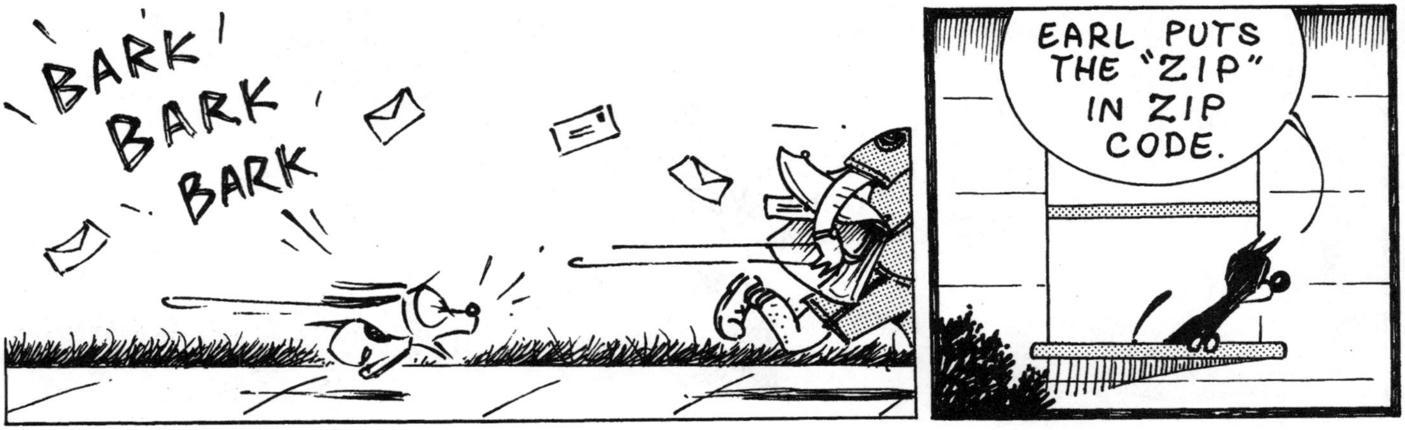
BARK
BARK
BARK
EARL PUTS THE "ZIP" IN ZIP CODE.

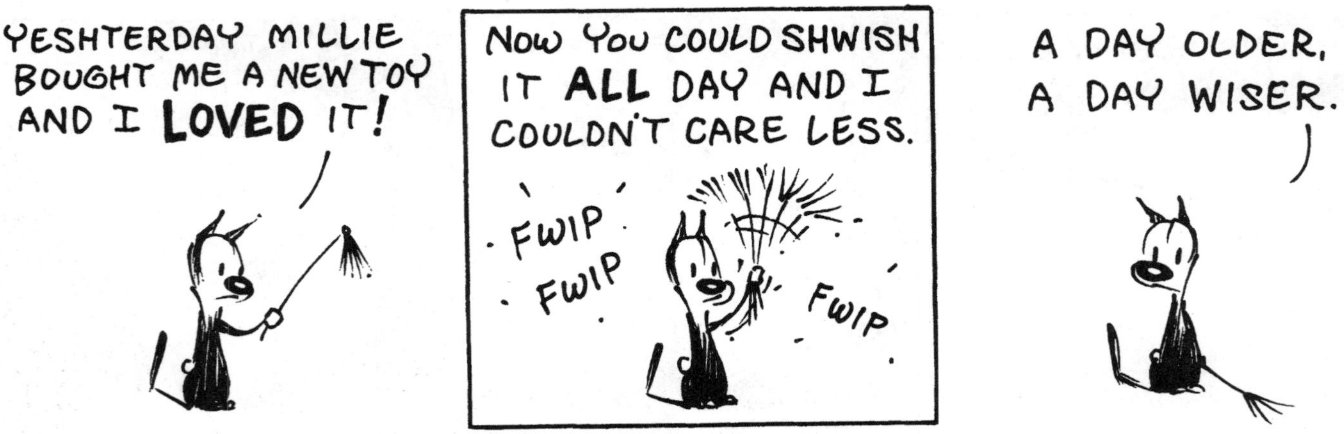
YESHTERDAY MILLIE BOUGHT ME A NEW TOY AND I LOVED IT!
NOW YOU COULD SHWISH IT ALL DAY AND I COULDN'T CARE LESS.
FWIP
FWIP
FWIP
A DAY OLDER, A DAY WISER.

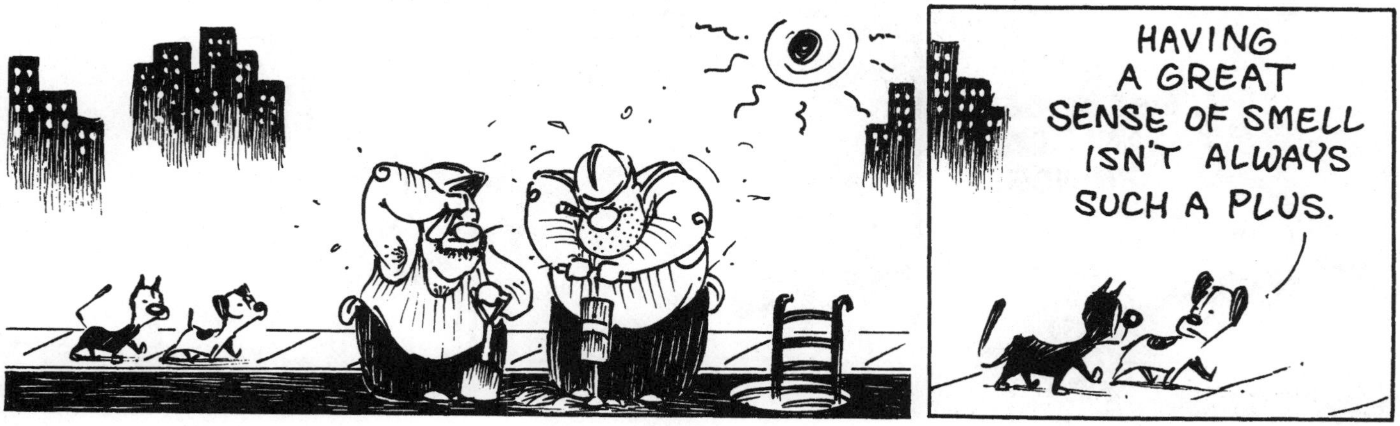
HAVING A GREAT SENSE OF SMELL ISN'T ALWAYS SUCH A PLUS.

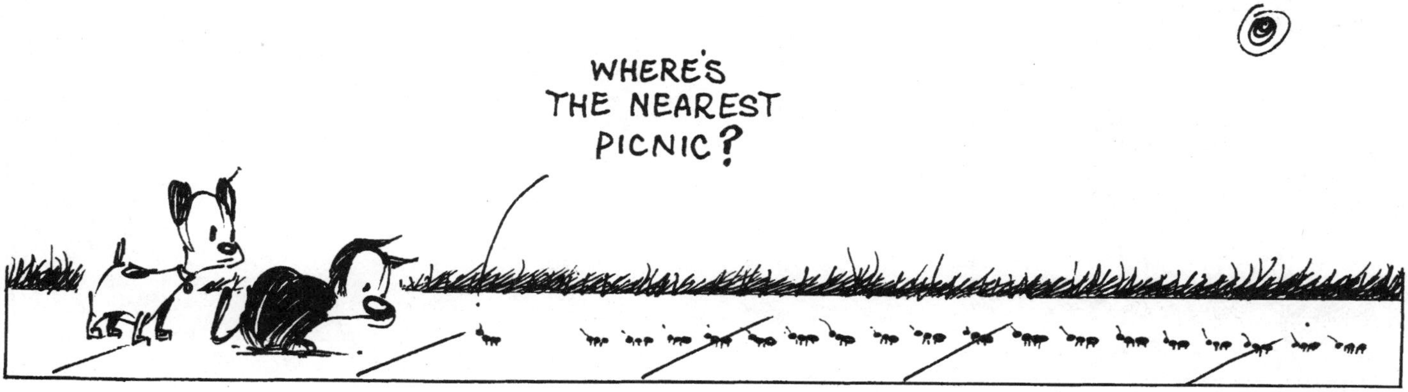
WHERE'S THE NEAREST PICNIC?

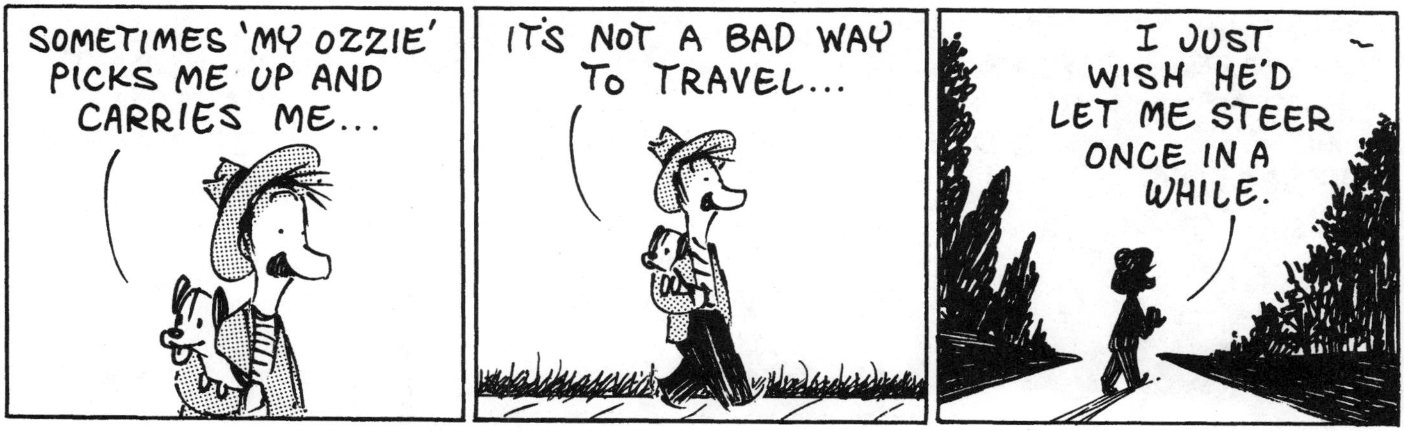
SOMETIMES 'MY OZZIE' PICKS ME UP AND CARRIES ME...
IT'S NOT A BAD WAY TO TRAVEL...
I JUST WISH HE'D LET ME STEER ONCE IN A WHILE.

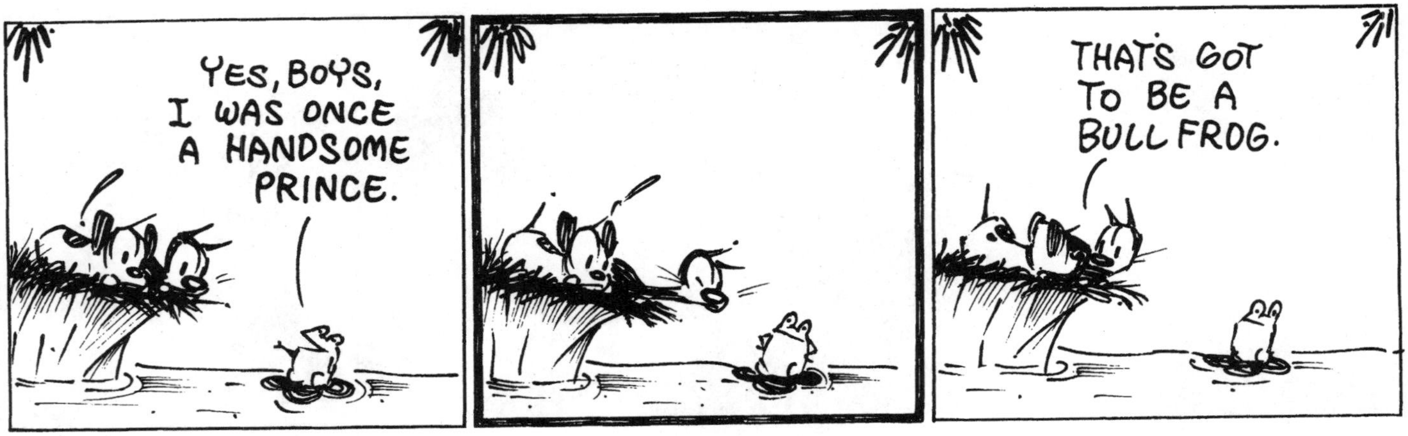
YES, BOYS, I WAS ONCE A HANDSOME PRINCE.
THAT'S GOT TO BE A BULL FROG.

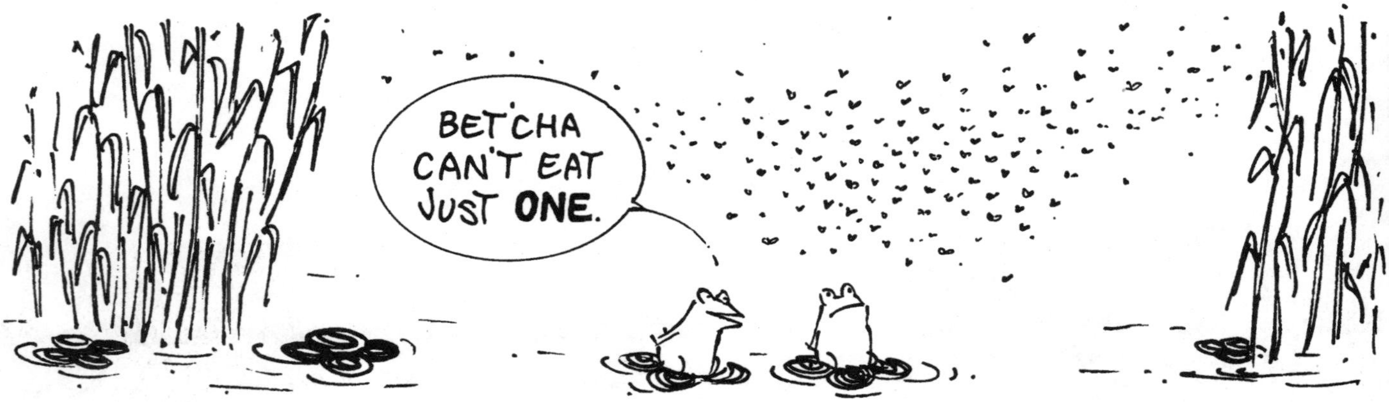
BET'CHA CAN'T EAT JUST **ONE**.

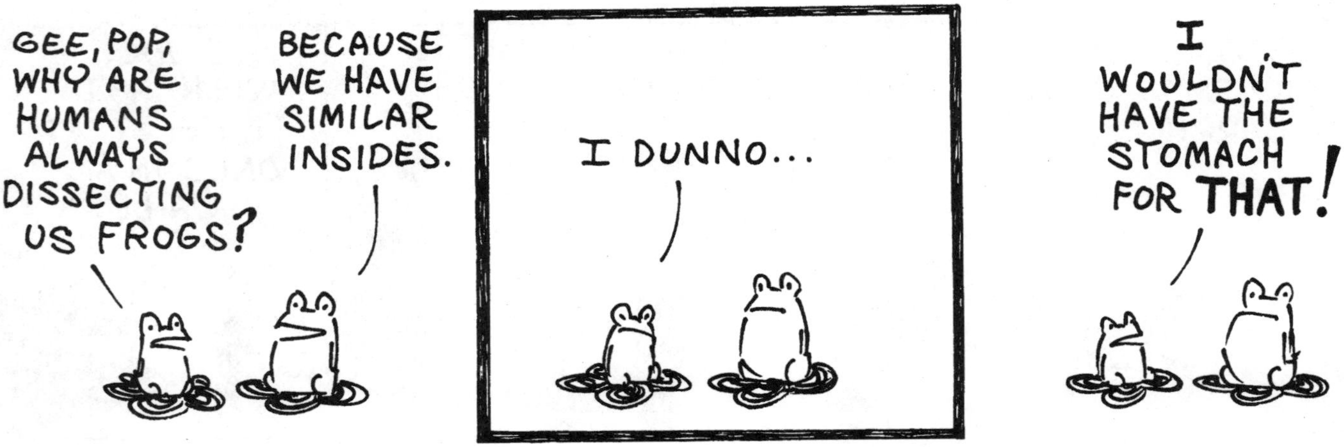
GEE, POP, WHY ARE HUMANS ALWAYS DISSECTING US FROGS?
BECAUSE WE HAVE SIMILAR INSIDES.
I DUNNO...
I WOULDN'T HAVE THE STOMACH FOR **THAT**!

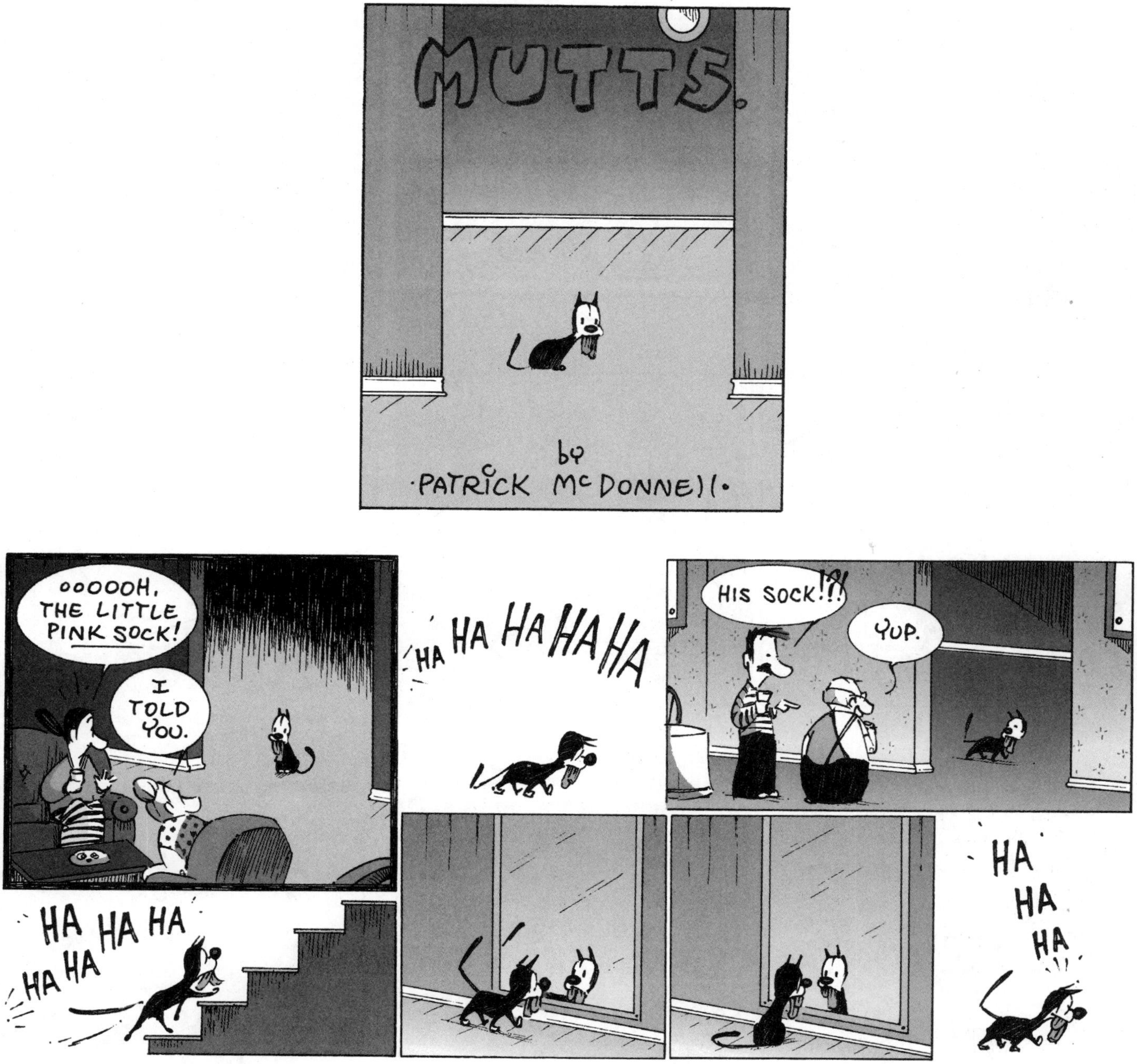
MUTTS
by
PATRICK McDONNELL
OOOOOH, THE LITTLE PINK SOCK!
I TOLD YOU.
HA HA HA HA HA
HIS SOCK!?!
YUP.
HA HA HA HA HA HA
HA HA HA

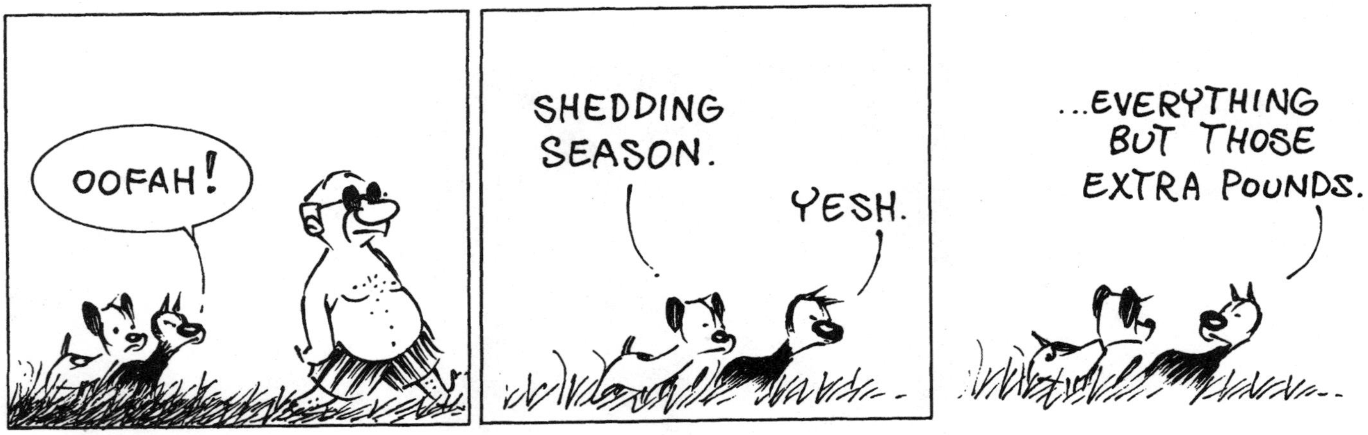
OOFAH!
SHEDDING SEASON.
YESH.
...EVERYTHING BUT THOSE EXTRA POUNDS.

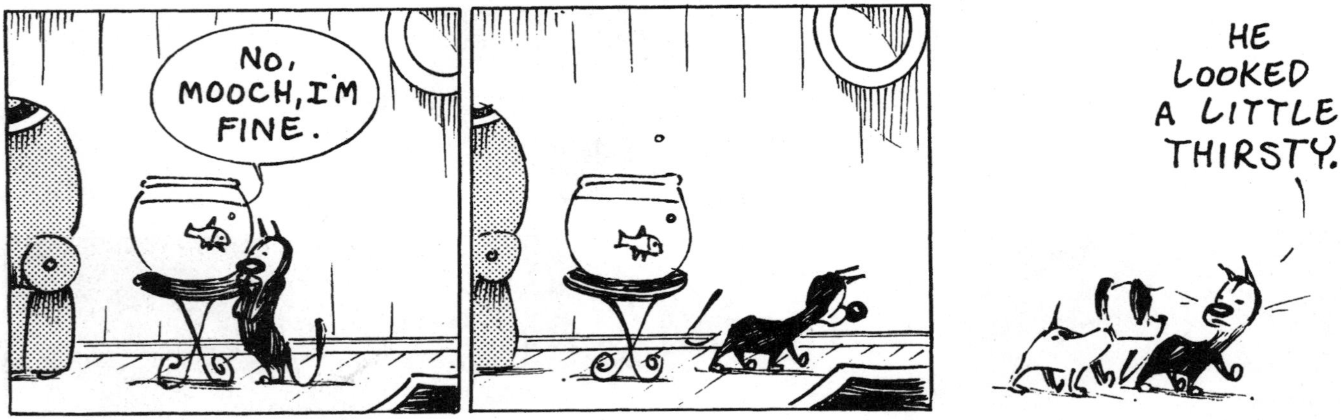
NO, MOOCH, I'M FINE.
HE LOOKED A LITTLE THIRSTY.

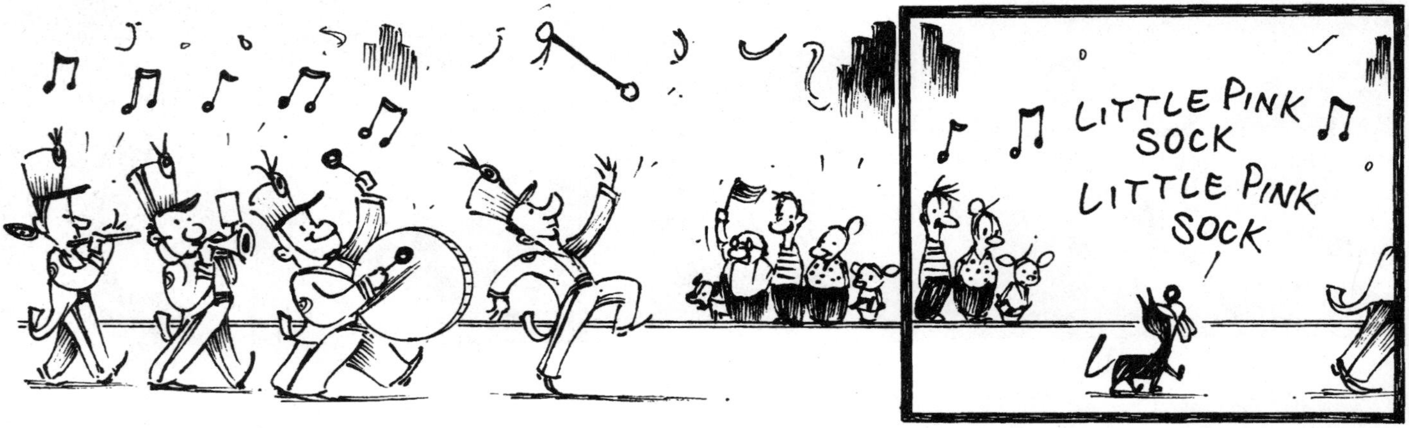
LITTLE PINK SOCK LITTLE PINK SOCK

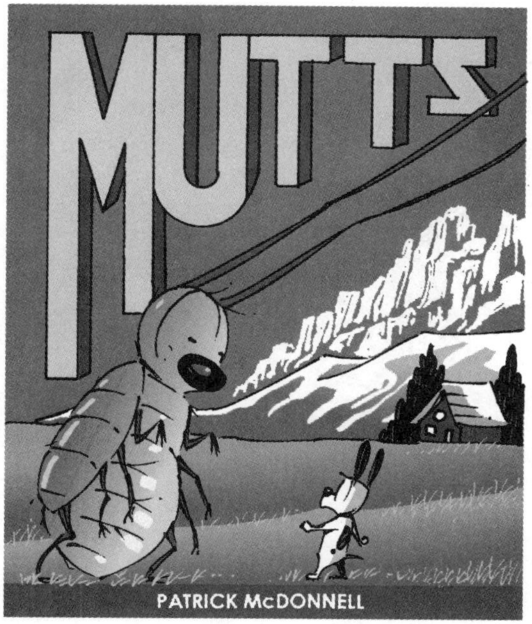
MUTTS
PATRICK McDONNELL

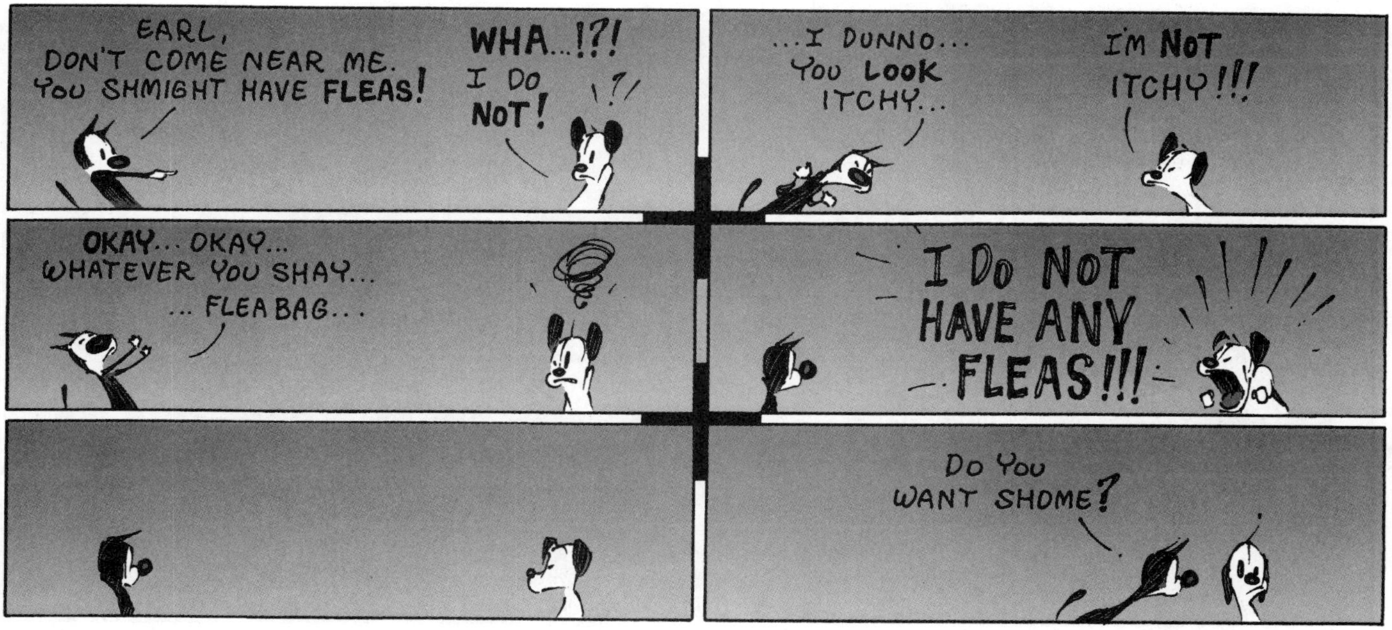
EARL, DON'T COME NEAR ME. YOU SHMIGHT HAVE FLEAS!
WHA...!?!
I DO NOT!
...I DUNNO... YOU LOOK ITCHY...
I'M NOT ITCHY!!!
OKAY... OKAY... WHATEVER YOU SHAY...
... FLEABAG...
I DO NOT HAVE ANY FLEAS!!!
DO YOU WANT SHOME?

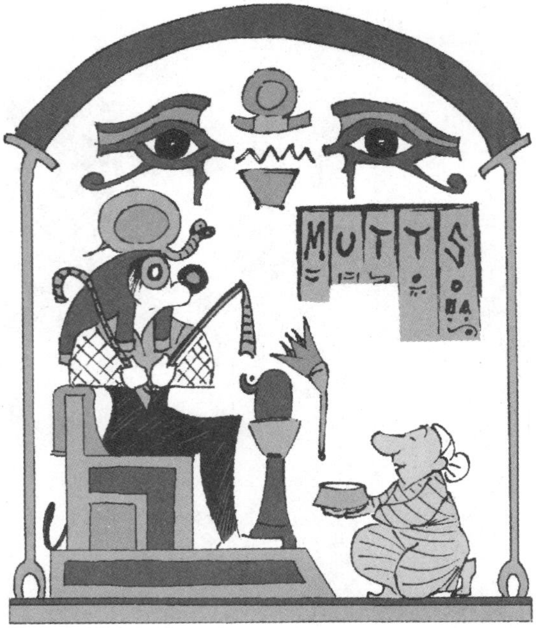
MUTTS

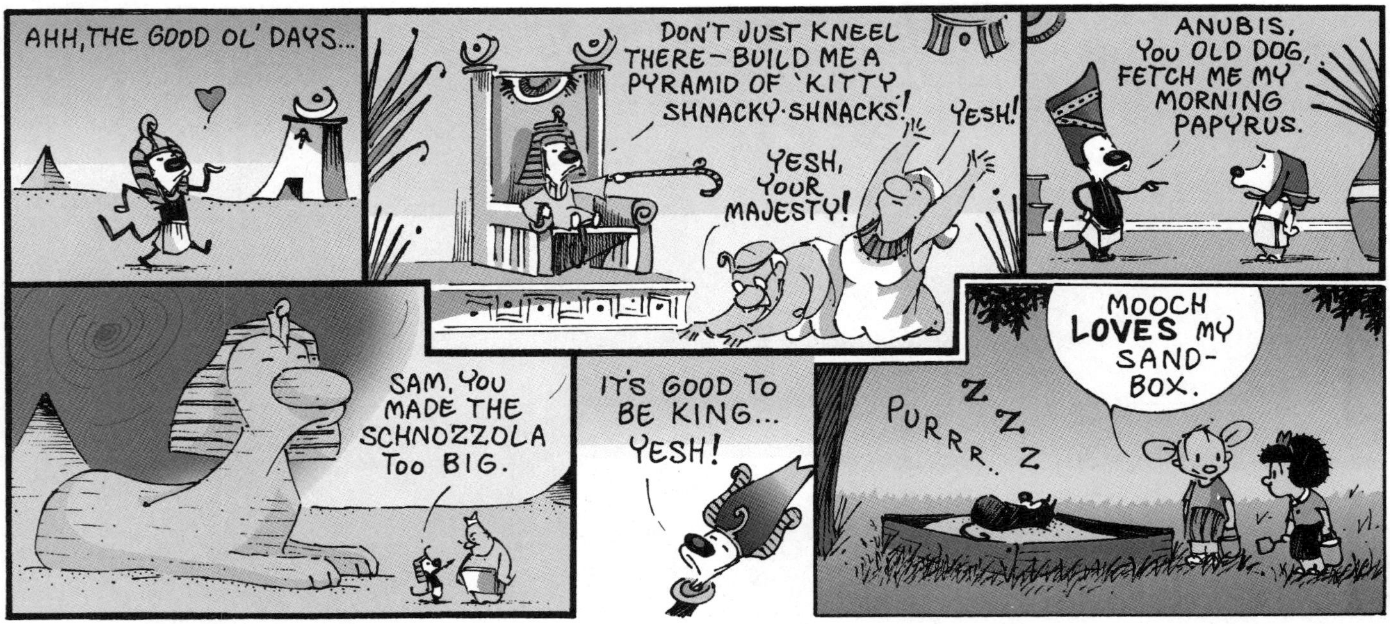
AHH, THE GOOD OL' DAYS...
DON'T JUST KNEEL THERE—BUILD ME A PYRAMID OF 'KITTY SHNACKY·SHNACKS'!
YESH!
YESH, YOUR MAJESTY!
ANUBIS, YOU OLD DOG, FETCH ME MY MORNING PAPYRUS.
SAM, YOU MADE THE SCHNOZZOLA TOO BIG.
IT'S GOOD TO BE KING... YESH!
MOOCH LOVES MY SAND-BOX.
PURRRR..
Z Z Z

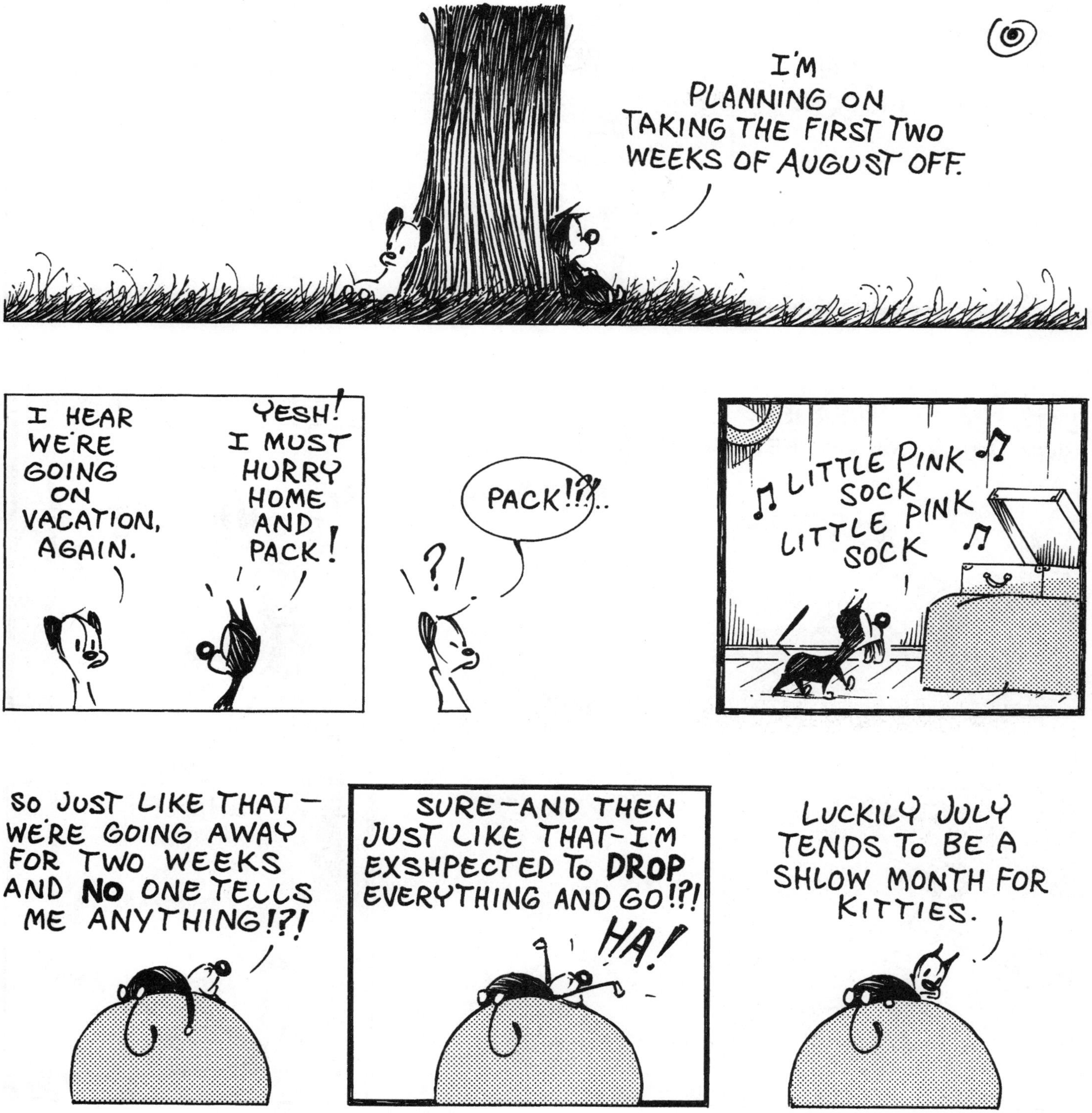

I'M PLANNING ON TAKING THE FIRST TWO WEEKS OF AUGUST OFF.
I HEAR WE'RE GOING ON VACATION, AGAIN.
YESH! I MUST HURRY HOME AND PACK!
PACK!?!..
♫ LITTLE PINK SOCK LITTLE PINK SOCK ♫
SO JUST LIKE THAT— WE'RE GOING AWAY FOR TWO WEEKS AND NO ONE TELLS ME ANYTHING!?!
SURE—AND THEN JUST LIKE THAT—I'M EXSHPECTED TO DROP EVERYTHING AND GO!?!
HA!
LUCKILY JULY TENDS TO BE A SHLOW MONTH FOR KITTIES.

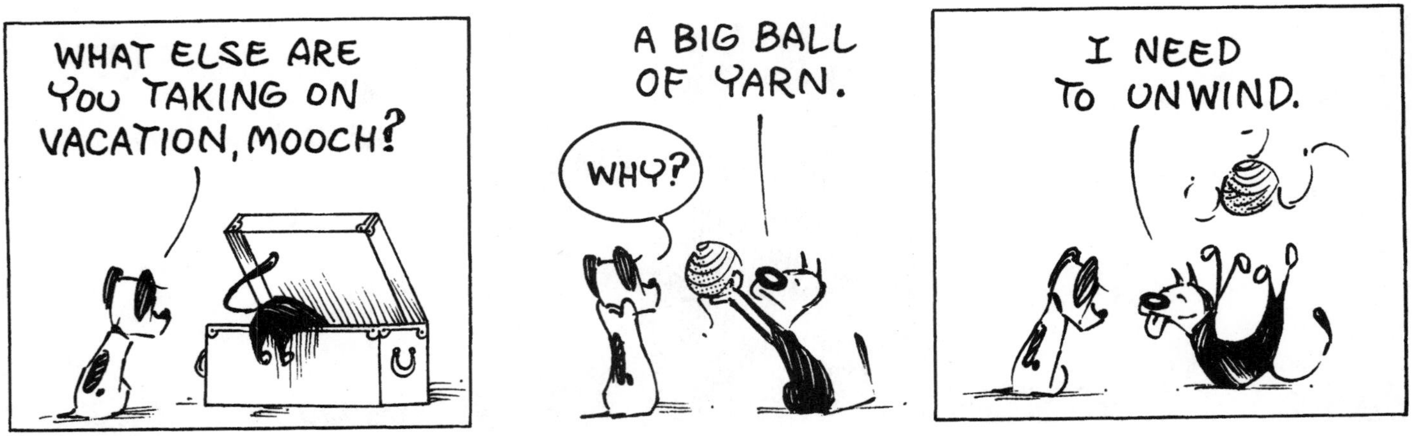
WHAT ELSE ARE YOU TAKING ON VACATION, MOOCH?
A BIG BALL OF YARN.
WHY?
I NEED TO UNWIND.

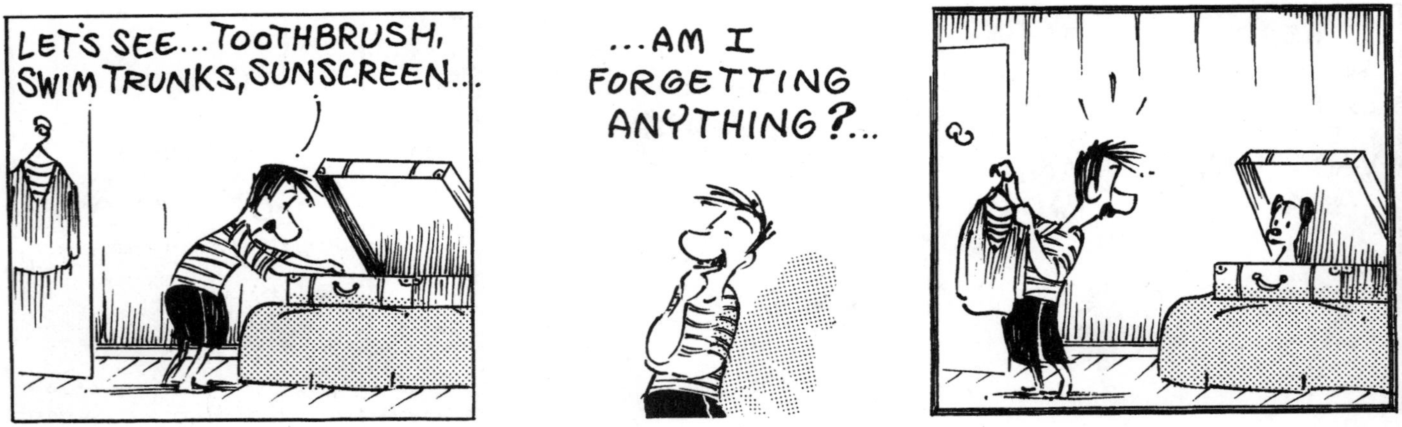
LET'S SEE... TOOTHBRUSH, SWIM TRUNKS, SUNSCREEN...
...AM I FORGETTING ANYTHING?...

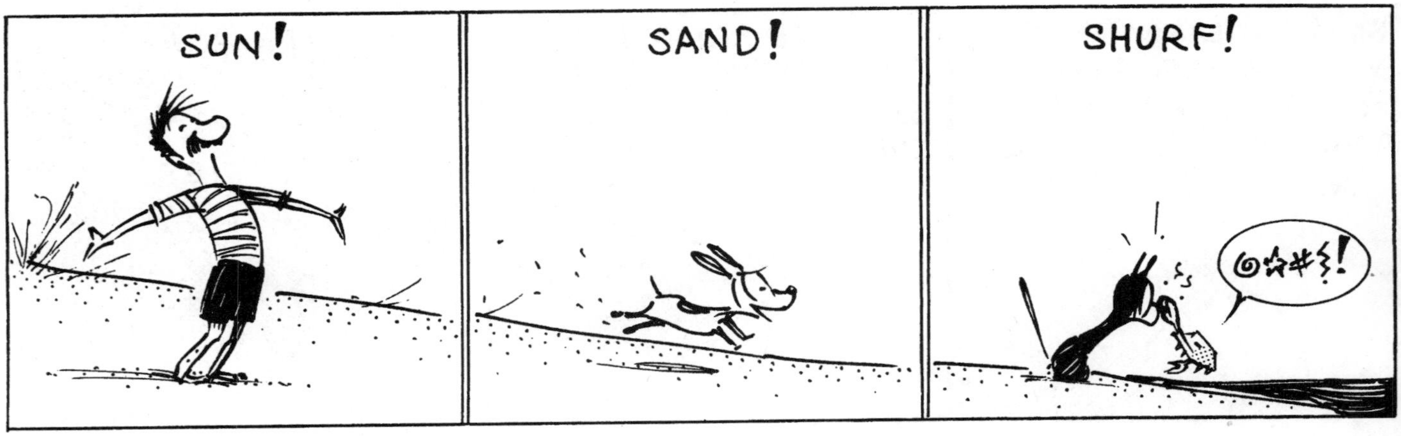
SUN!
SAND!
SHURF!
@☆#$!

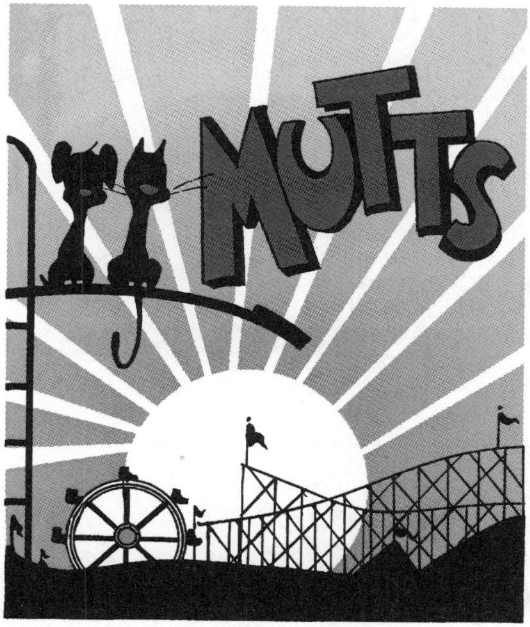

MUTTS

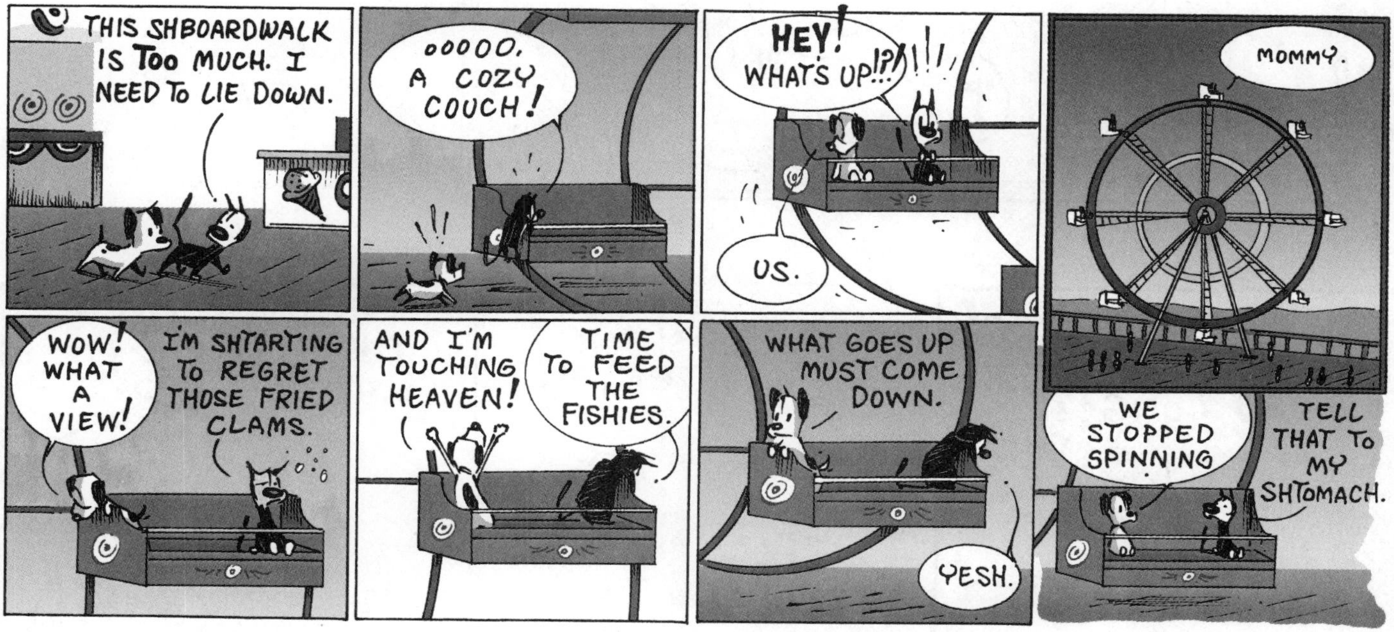

THIS SHBOARDWALK IS TOO MUCH. I NEED TO LIE DOWN.
OOOOO, A COZY COUCH!
HEY! WHAT'S UP!?!
US.
MOMMY.
WOW! WHAT A VIEW!
I'M SHTARTING TO REGRET THOSE FRIED CLAMS.
AND I'M TOUCHING HEAVEN!
TIME TO FEED THE FISHIES.
WHAT GOES UP MUST COME DOWN.
YESH.
WE STOPPED SPINNING
TELL THAT TO MY SHTOMACH.

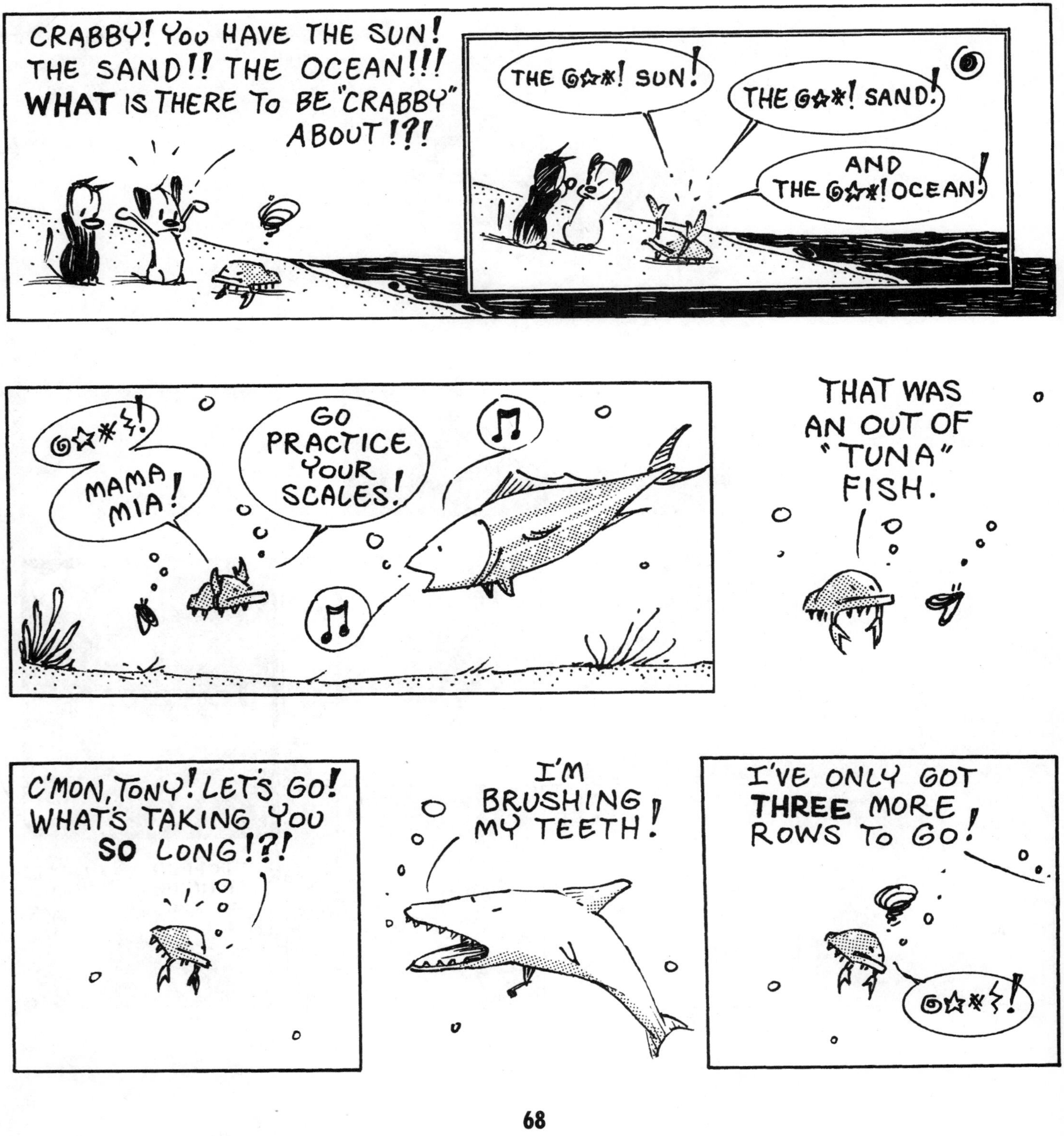
CRABBY! YOU HAVE THE SUN! THE SAND!! THE OCEAN!!! WHAT IS THERE TO BE "CRABBY" ABOUT!?!
THE @☆*! SUN!
THE @☆*! SAND!
AND THE @☆*! OCEAN!
@☆*~!
MAMA MIA!
GO PRACTICE YOUR SCALES!
THAT WAS AN OUT OF "TUNA" FISH.
C'MON, TONY! LET'S GO! WHAT'S TAKING YOU SO LONG!?!
I'M BRUSHING MY TEETH!
I'VE ONLY GOT THREE MORE ROWS TO GO!
@☆*~!

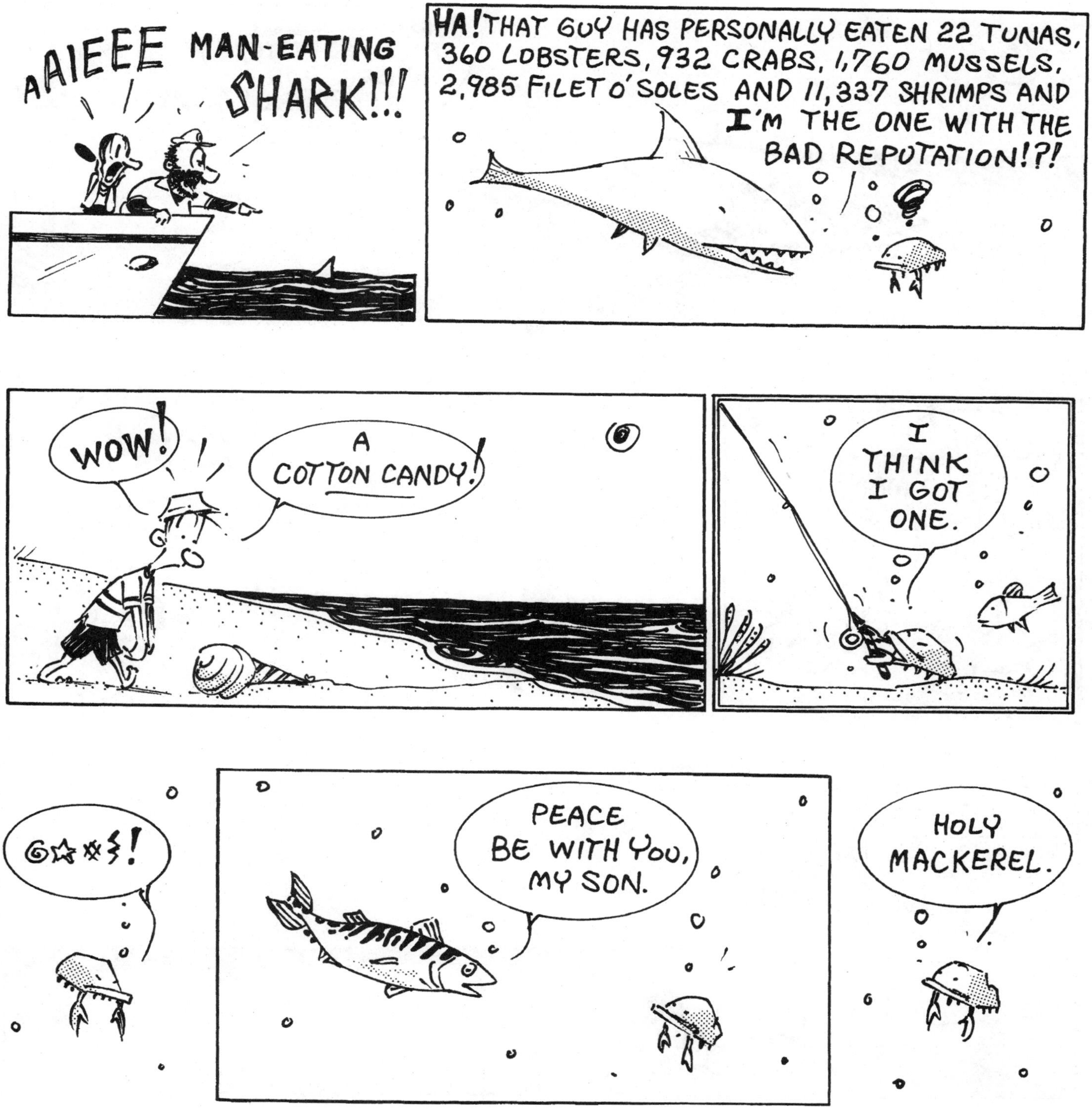
AAIEEE MAN-EATING SHARK!!!
HA! THAT GUY HAS PERSONALLY EATEN 22 TUNAS, 360 LOBSTERS, 932 CRABS, 1,760 MUSSELS, 2,985 FILET O' SOLES AND 11,337 SHRIMPS AND I'M THE ONE WITH THE BAD REPUTATION!?!
WOW!
A COTTON CANDY!
I THINK I GOT ONE.
PEACE BE WITH YOU, MY SON.
HOLY MACKEREL.

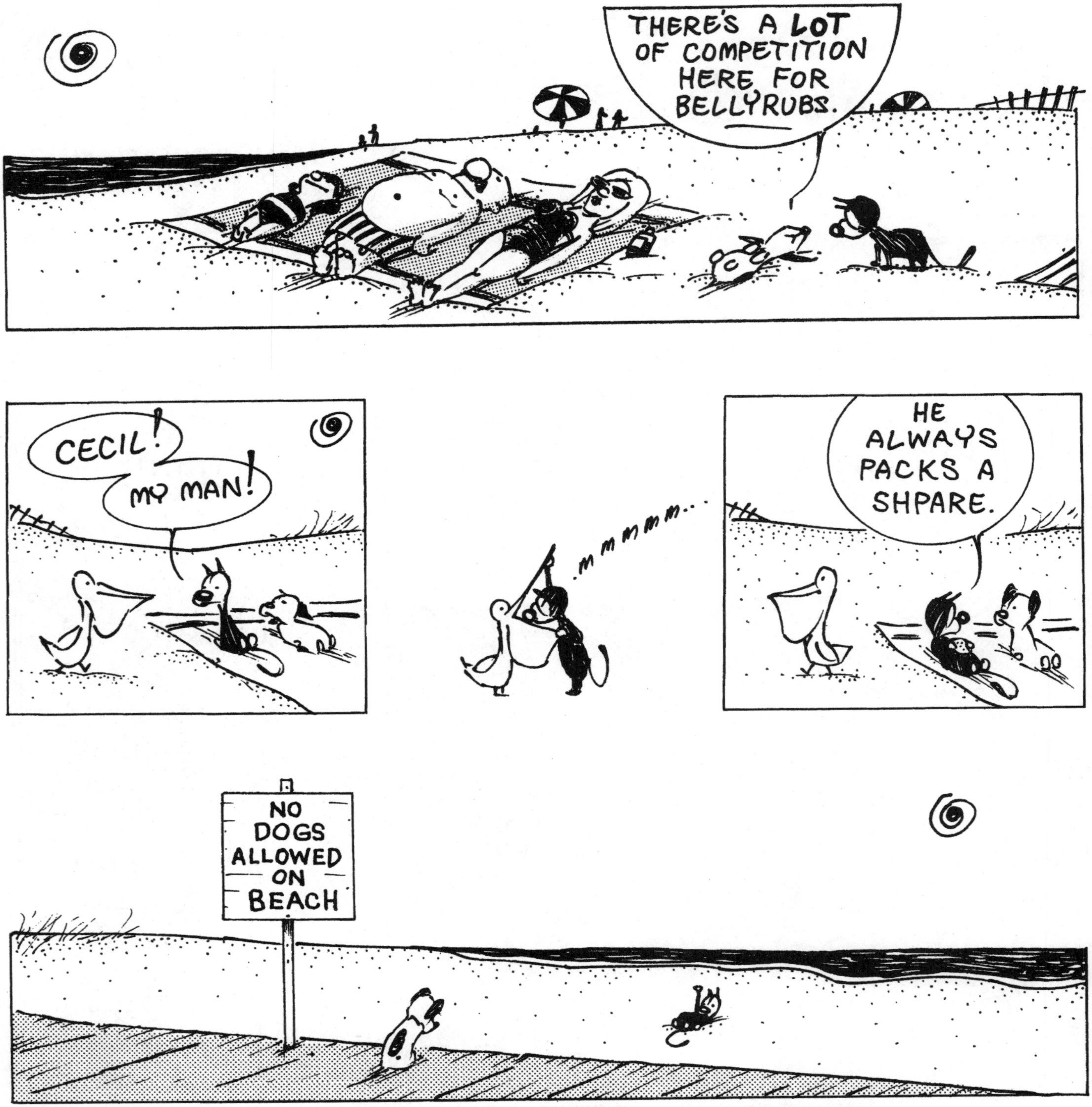
THERE'S A LOT OF COMPETITION HERE FOR BELLYRUBS.
CECIL!
MY MAN!
...MMMMMM...
HE ALWAYS PACKS A SHPARE.
NO DOGS ALLOWED ON BEACH

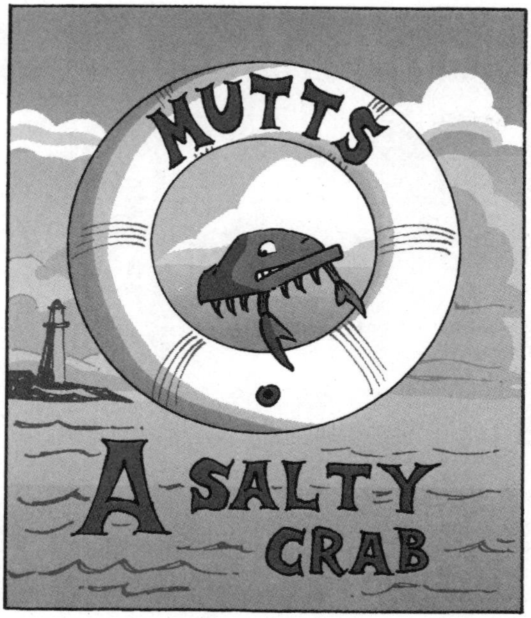
MUTTS
A SALTY CRAB

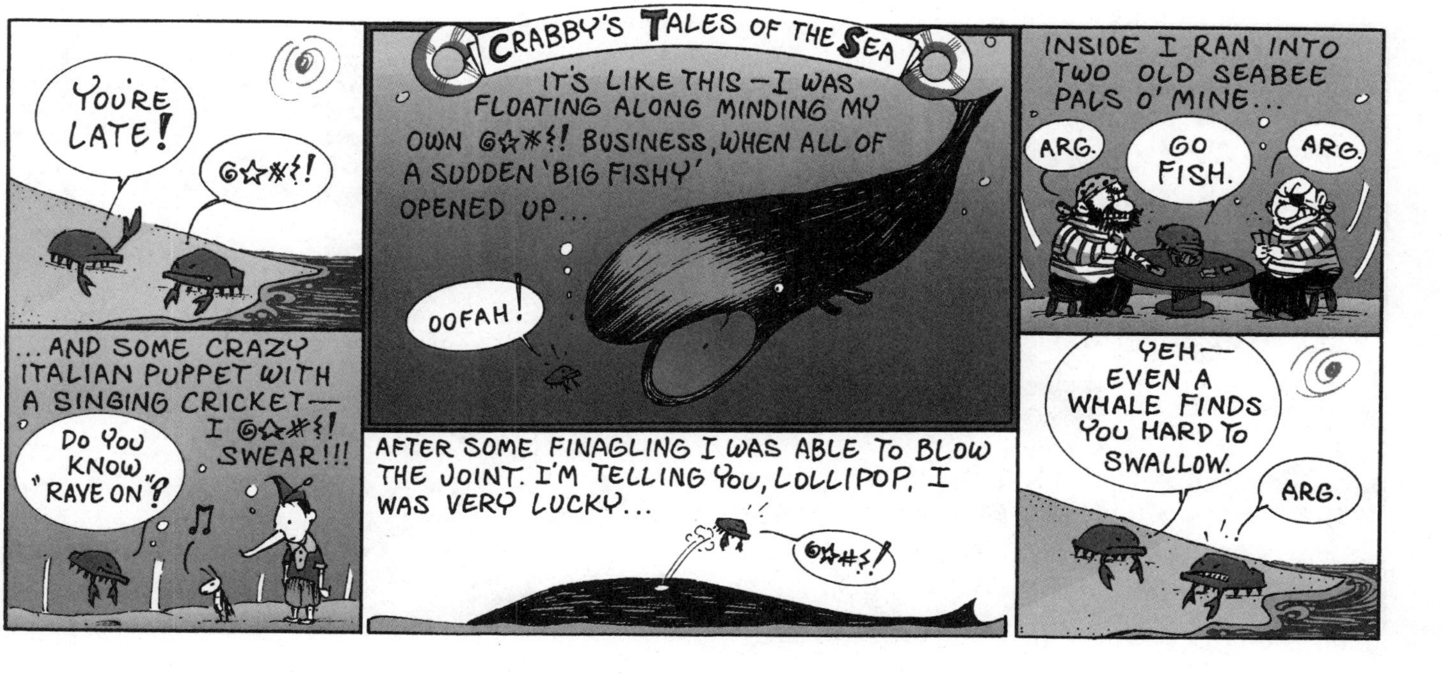
YOU'RE LATE!
G☆*$!
CRABBY'S TALES OF THE SEA
IT'S LIKE THIS—I WAS FLOATING ALONG MINDING MY OWN G☆*$! BUSINESS, WHEN ALL OF A SUDDEN 'BIG FISHY' OPENED UP...
OOFAH!
INSIDE I RAN INTO TWO OLD SEABEE PALS O' MINE...
ARG.
GO FISH.
ARG.
...AND SOME CRAZY ITALIAN PUPPET WITH A SINGING CRICKET— I G☆*$! SWEAR!!!
DO YOU KNOW "RAVE ON"?
AFTER SOME FINAGLING I WAS ABLE TO BLOW THE JOINT. I'M TELLING YOU, LOLLIPOP, I WAS VERY LUCKY...
G☆#$!
YEH— EVEN A WHALE FINDS YOU HARD TO SWALLOW.
ARG.

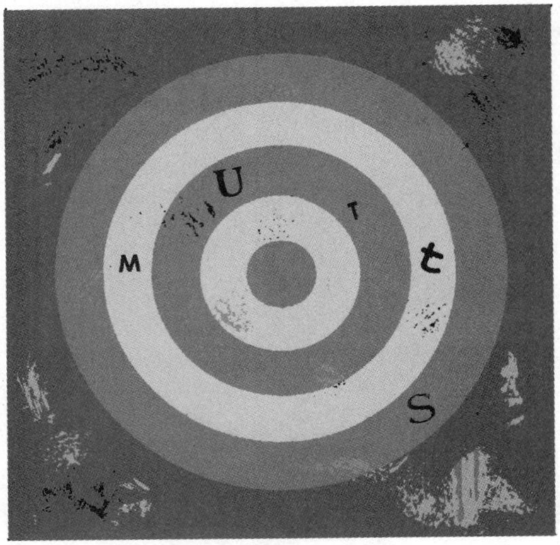
M U T t S

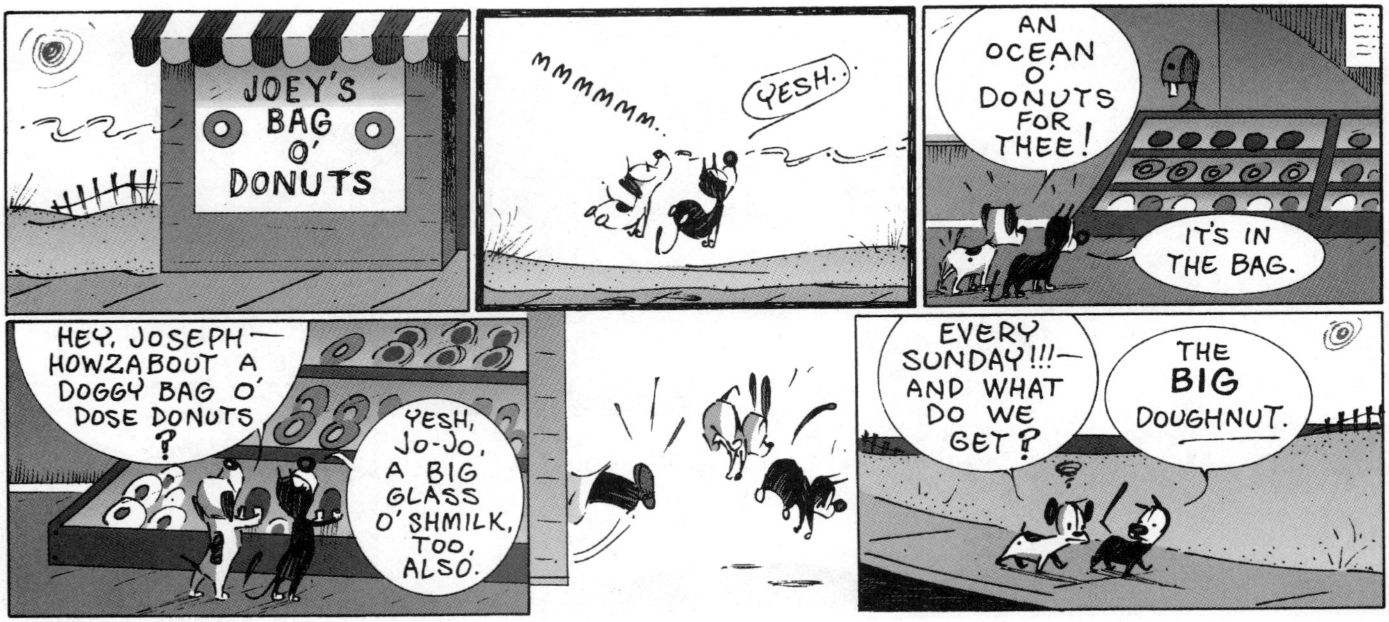
JOEY'S BAG O' DONUTS
MMMMMMM..
YESH..
AN OCEAN O' DONUTS FOR THEE!
IT'S IN THE BAG.
HEY, JOSEPH— HOWZABOUT A DOGGY BAG O' DOSE DONUTS ?
YESH, JO-JO, A BIG GLASS O'SHMILK, TOO, ALSO.
EVERY SUNDAY!!!— AND WHAT DO WE GET?
THE BIG DOUGHNUT.

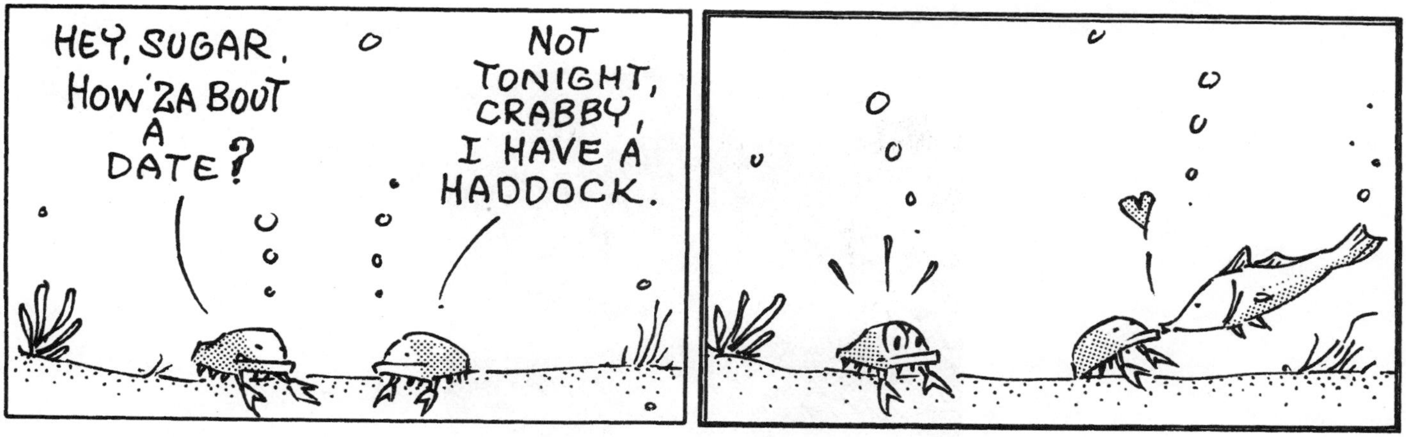
HEY, SUGAR. HOW'ZA BOUT A DATE?
NOT TONIGHT, CRABBY, I HAVE A HADDOCK.

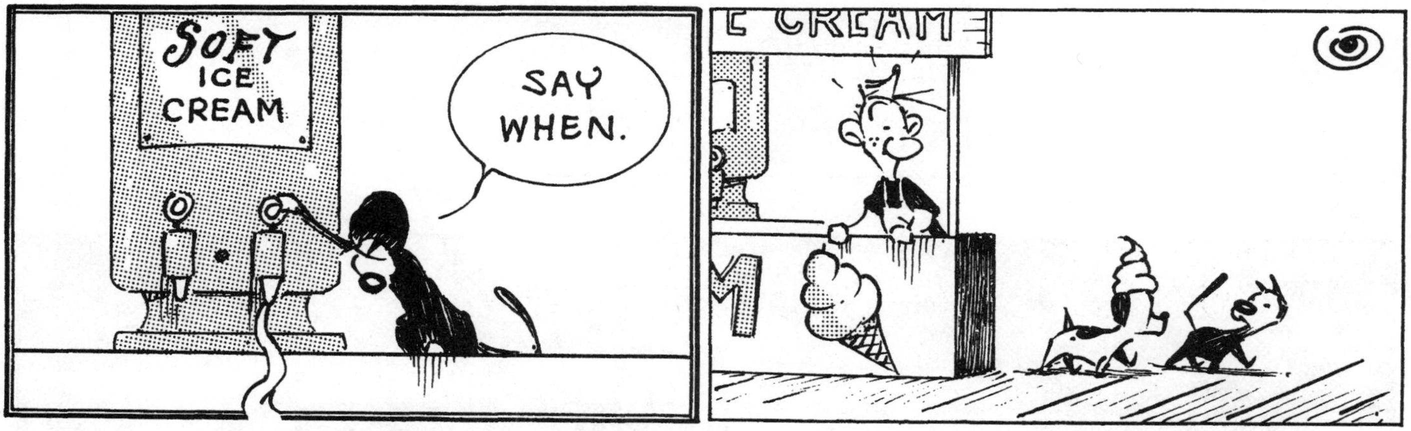
SOFT ICE CREAM
SAY WHEN.
E CREAM

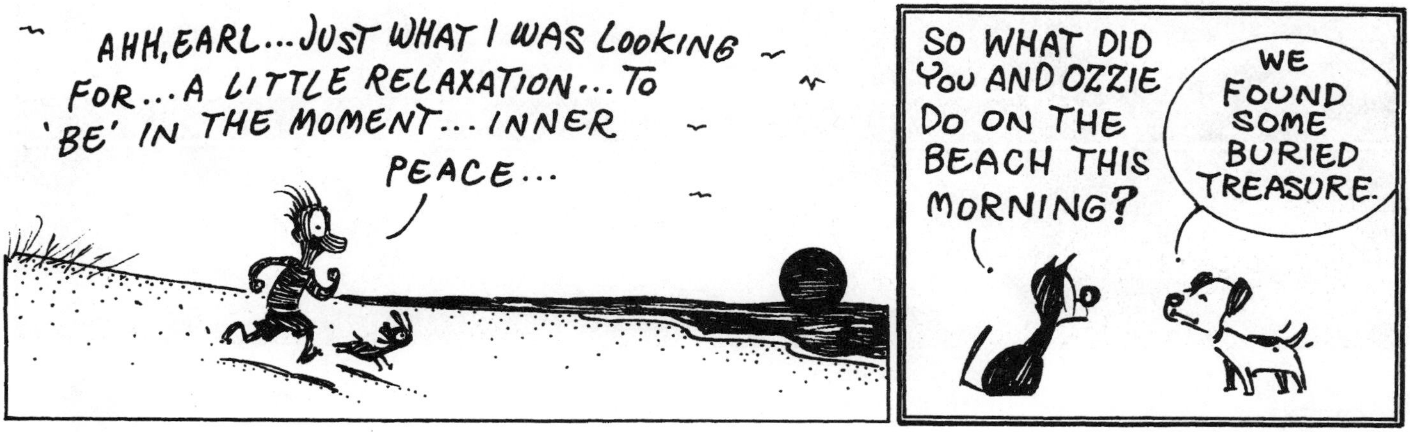
AHH, EARL... JUST WHAT I WAS LOOKING FOR... A LITTLE RELAXATION... TO 'BE' IN THE MOMENT... INNER PEACE...
SO WHAT DID YOU AND OZZIE DO ON THE BEACH THIS MORNING?
WE FOUND SOME BURIED TREASURE.

MUTTS

DO YOU MISS HOME, EARL?
?
HOME IS WHERE THE OZZIE IS.

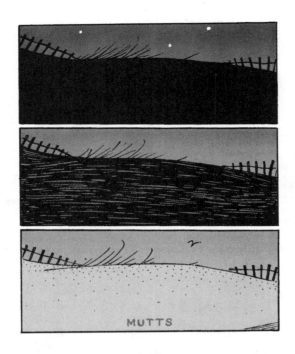

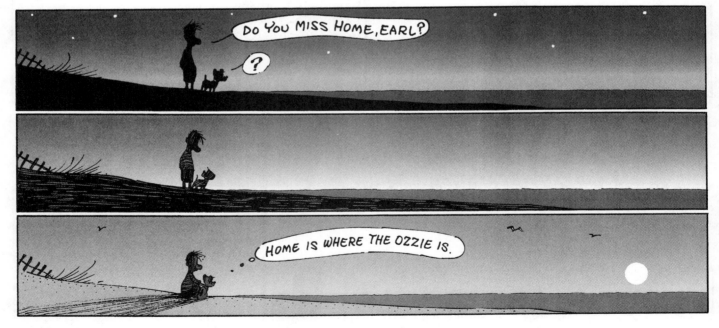

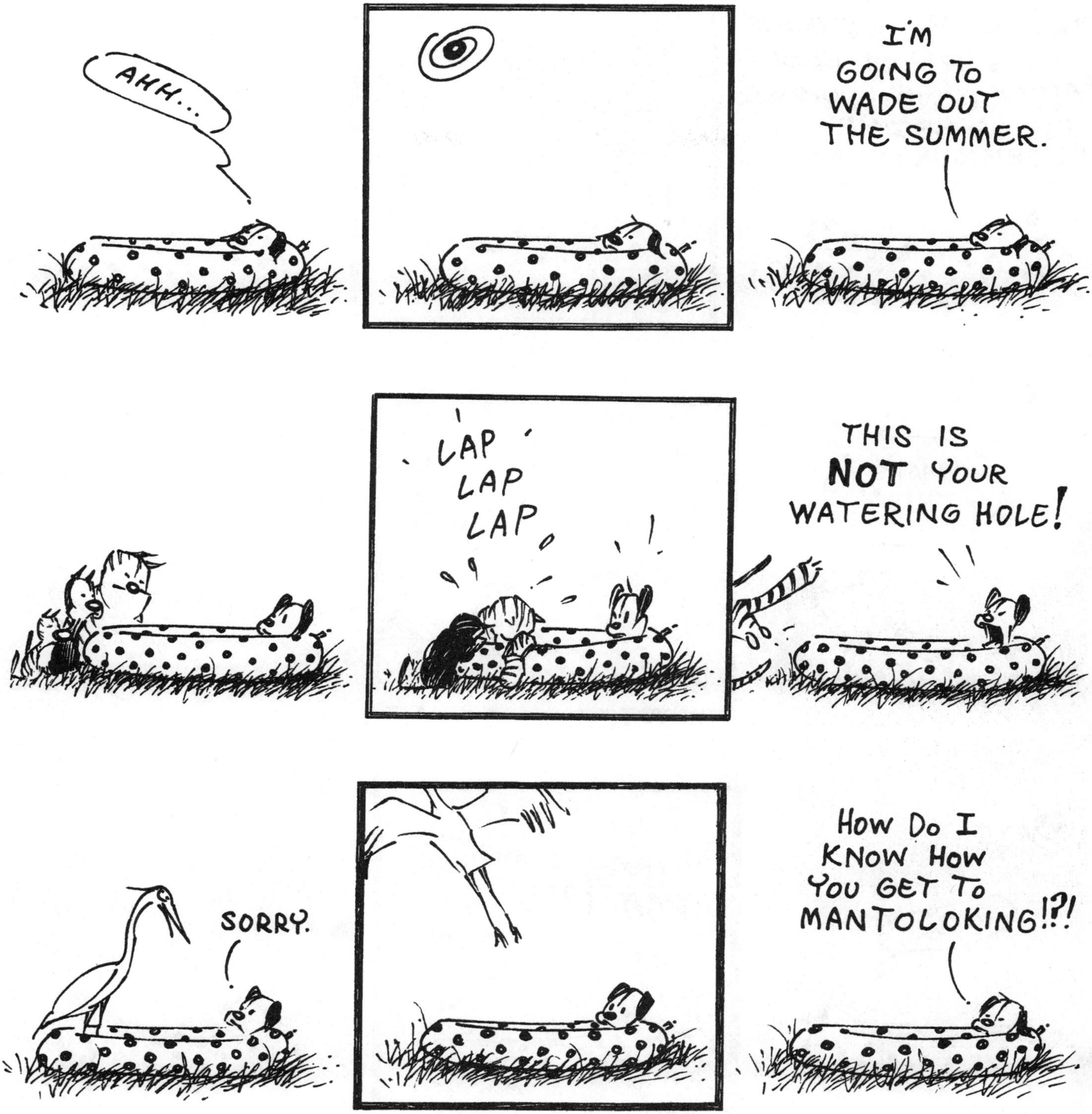
AHH...
I'M GOING TO WADE OUT THE SUMMER.
LAP LAP LAP
THIS IS **NOT** YOUR WATERING HOLE!
SORRY.
HOW DO I KNOW HOW YOU GET TO MANTOLOKING!?!

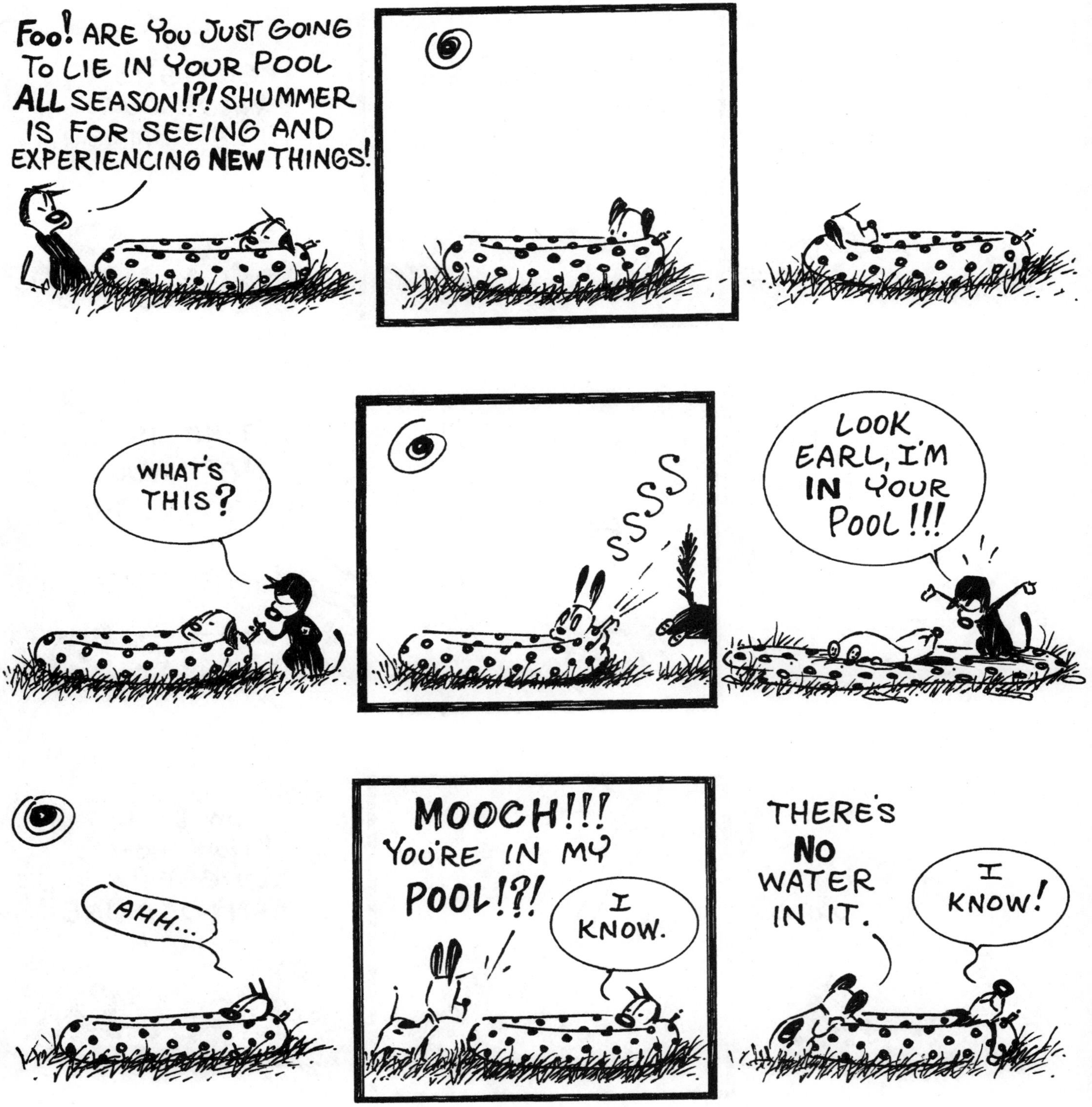
FOO! ARE YOU JUST GOING TO LIE IN YOUR POOL ALL SEASON!?! SHUMMER IS FOR SEEING AND EXPERIENCING NEW THINGS!
WHAT'S THIS?
SSSS
LOOK EARL, I'M IN YOUR POOL!!!
AHH...
MOOCH!!! YOU'RE IN MY POOL!?!
I KNOW.
THERE'S NO WATER IN IT.
I KNOW!

MUTTS

HOW Do WORMS TRAVEL, EARL!?!
THEY WIGGLE.
UMF.
UGH.
ARG.
GA·GA.
HOW AM I DOIN'?
IS THAT CAT DUE FOR SOME SHOTS?

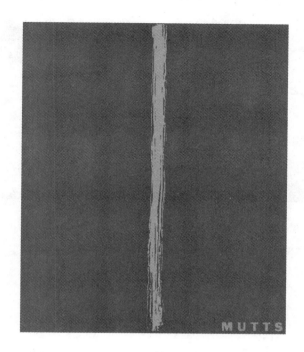

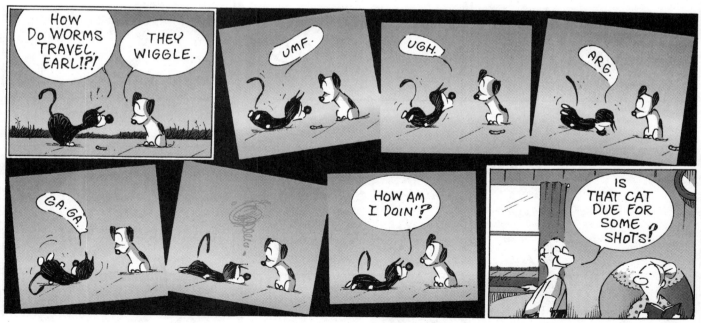

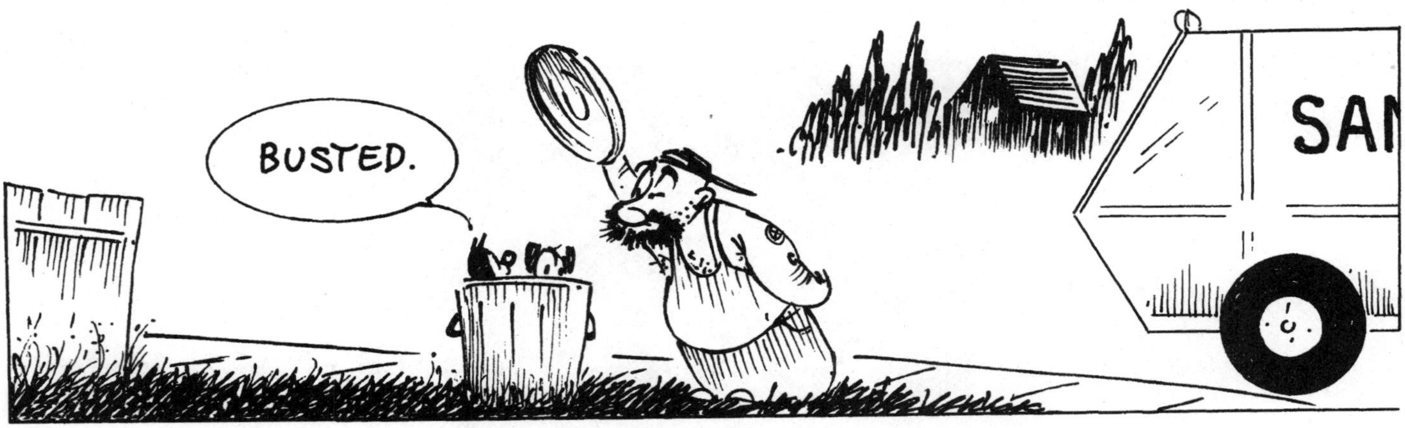
BUSTED.
SA

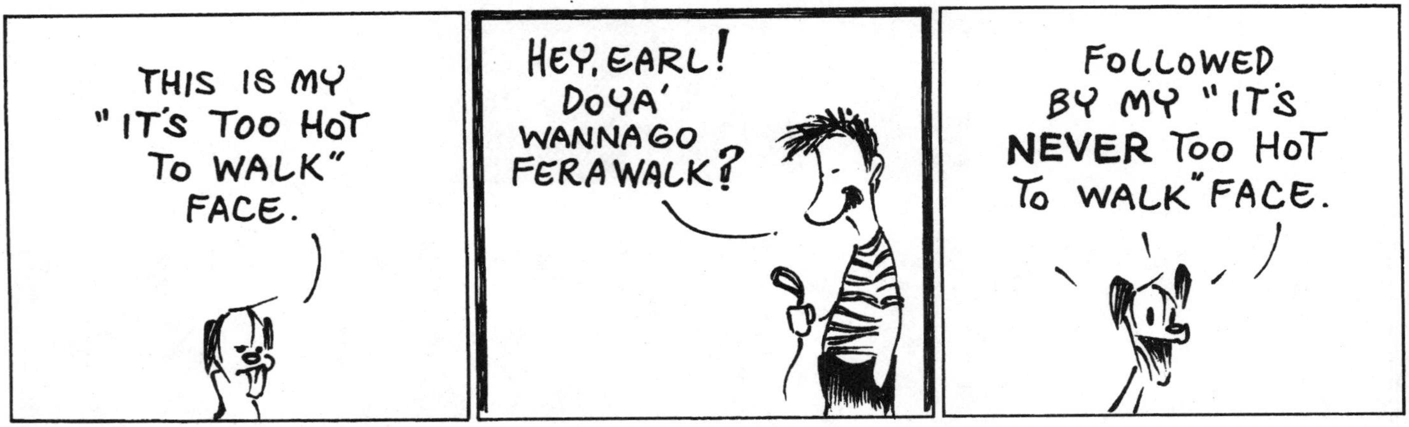
THIS IS MY "IT'S TOO HOT TO WALK" FACE.
HEY, EARL! DOYA' WANNAGO FERAWALK?
FOLLOWED BY MY "IT'S NEVER TOO HOT TO WALK" FACE.

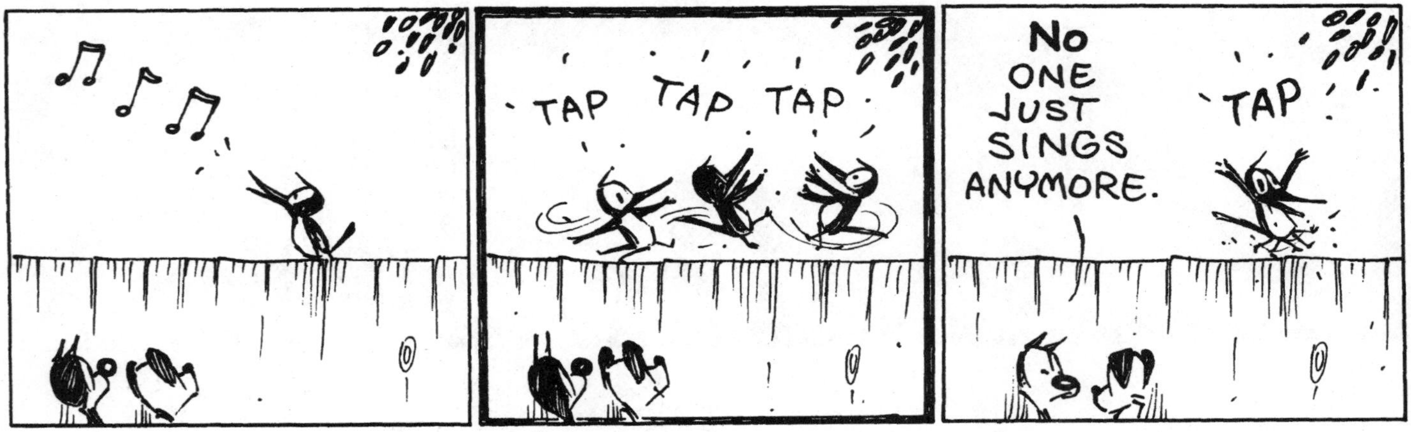
TAP TAP TAP
NO ONE JUST SINGS ANYMORE.
TAP

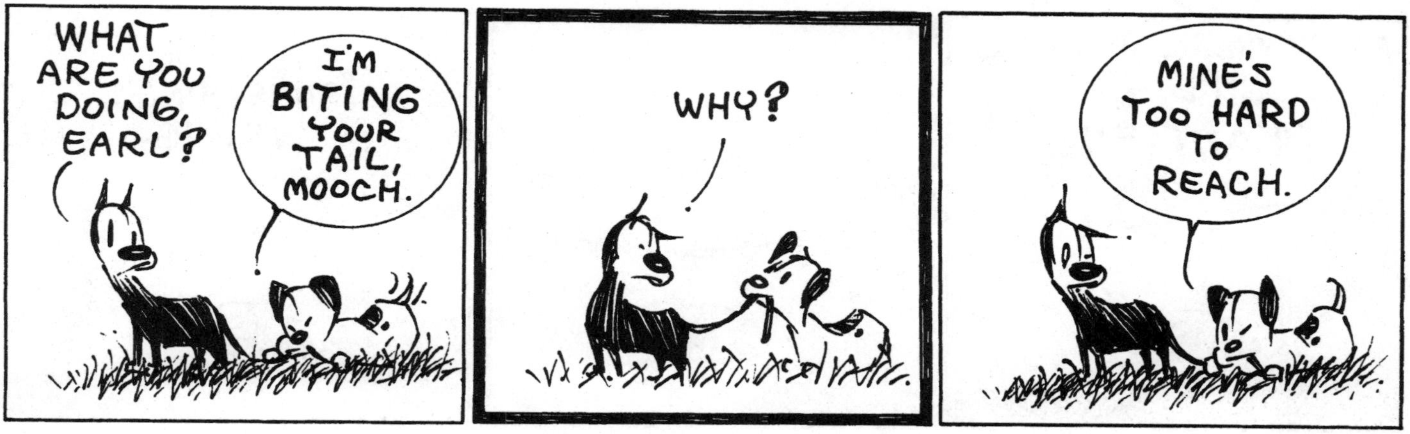
WHAT ARE YOU DOING, EARL?
I'M BITING YOUR TAIL, MOOCH.
WHY?
MINE'S TOO HARD TO REACH.

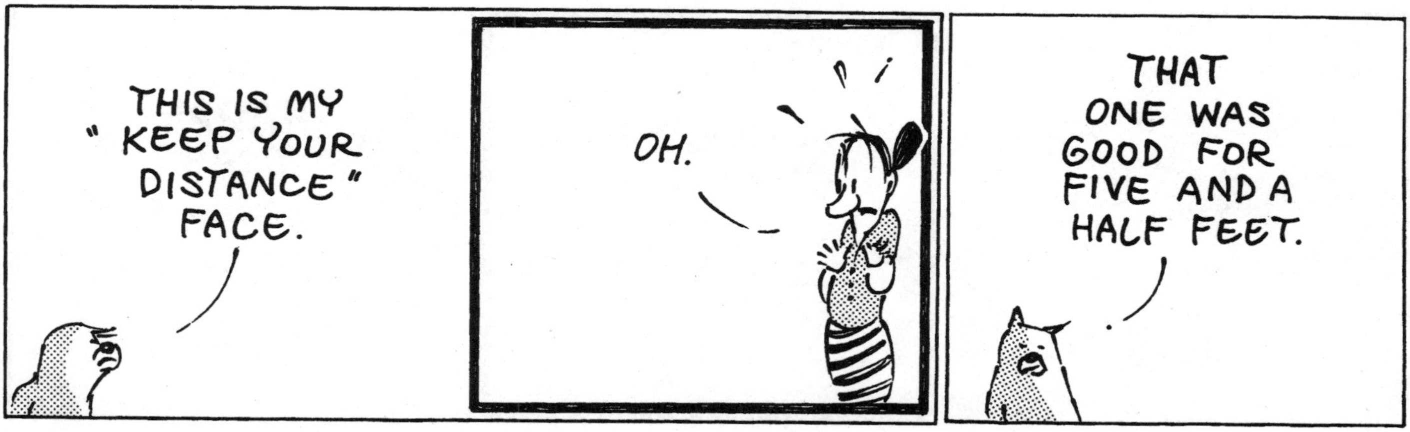
THIS IS MY "KEEP YOUR DISTANCE" FACE.
OH.
THAT ONE WAS GOOD FOR FIVE AND A HALF FEET.

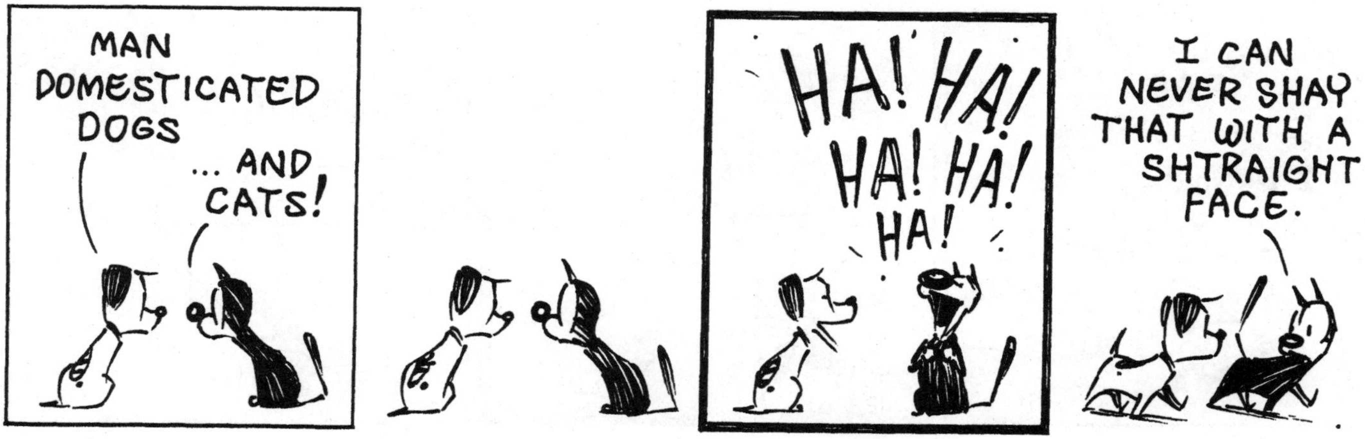
MAN DOMESTICATED DOGS
... AND CATS!
HA! HA! HA! HA! HA!
I CAN NEVER SHAY THAT WITH A SHTRAIGHT FACE.

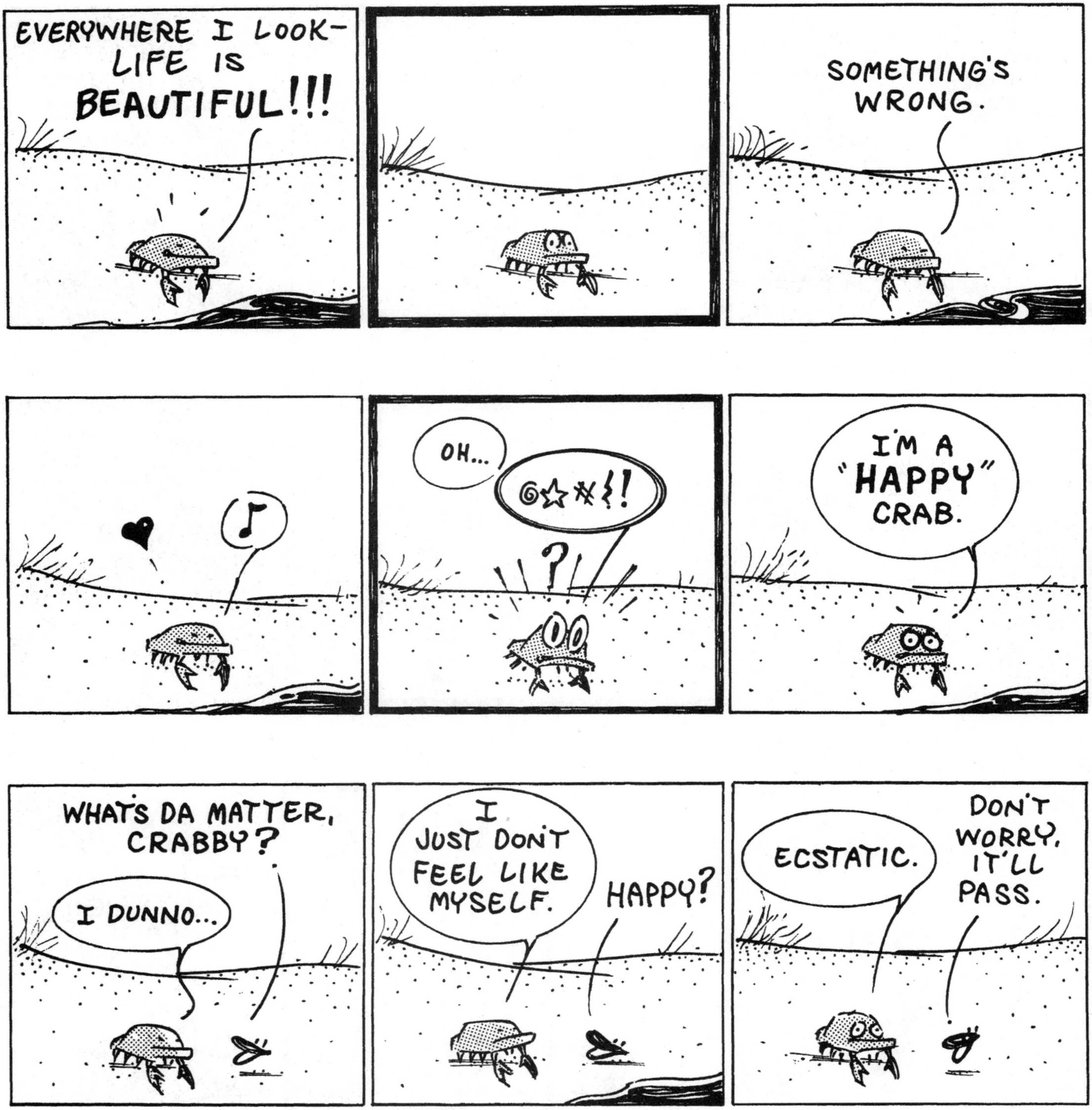
EVERYWHERE I LOOK- LIFE IS BEAUTIFUL!!!
SOMETHING'S WRONG.
OH...
I'M A "HAPPY" CRAB.
WHAT'S DA MATTER, CRABBY?
I DUNNO...
I JUST DON'T FEEL LIKE MYSELF.
HAPPY?
ECSTATIC.
DON'T WORRY, IT'LL PASS.

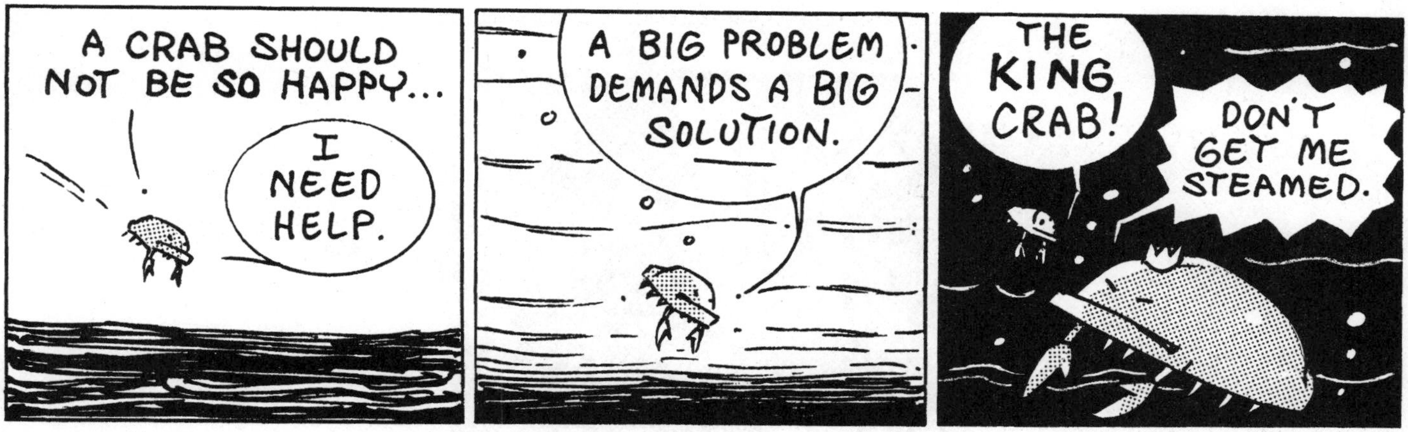
A CRAB SHOULD NOT BE SO HAPPY...
I NEED HELP.
A BIG PROBLEM DEMANDS A BIG SOLUTION.
THE KING CRAB!
DON'T GET ME STEAMED.

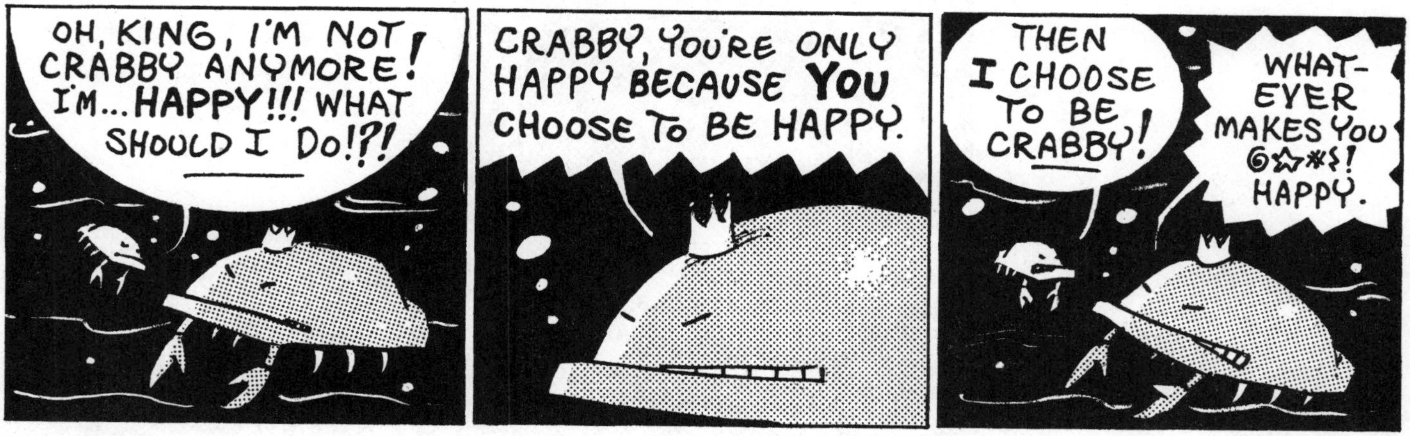
OH, KING, I'M NOT CRABBY ANYMORE! I'M... HAPPY!!! WHAT SHOULD I DO!?!
CRABBY, YOU'RE ONLY HAPPY BECAUSE YOU CHOOSE TO BE HAPPY.
THEN I CHOOSE TO BE CRABBY!
WHAT-EVER MAKES YOU @☆*$! HAPPY.

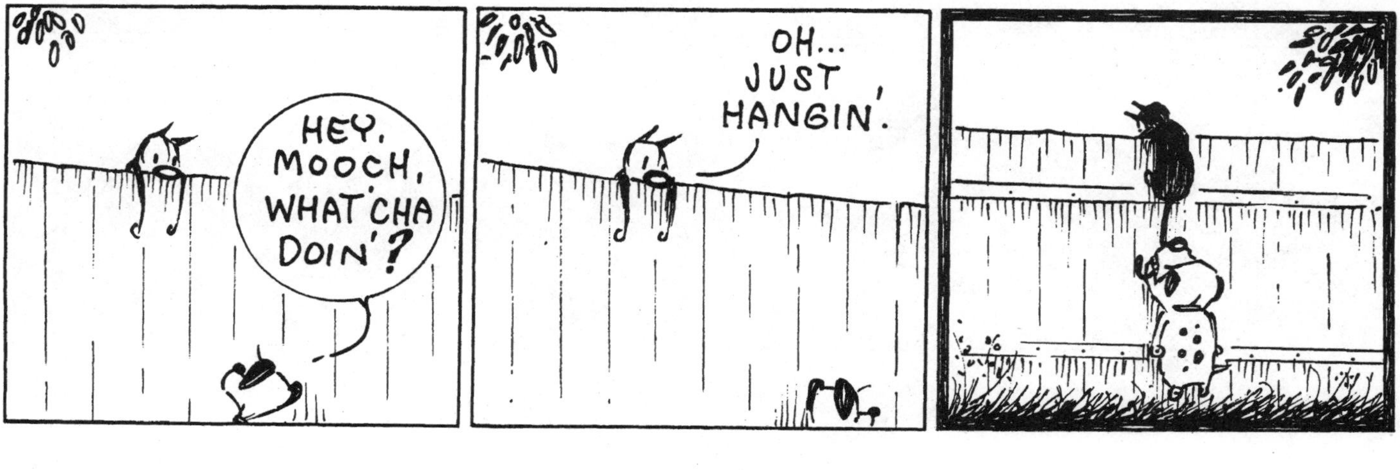
HEY, MOOCH, WHAT'CHA DOIN'?
OH... JUST HANGIN'.

SODA CAN.
SHOE BOX.
JUICE BOTTLE.
CIGARETTE PACK.
FAST-FOOD BAG.
PLASTIC CUP.
OOOOH. A FISH!
CANDY WRAPPER.
NEWSPAPER.

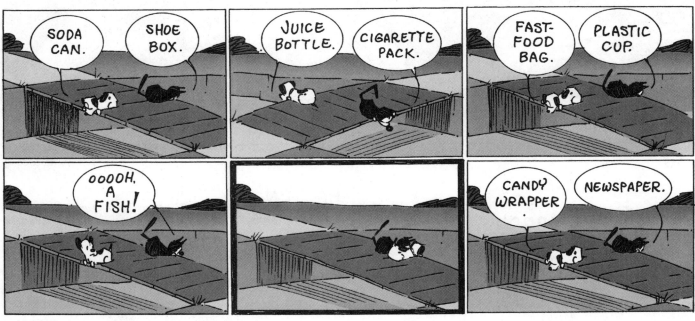

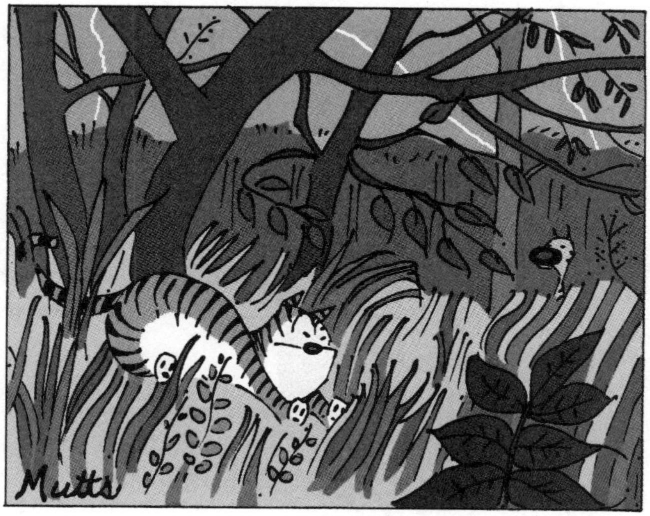
Mutts

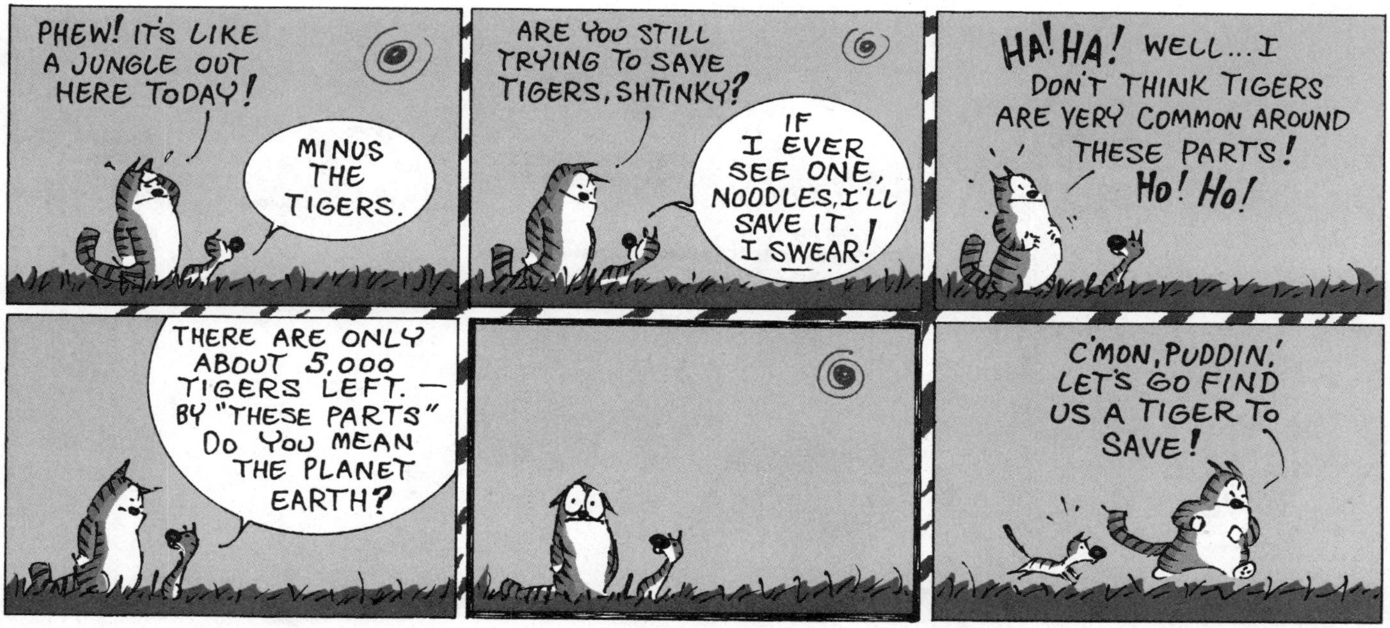
PHEW! IT'S LIKE A JUNGLE OUT HERE TODAY!
MINUS THE TIGERS.
ARE YOU STILL TRYING TO SAVE TIGERS, SHTINKY?
IF I EVER SEE ONE, NOODLES, I'LL SAVE IT. I SWEAR!
HA! HA! WELL... I DON'T THINK TIGERS ARE VERY COMMON AROUND THESE PARTS! HO! HO!
THERE ARE ONLY ABOUT 5,000 TIGERS LEFT. — BY "THESE PARTS" DO YOU MEAN THE PLANET EARTH?
C'MON, PUDDIN.' LET'S GO FIND US A TIGER TO SAVE!

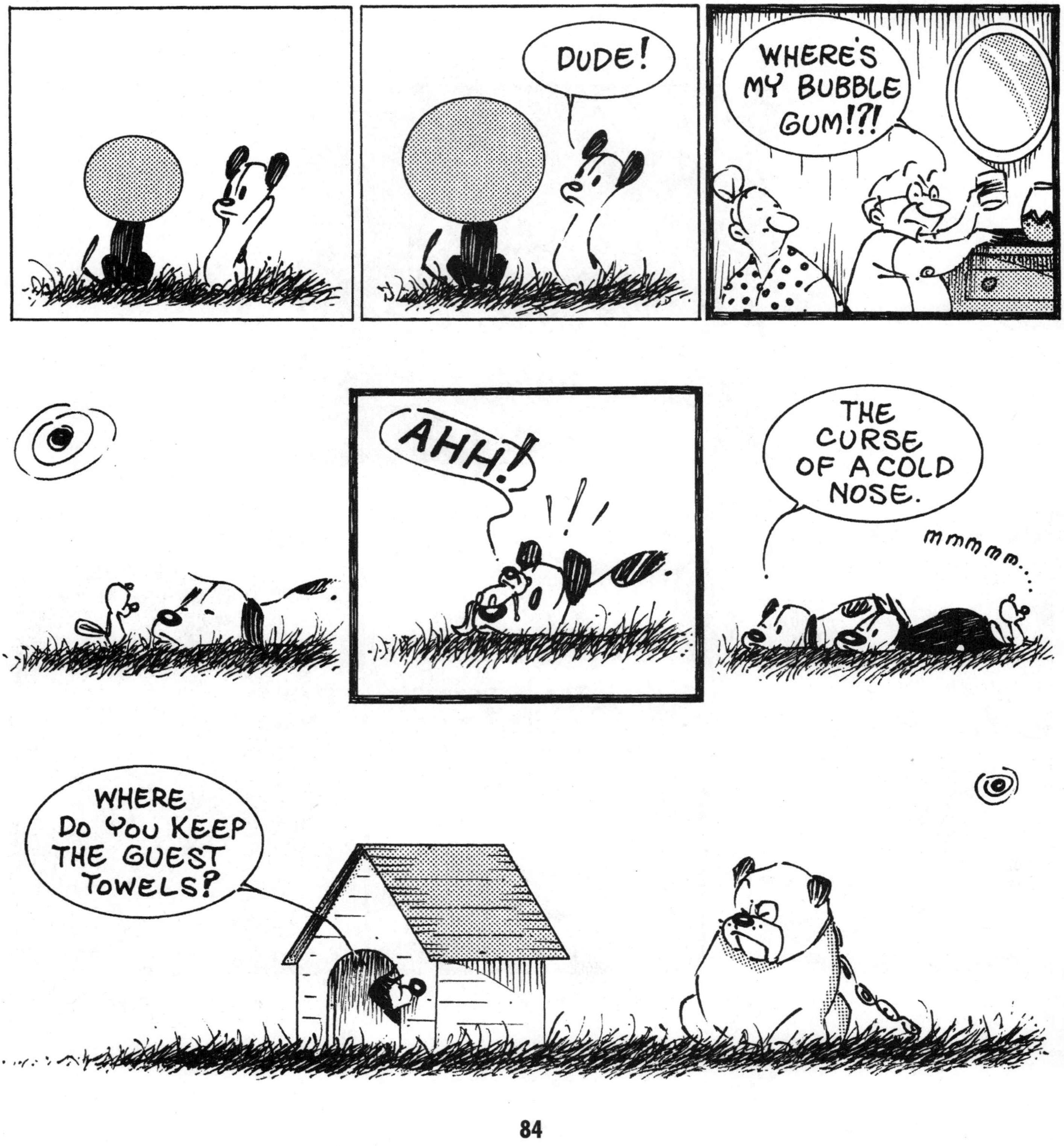
DUDE!
WHERE'S MY BUBBLE GUM!?!
AHH!
THE CURSE OF A COLD NOSE.
mmmmm...
WHERE DO YOU KEEP THE GUEST TOWELS?

MUTTS

THE "MOONDOGS" ARE AT IT AGAIN–MONITORING ALL DOGGY TRANSMISSIONS FROM PLANET EARTH...
HOWL
HOWLWOOO
HOWL
EARL'S BEEN LEFT HOME ALONE, SIR.
WOOOOO
PETE IS STILL WAITING TO BE ADOPTED.
HOWL
AND GUARD DOG REMAINS CHAINED IN HIS YARD.
WHAT KIND OF UNCIVILIZED WORLD IS THIS!?!
HOWL
BUT NOT ALL THE NEWS IS BAD...
HOWLWOOO
WOOFIE LOVES A FULL MOON.
DON'T WE ALL, SIR.

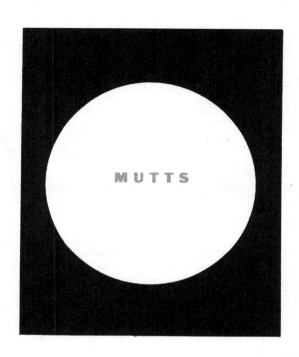

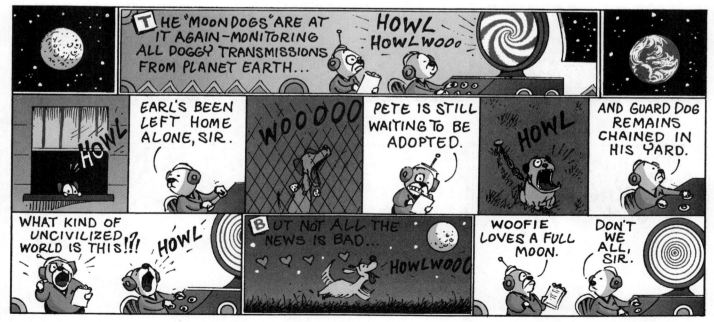

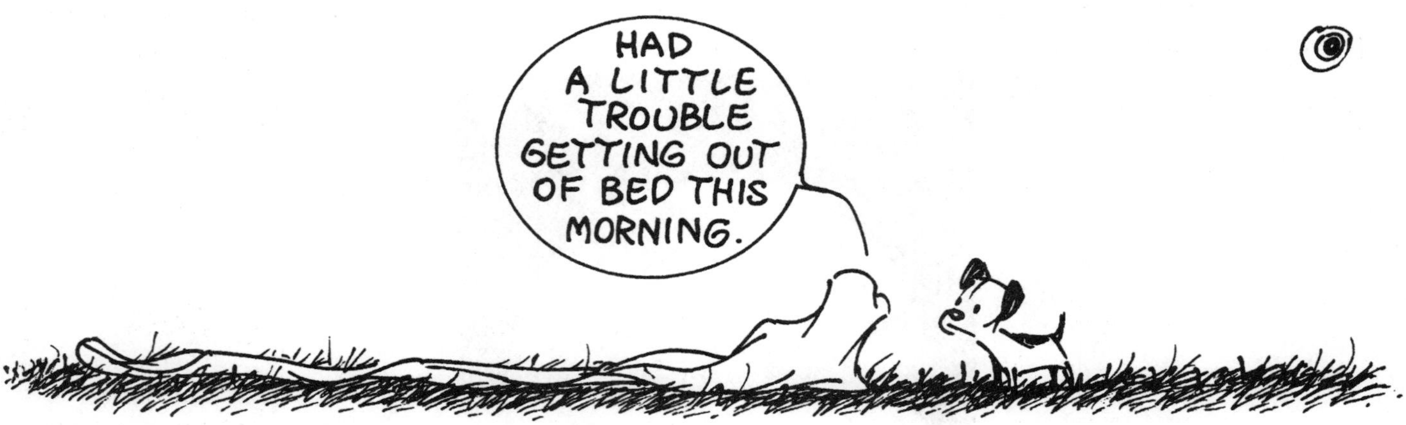
HAD A LITTLE TROUBLE GETTING OUT OF BED THIS MORNING.

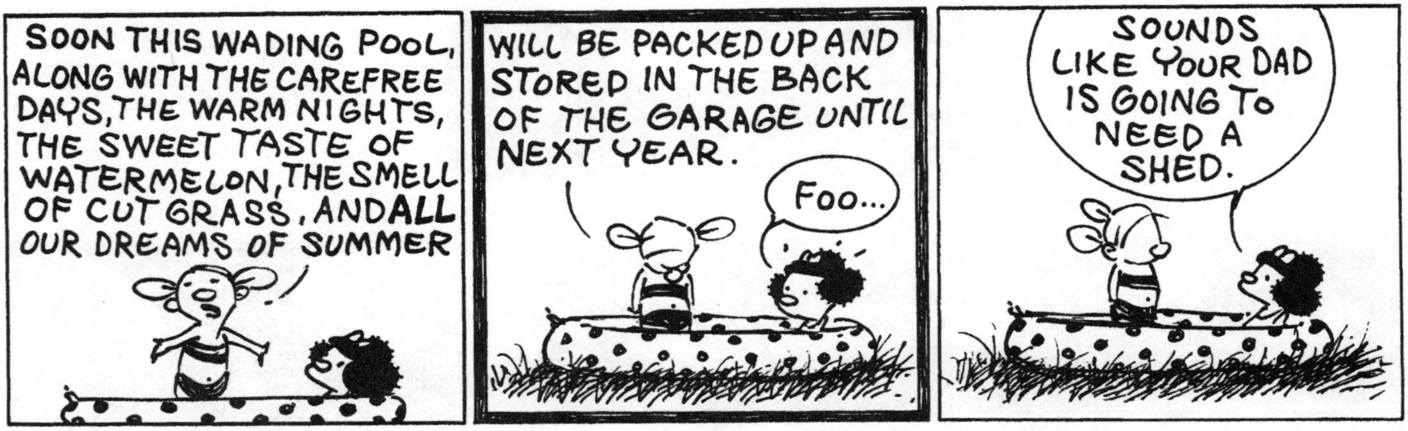
SOON THIS WADING POOL, ALONG WITH THE CAREFREE DAYS, THE WARM NIGHTS, THE SWEET TASTE OF WATERMELON, THE SMELL OF CUT GRASS, AND ALL OUR DREAMS OF SUMMER
WILL BE PACKED UP AND STORED IN THE BACK OF THE GARAGE UNTIL NEXT YEAR.
FOO...
SOUNDS LIKE YOUR DAD IS GOING TO NEED A SHED.

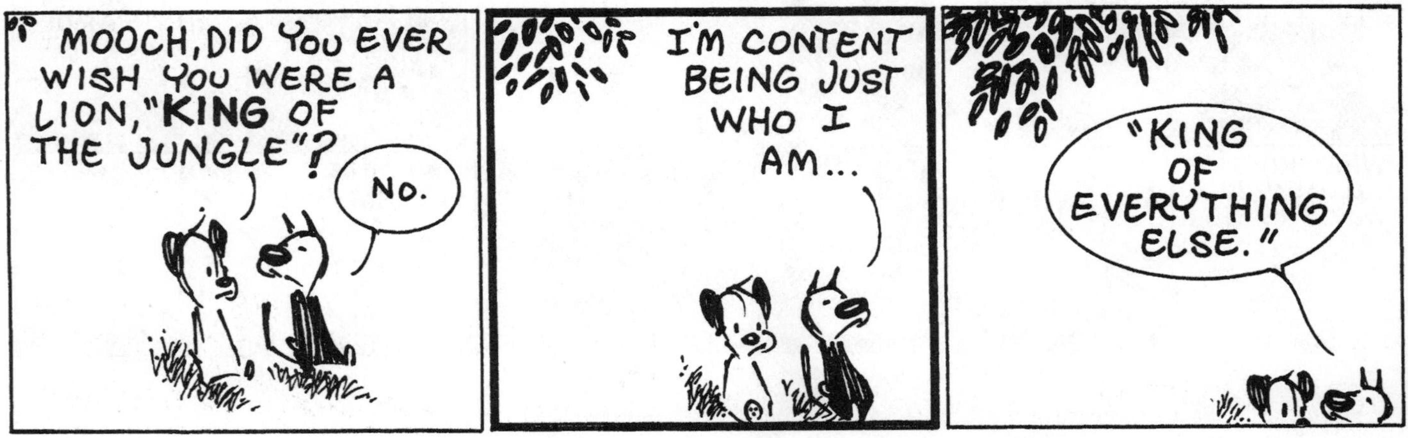
MOOCH, DID YOU EVER WISH YOU WERE A LION, "KING OF THE JUNGLE"?
NO.
I'M CONTENT BEING JUST WHO I AM...
"KING OF EVERYTHING ELSE."

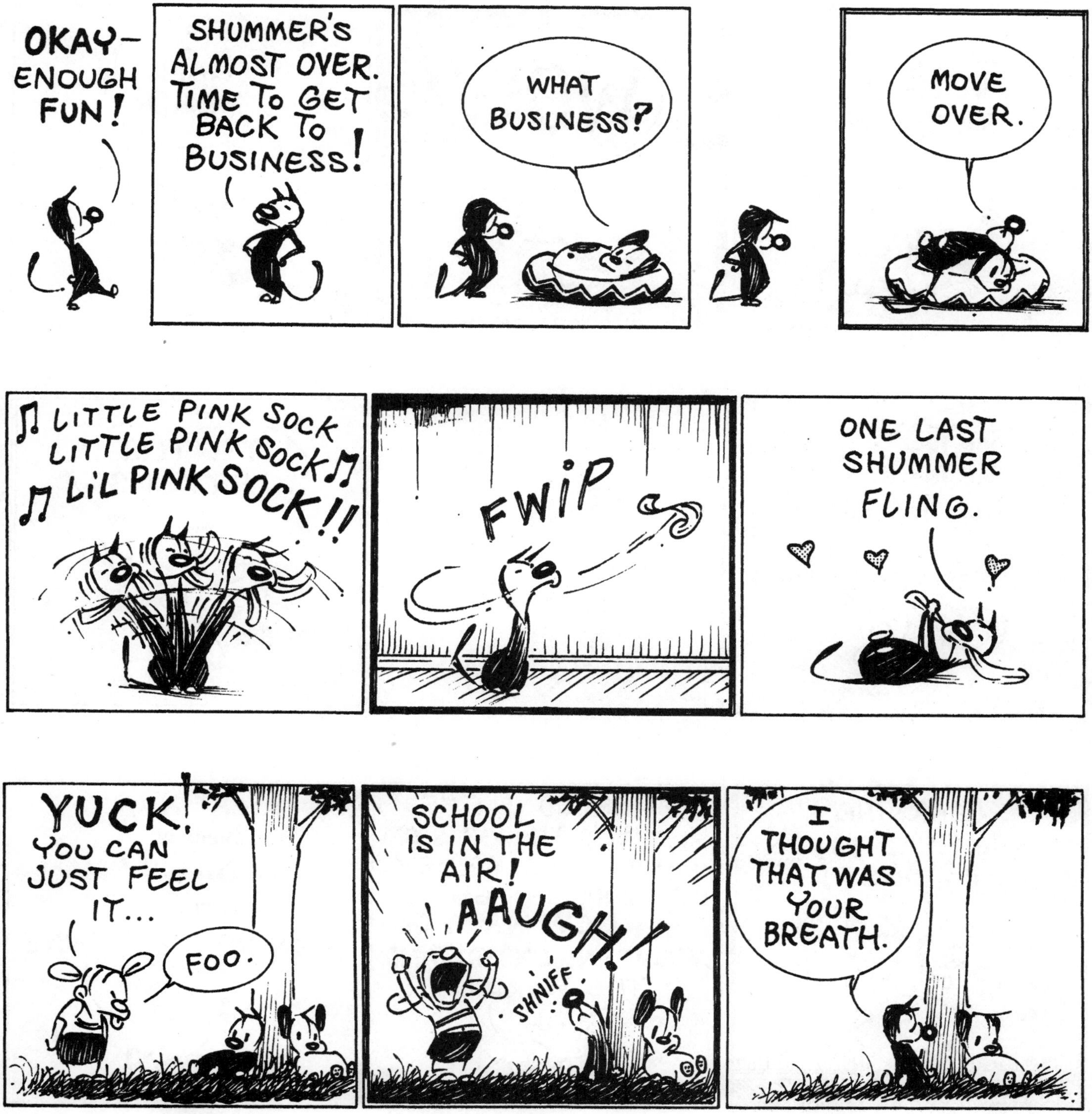
OKAY— ENOUGH FUN!
SHUMMER'S ALMOST OVER. TIME TO GET BACK TO BUSINESS!
WHAT BUSINESS?
MOVE OVER.
♫ LITTLE PINK SOCK LITTLE PINK SOCK ♫
♫ LIL PINK SOCK!!
FWIP
ONE LAST SHUMMER FLING.
YUCK! YOU CAN JUST FEEL IT...
FOO.
SCHOOL IS IN THE AIR!
AAUGH!
SHNIFF
I THOUGHT THAT WAS YOUR BREATH.

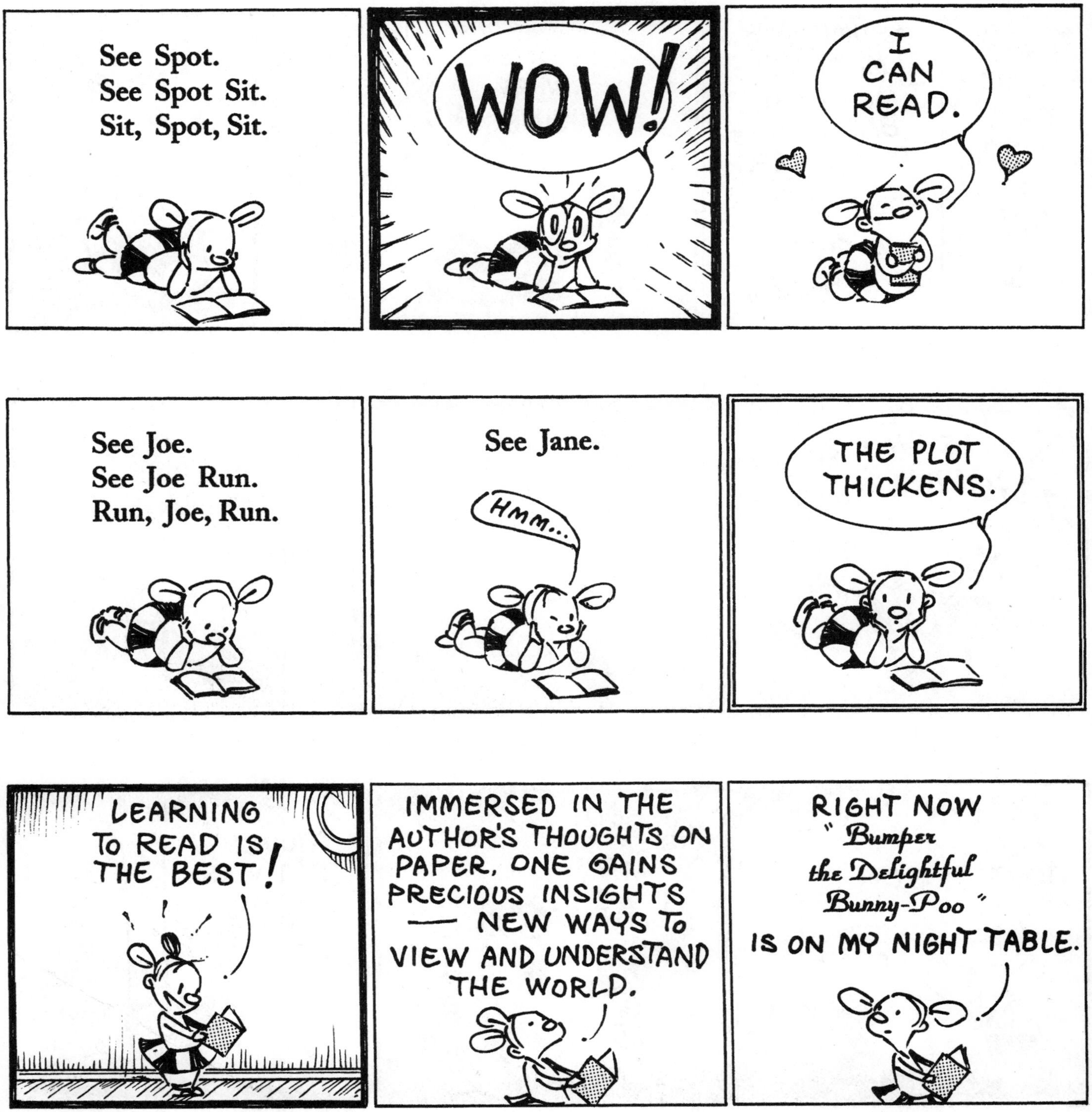
See Spot.
See Spot Sit.
Sit, Spot, Sit.
WOW!
I CAN READ.
See Joe.
See Joe Run.
Run, Joe, Run.
See Jane.
HMM...
THE PLOT THICKENS.
LEARNING TO READ IS THE BEST!
IMMERSED IN THE AUTHOR'S THOUGHTS ON PAPER, ONE GAINS PRECIOUS INSIGHTS — NEW WAYS TO VIEW AND UNDERSTAND THE WORLD.
RIGHT NOW "Bumper the Delightful Bunny-Poo" IS ON MY NIGHT TABLE.

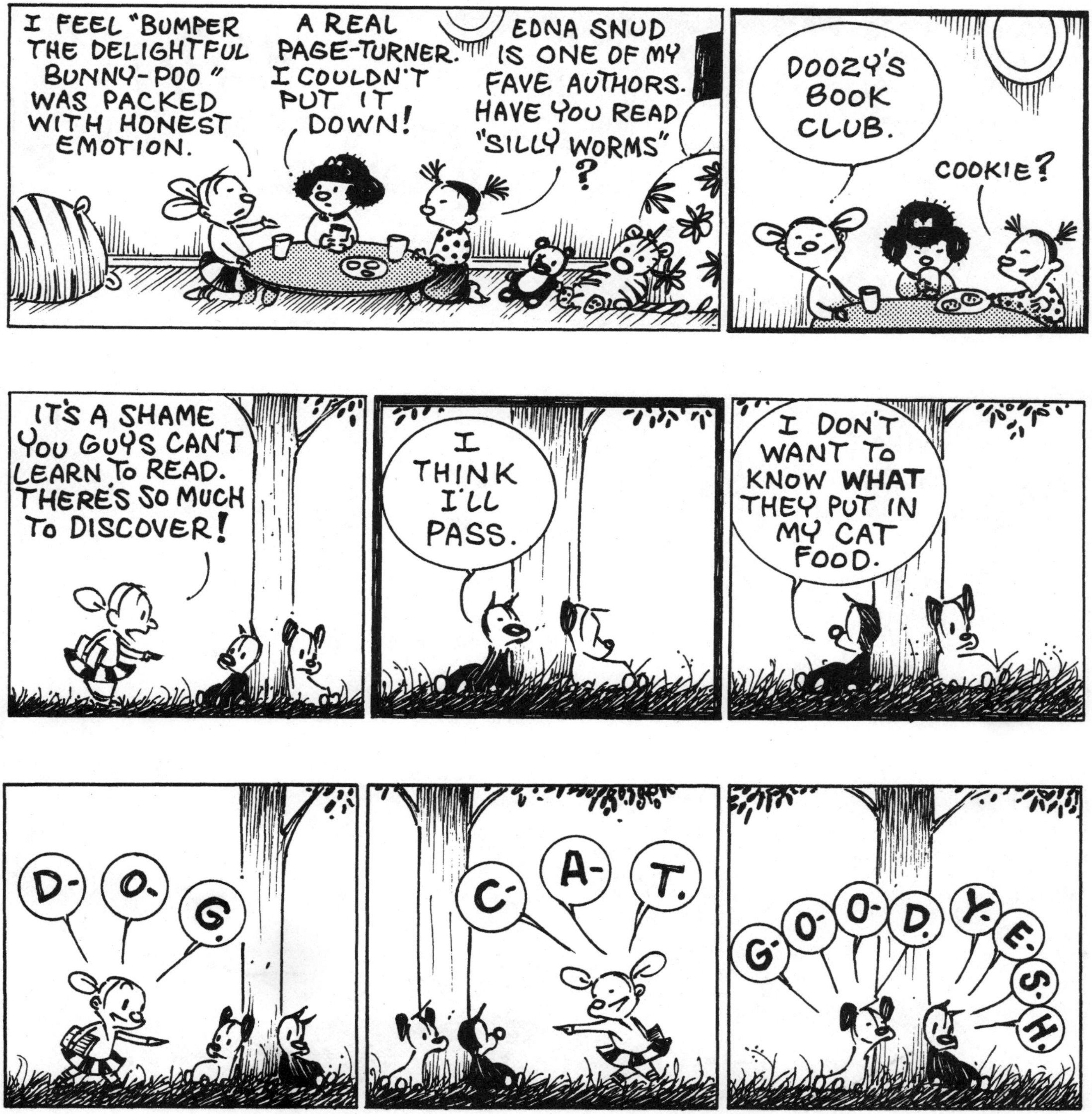
I FEEL "BUMPER THE DELIGHTFUL BUNNY-POO" WAS PACKED WITH HONEST EMOTION.
A REAL PAGE-TURNER. I COULDN'T PUT IT DOWN!
EDNA SNUD IS ONE OF MY FAVE AUTHORS. HAVE YOU READ "SILLY WORMS"?
DOOZY'S BOOK CLUB.
COOKIE?
IT'S A SHAME YOU GUYS CAN'T LEARN TO READ. THERE'S SO MUCH TO DISCOVER!
I THINK I'LL PASS.
I DON'T WANT TO KNOW WHAT THEY PUT IN MY CAT FOOD.
D-
O-
G.
C-
A-
T.
G-
O-
O-
D.
Y-
E-
S-
H.

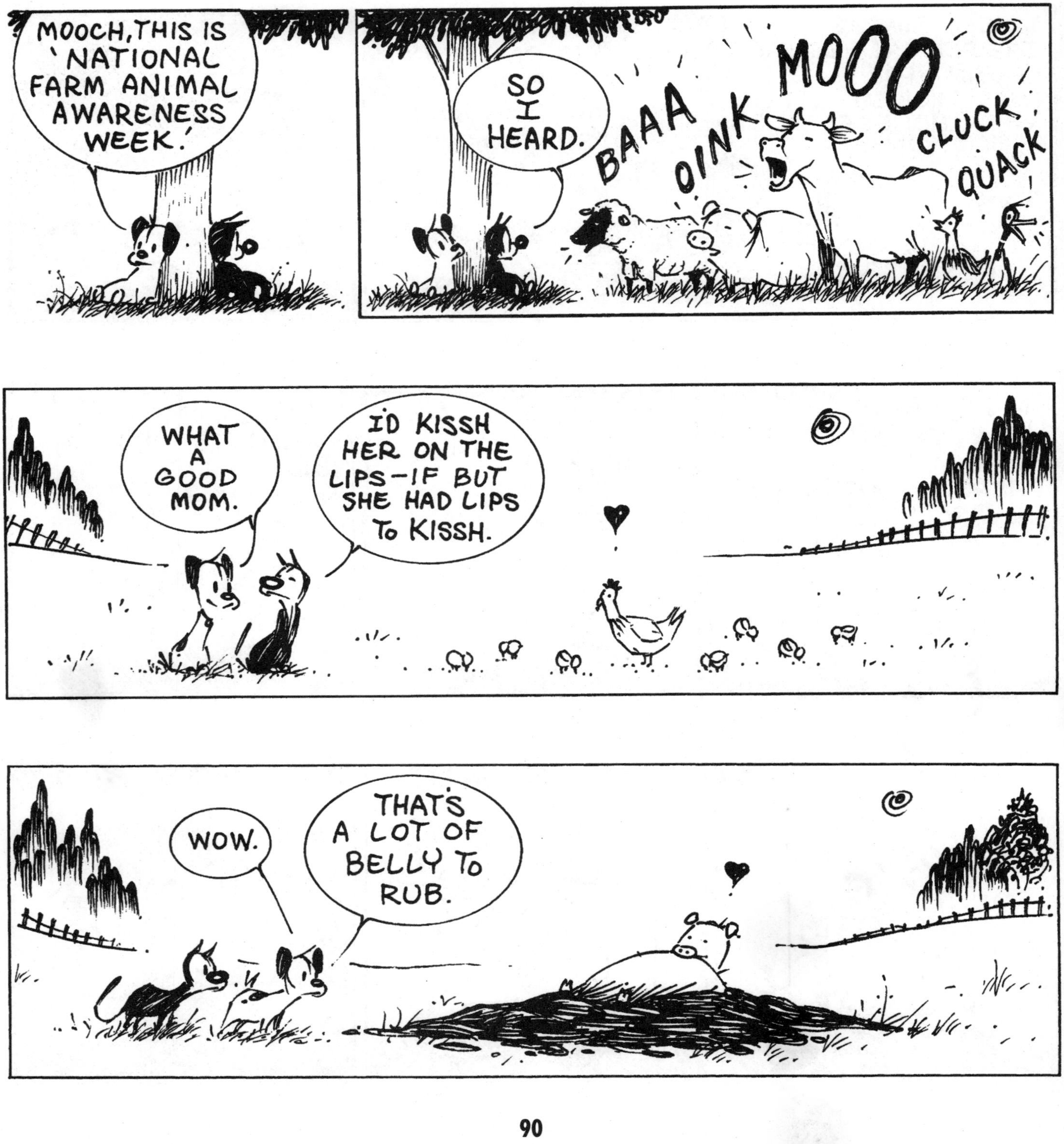
MOOCH, THIS IS 'NATIONAL FARM ANIMAL AWARENESS WEEK.'
SO I HEARD.
BAAA
OINK
MOOO
CLUCK
QUACK
WHAT A GOOD MOM.
I'D KISSH HER ON THE LIPS—IF BUT SHE HAD LIPS TO KISSH.
WOW.
THAT'S A LOT OF BELLY TO RUB.

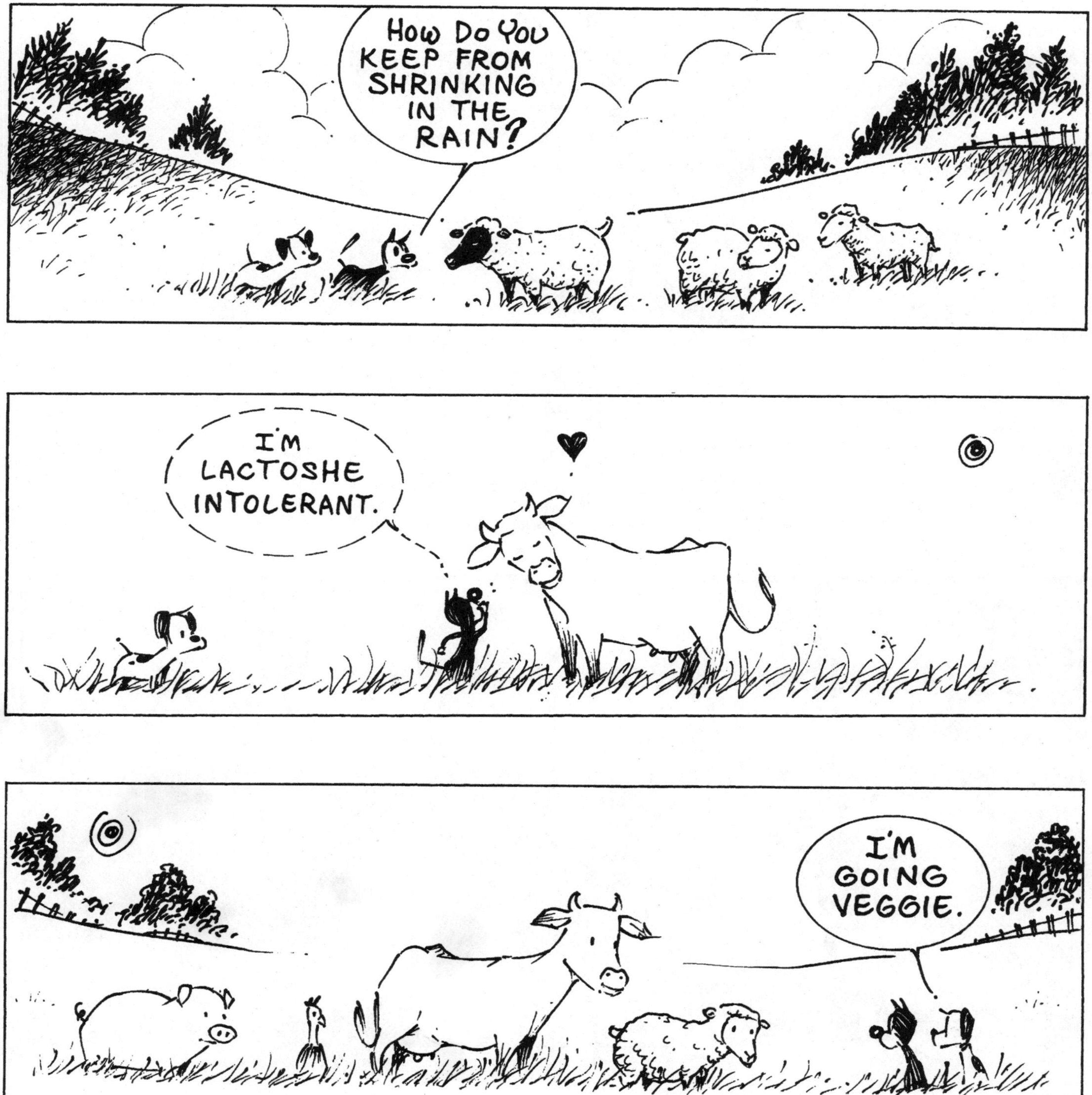
HOW DO YOU KEEP FROM SHRINKING IN THE RAIN?
I'M LACTOSHE INTOLERANT.
I'M GOING VEGGIE.

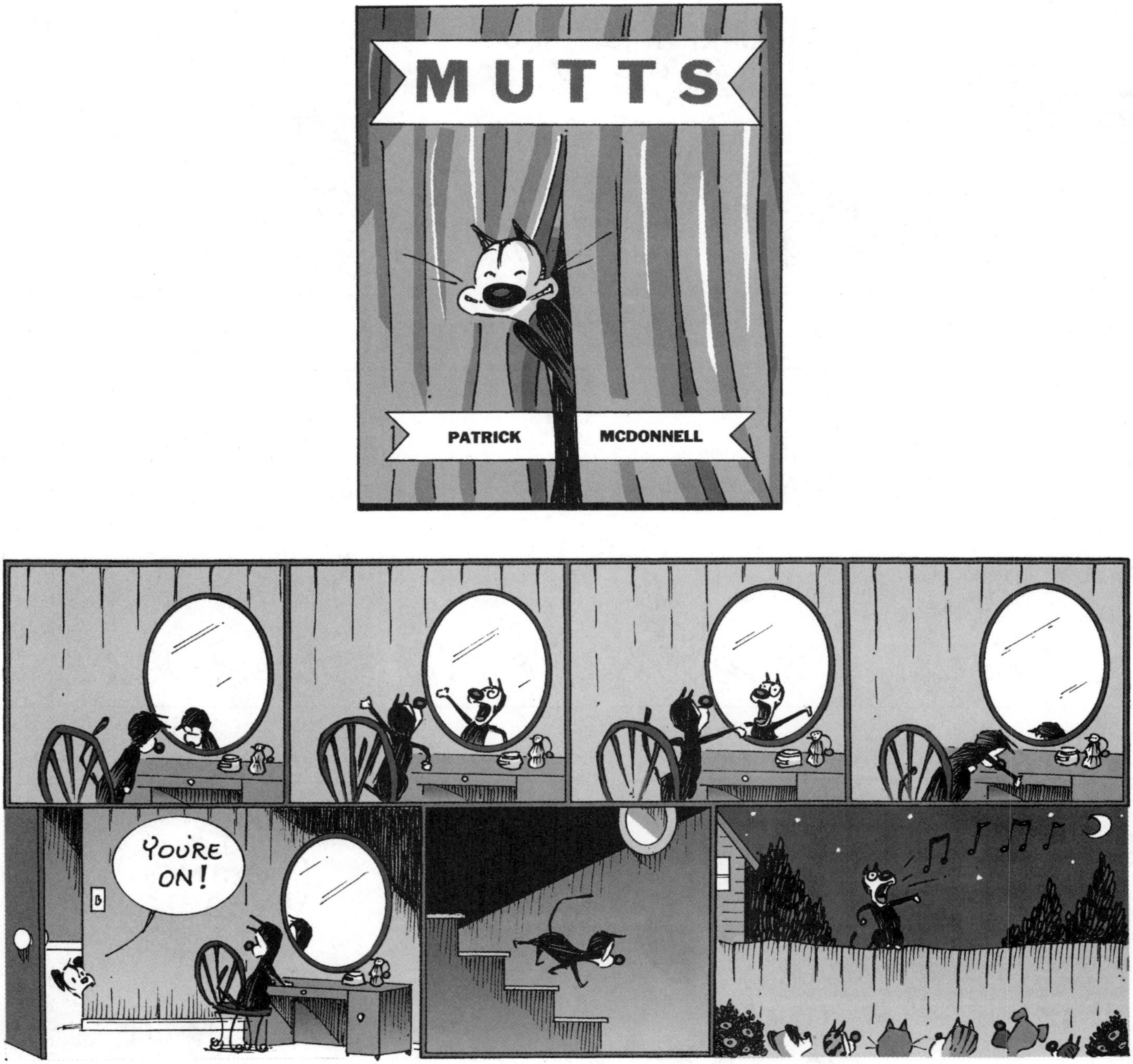
MUTTS
PATRICK
MCDONNELL
YOU'RE ON!

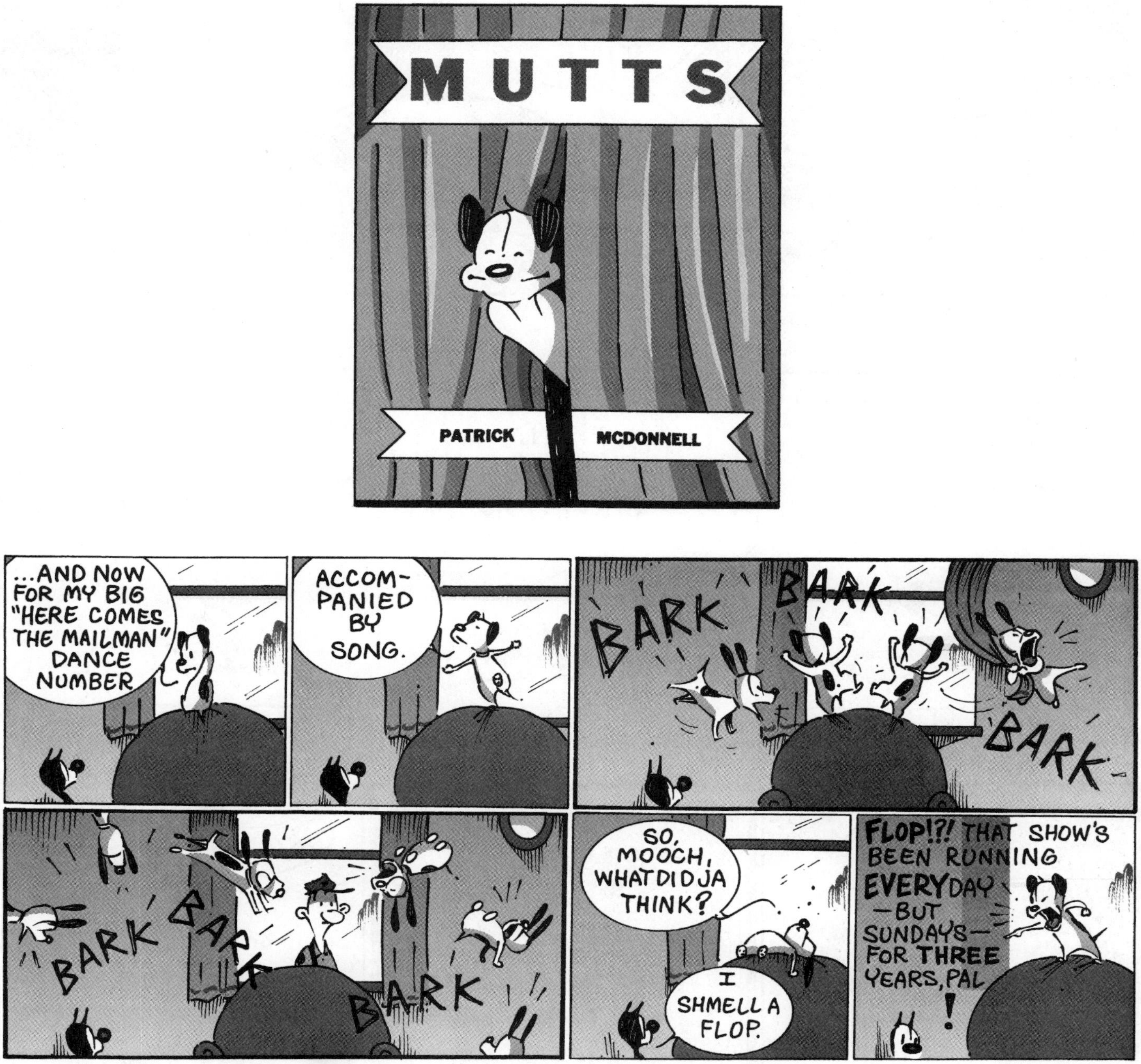
MUTTS
PATRICK MCDONNELL
...AND NOW FOR MY BIG "HERE COMES THE MAILMAN" DANCE NUMBER
ACCOM-PANIED BY SONG.
BARK
BARK
BARK
BARK
BARK
BARK
SO, MOOCH, WHATDIDJA THINK?
I SHMELL A FLOP.
FLOP!?! THAT SHOW'S BEEN RUNNING EVERYDAY —BUT SUNDAYS— FOR THREE YEARS, PAL!

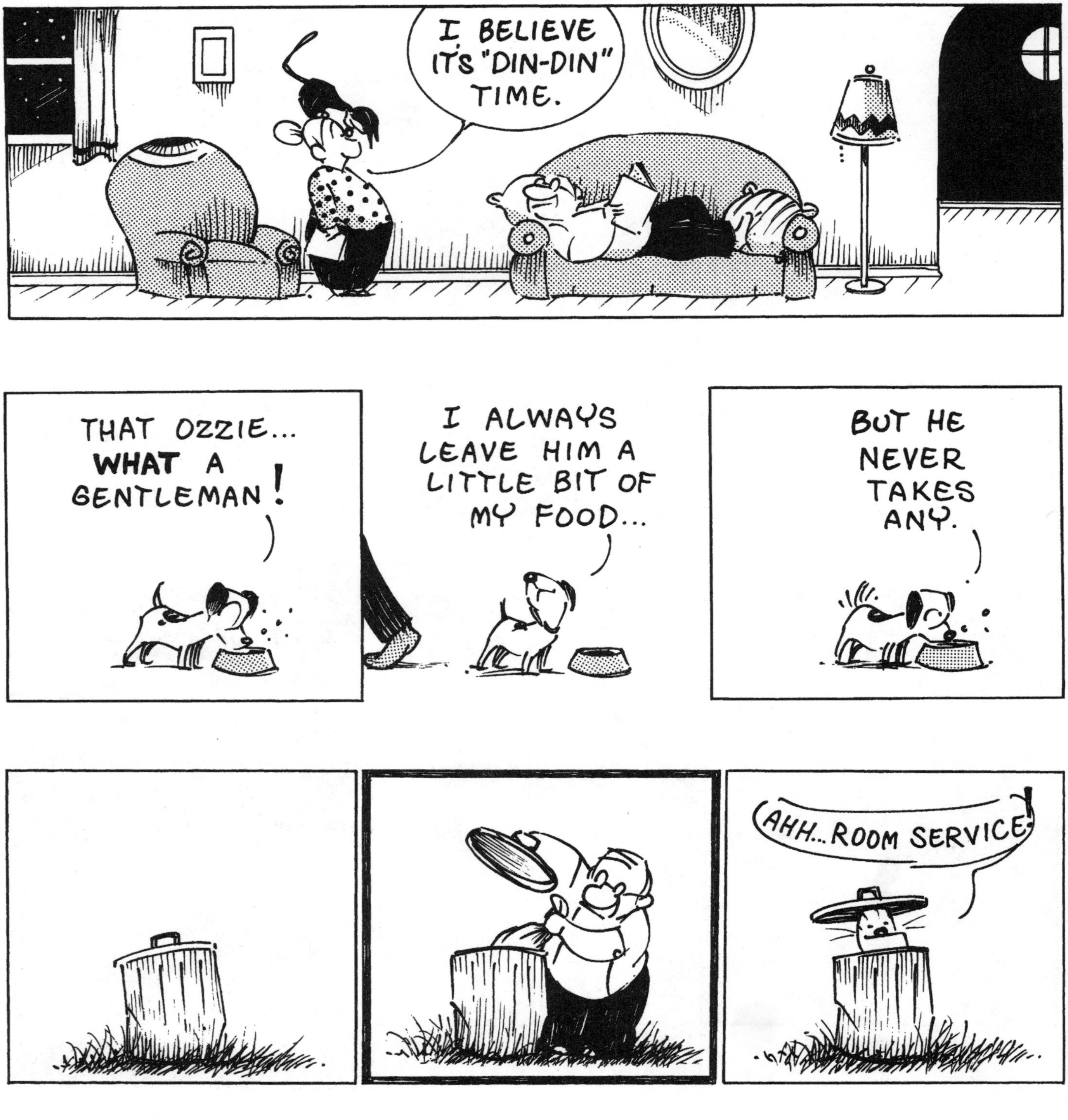
I BELIEVE IT'S "DIN-DIN" TIME.
THAT OZZIE... WHAT A GENTLEMAN!
I ALWAYS LEAVE HIM A LITTLE BIT OF MY FOOD...
BUT HE NEVER TAKES ANY.
AHH... ROOM SERVICE!

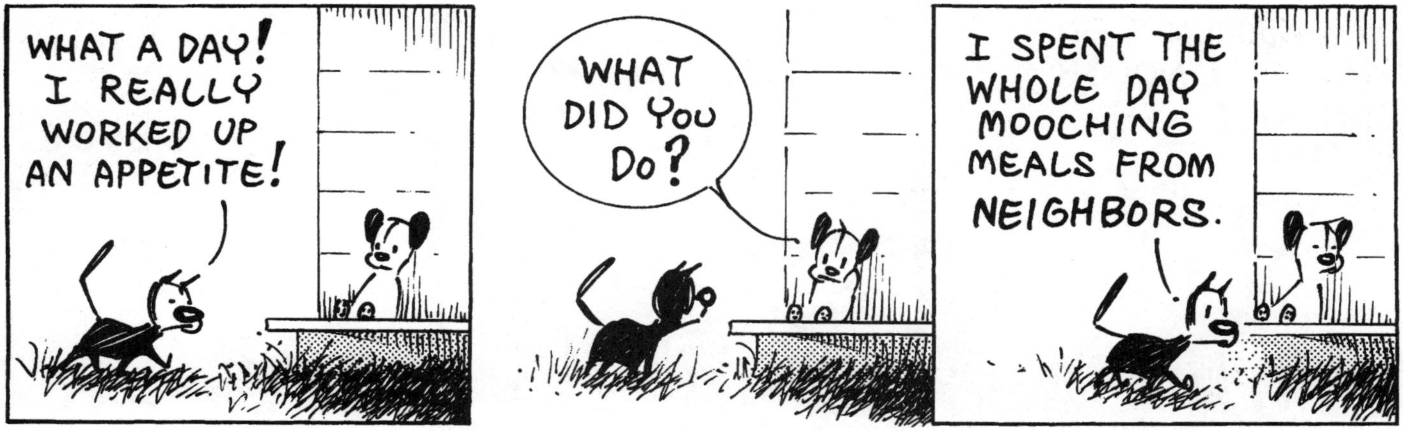
WHAT A DAY! I REALLY WORKED UP AN APPETITE!
WHAT DID YOU DO?
I SPENT THE WHOLE DAY MOOCHING MEALS FROM NEIGHBORS.

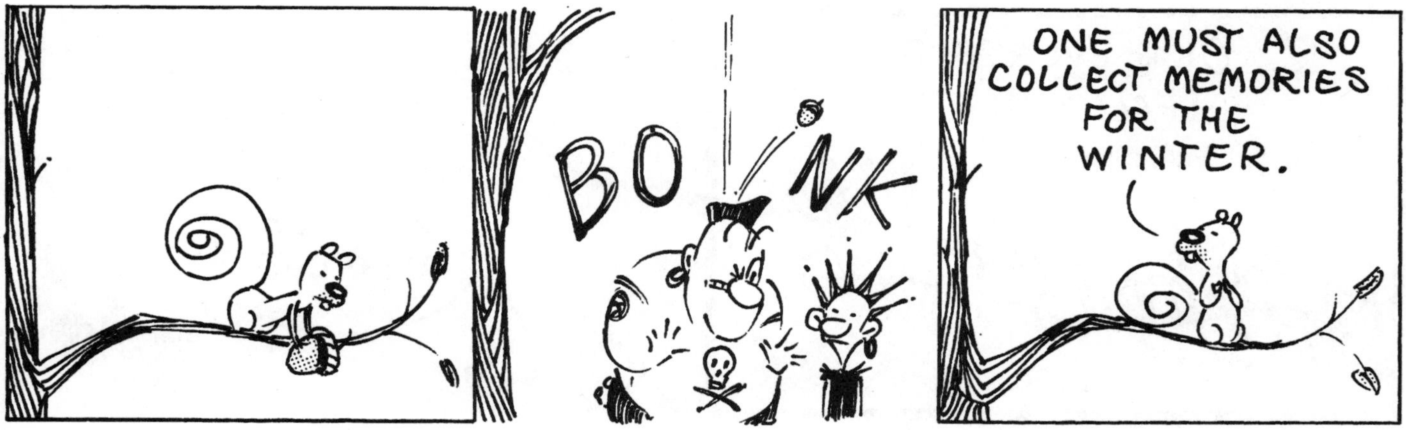
BONK
ONE MUST ALSO COLLECT MEMORIES FOR THE WINTER.

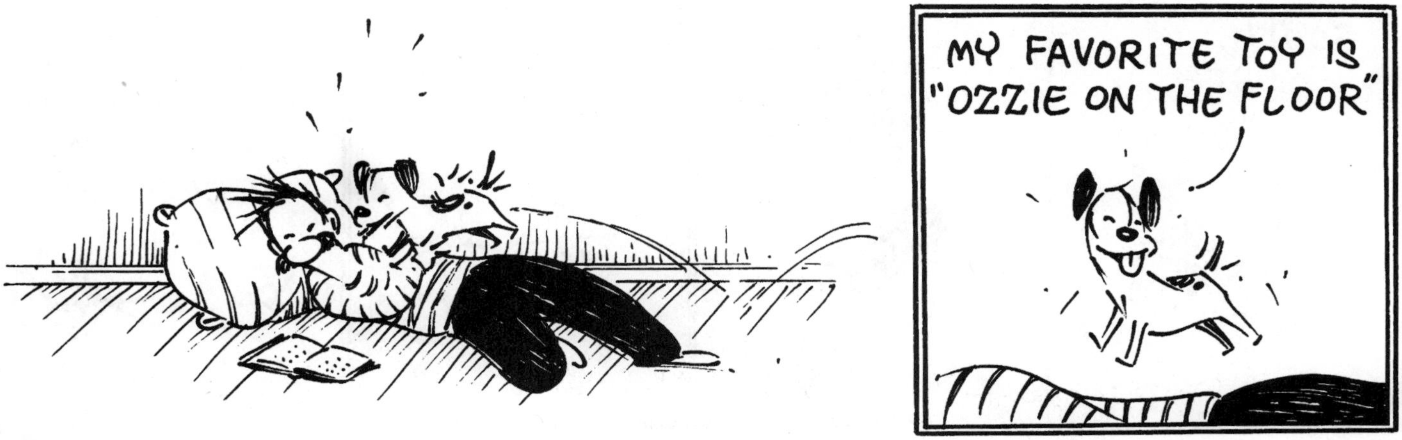
MY FAVORITE TOY IS "OZZIE ON THE FLOOR"

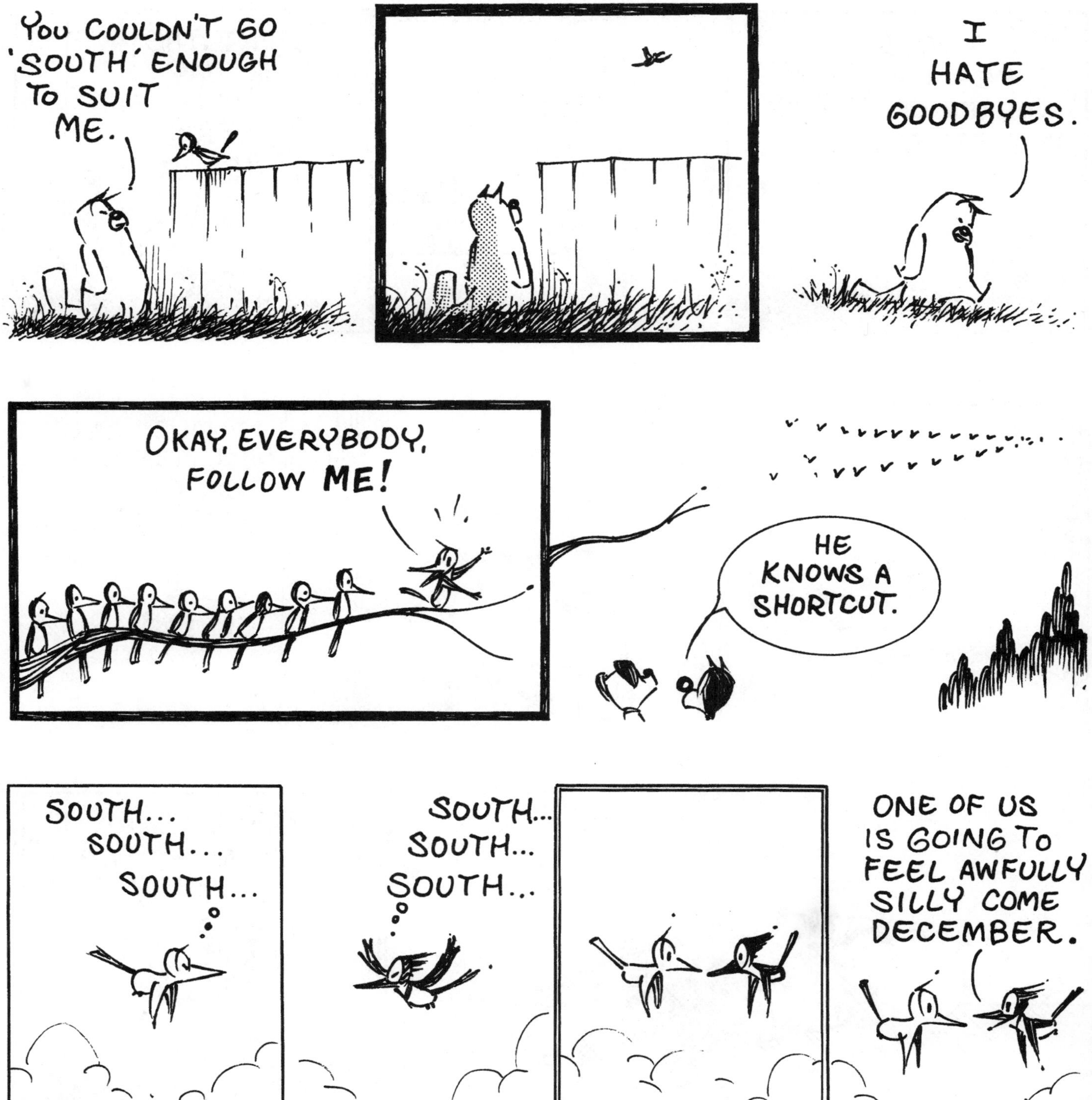
YOU COULDN'T GO 'SOUTH' ENOUGH TO SUIT ME.
I HATE GOODBYES.
OKAY, EVERYBODY, FOLLOW ME!
HE KNOWS A SHORTCUT.
SOUTH... SOUTH... SOUTH...
SOUTH... SOUTH... SOUTH...
ONE OF US IS GOING TO FEEL AWFULLY SILLY COME DECEMBER.

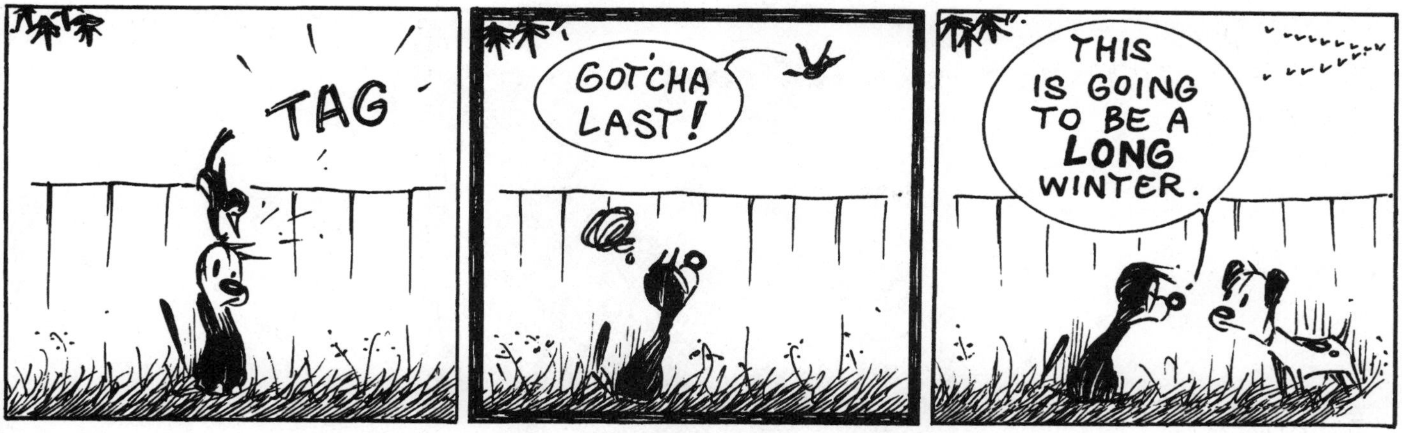
TAG
GOT'CHA LAST!
THIS IS GOING TO BE A LONG WINTER.

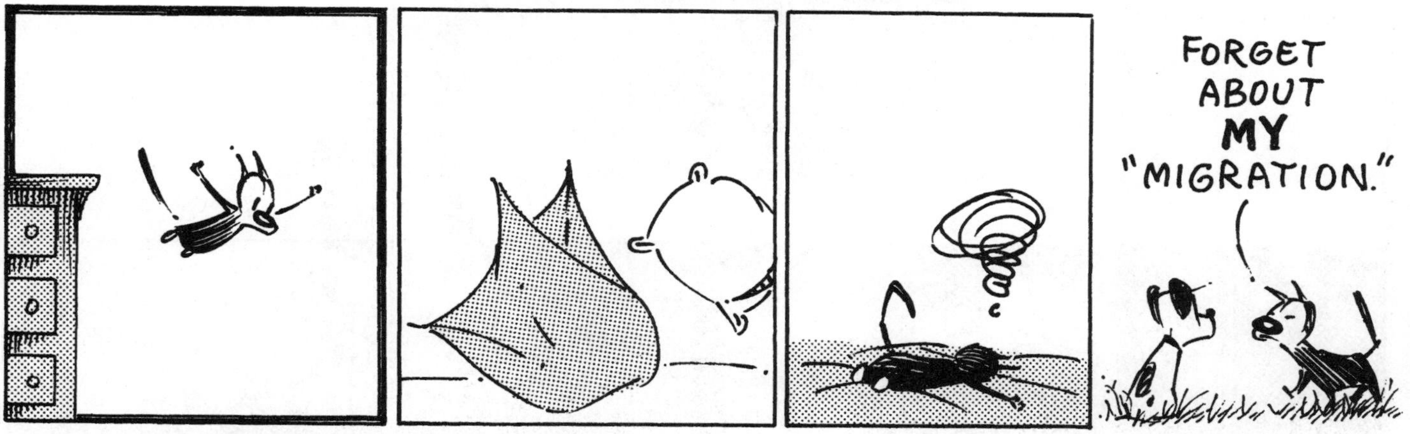
FORGET ABOUT MY "MIGRATION."

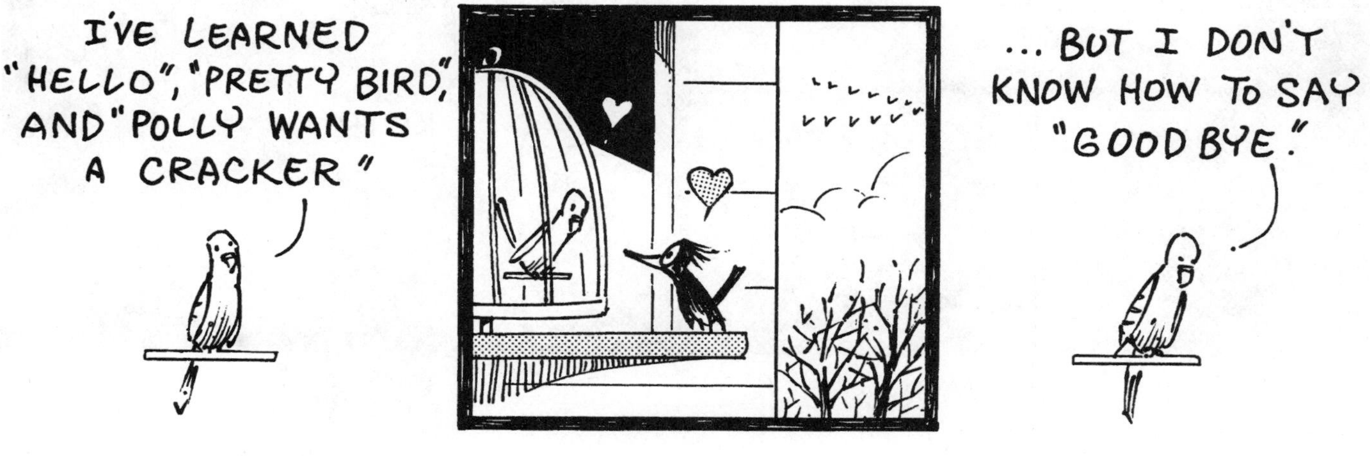
I'VE LEARNED "HELLO", "PRETTY BIRD", AND "POLLY WANTS A CRACKER"
... BUT I DON'T KNOW HOW TO SAY "GOOD BYE."

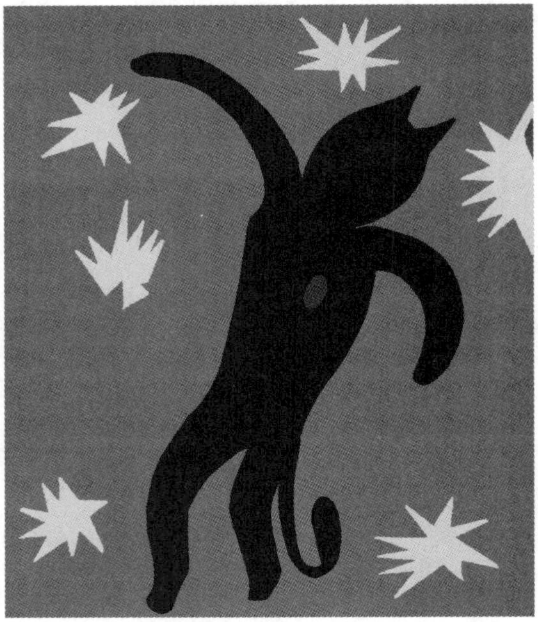

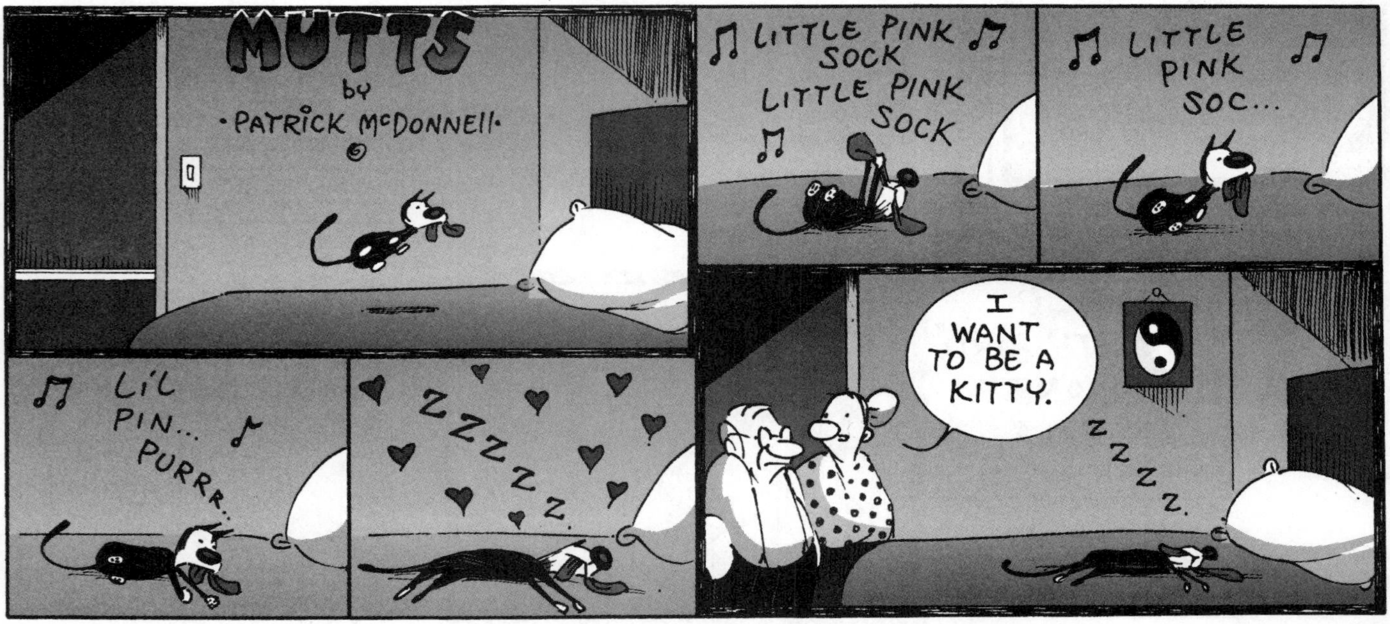
MUTTS
by
PATRICK McDONNELL
♫ LITTLE PINK SOCK LITTLE PINK SOCK ♫
♫ LITTLE PINK SOC... ♫
♫ LI'L PIN... ♪ PURRR...
ZZZZZZ.
I WANT TO BE A KITTY.
Z Z Z Z.

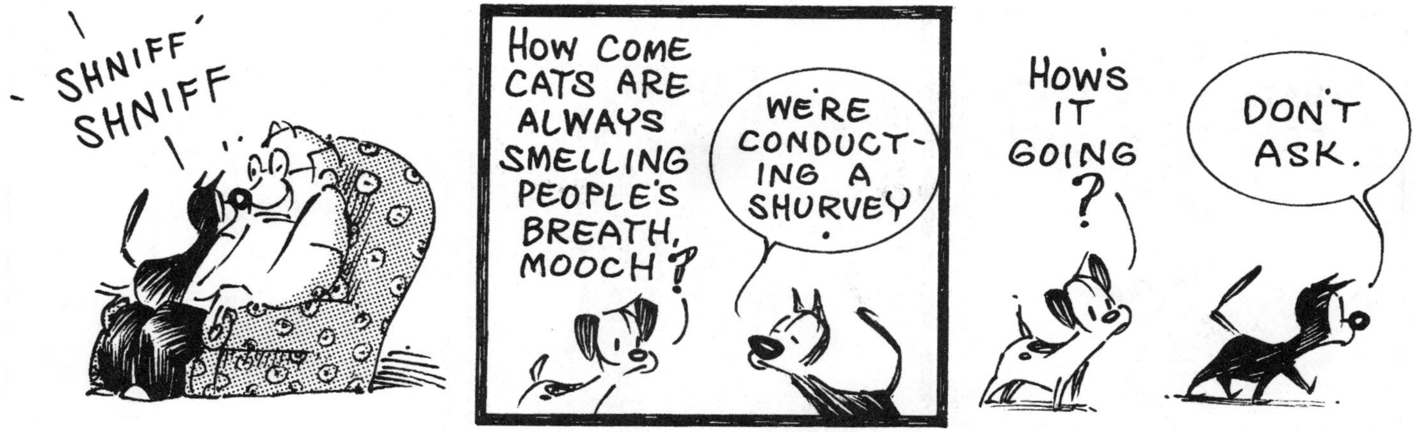
SHNIFF SHNIFF
HOW COME CATS ARE ALWAYS SMELLING PEOPLE'S BREATH, MOOCH?
WE'RE CONDUCTING A SHURVEY.
HOW'S IT GOING?
DON'T ASK.

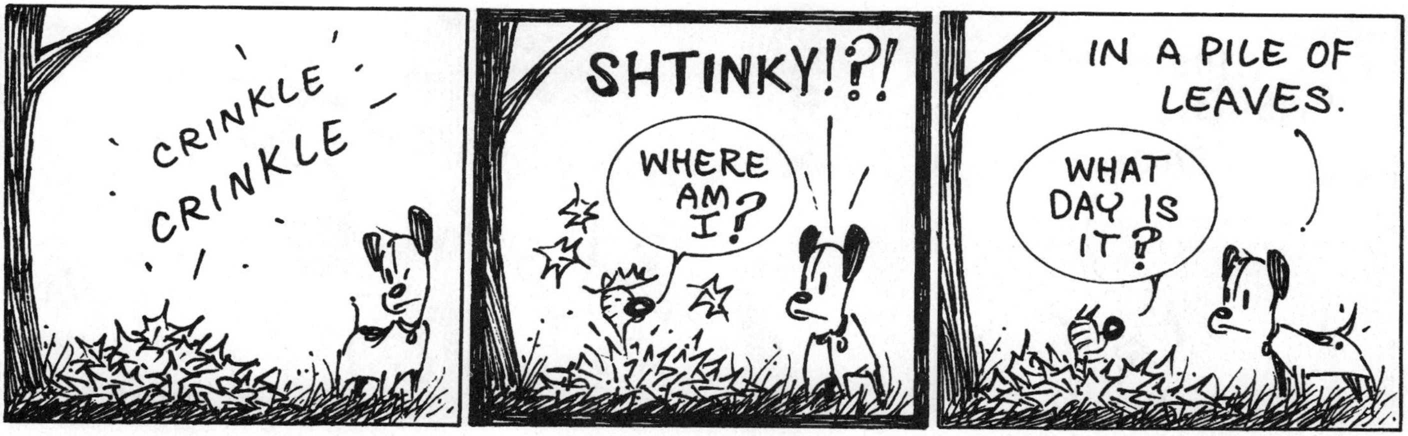
CRINKLE CRINKLE
SHTINKY!?!
WHERE AM I?
IN A PILE OF LEAVES.
WHAT DAY IS IT?

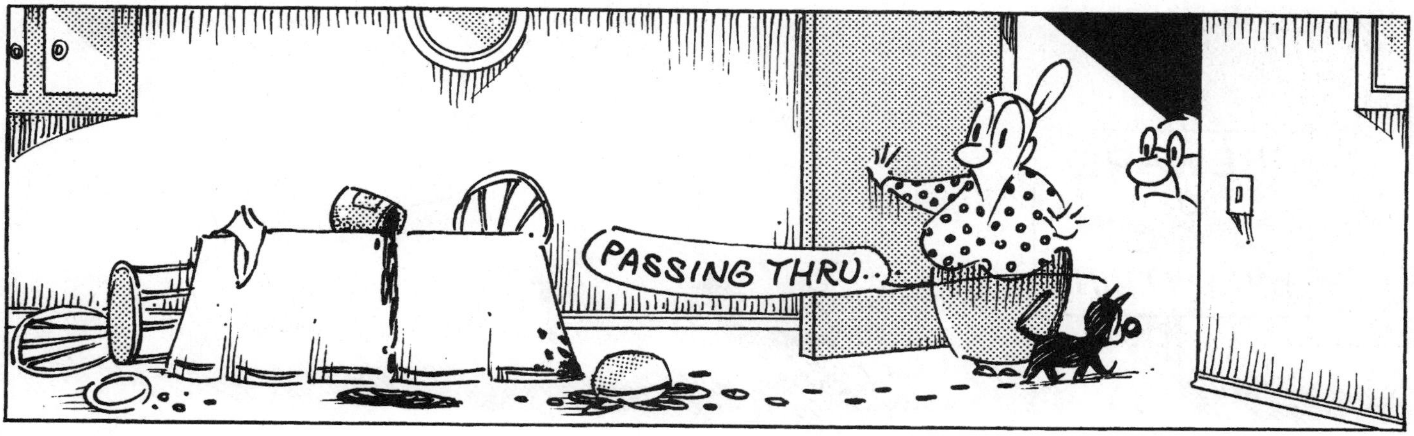
PASSING THRU...

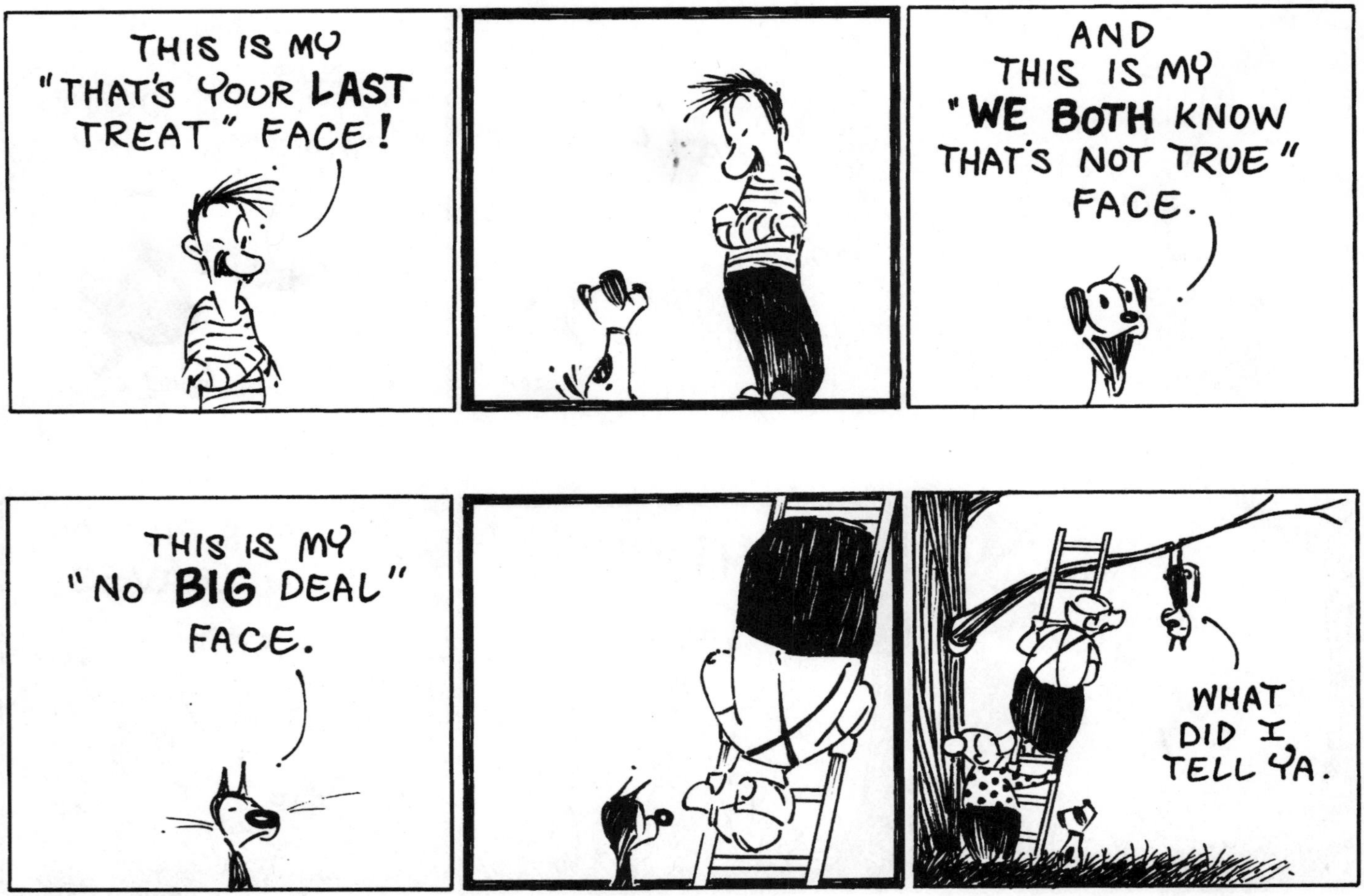
THIS IS MY "THAT'S YOUR **LAST** TREAT" FACE!
AND THIS IS MY "**WE BOTH** KNOW THAT'S NOT TRUE" FACE.
THIS IS MY "NO **BIG** DEAL" FACE.
WHAT DID I TELL YA.

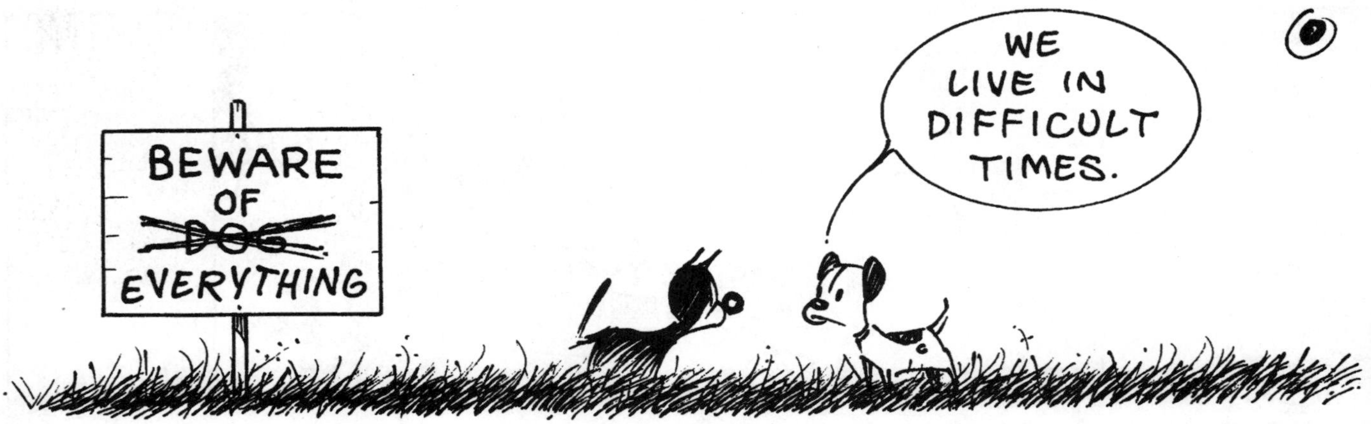
BEWARE OF ~~DOG~~ EVERYTHING
WE LIVE IN DIFFICULT TIMES.

MUTTS
COMICS
McDONNELL

LO! A PISTACHIO! ALL THE WAY FROM THE DESERTS OF IRAN!
MUST BE A MIRAGE.
SAY "ALOHA" TO THE MACADAMIA NUT. A LULU FROM HONOLULU.
ALOHA!
ONE CAN ALMOST FEEL THE PALM TREES SWAYING...
HULA·HULA
BOW TO OUR HONORABLE GUEST FROM THE ORIENT ...THE LITCHI NUT!
MR. LITCHI.
"GOOD GRIEF"! THE COMMON PEANUT— THE GOOBER!
HEE-HAW!
... AND FINALLY— TALL AND TAN, THE BRAZIL. ONE TOUGH NUT!!!
AHH..
BONK
BONK
BONK
I LIKE TO MIX IT UP.

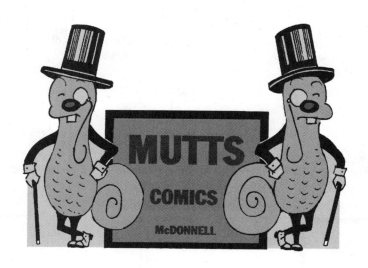

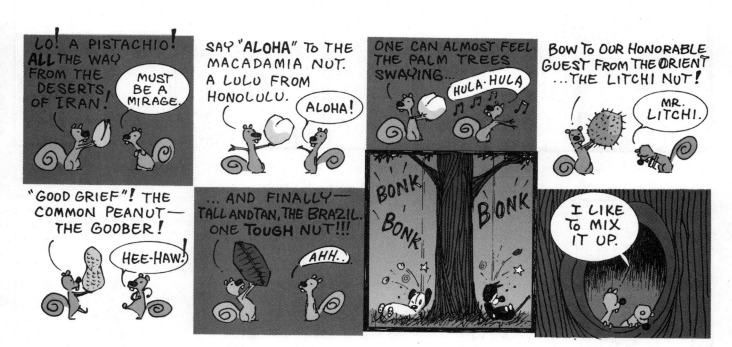

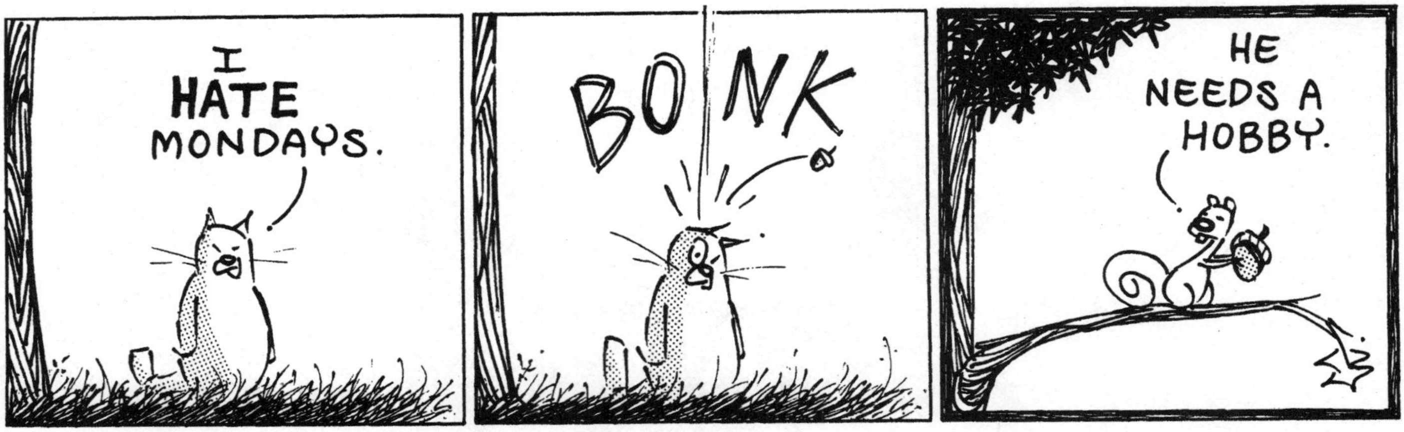
I HATE MONDAYS.
BONK
HE NEEDS A HOBBY.

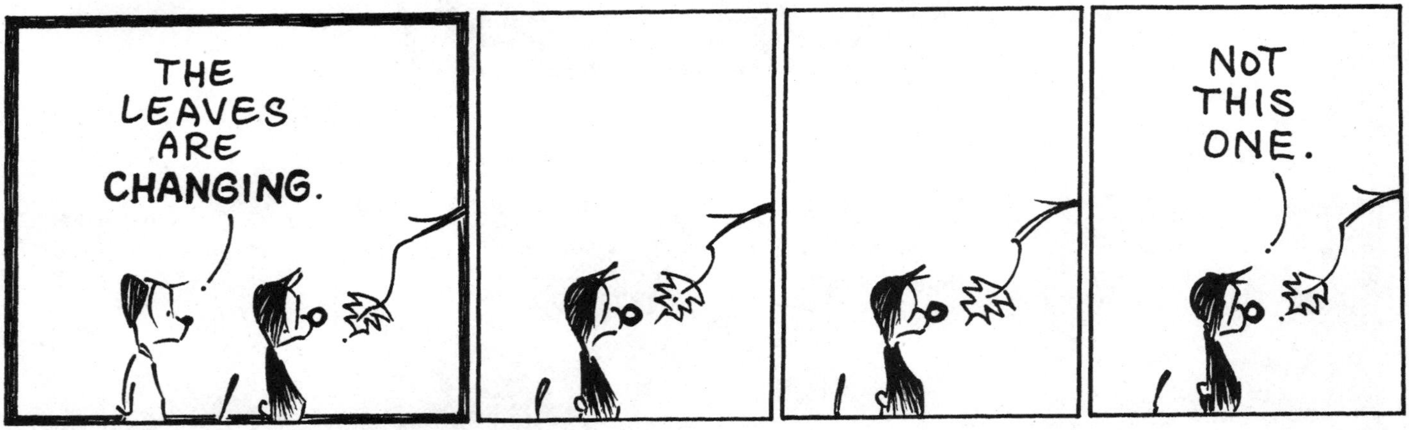
THE LEAVES ARE CHANGING.
NOT THIS ONE.

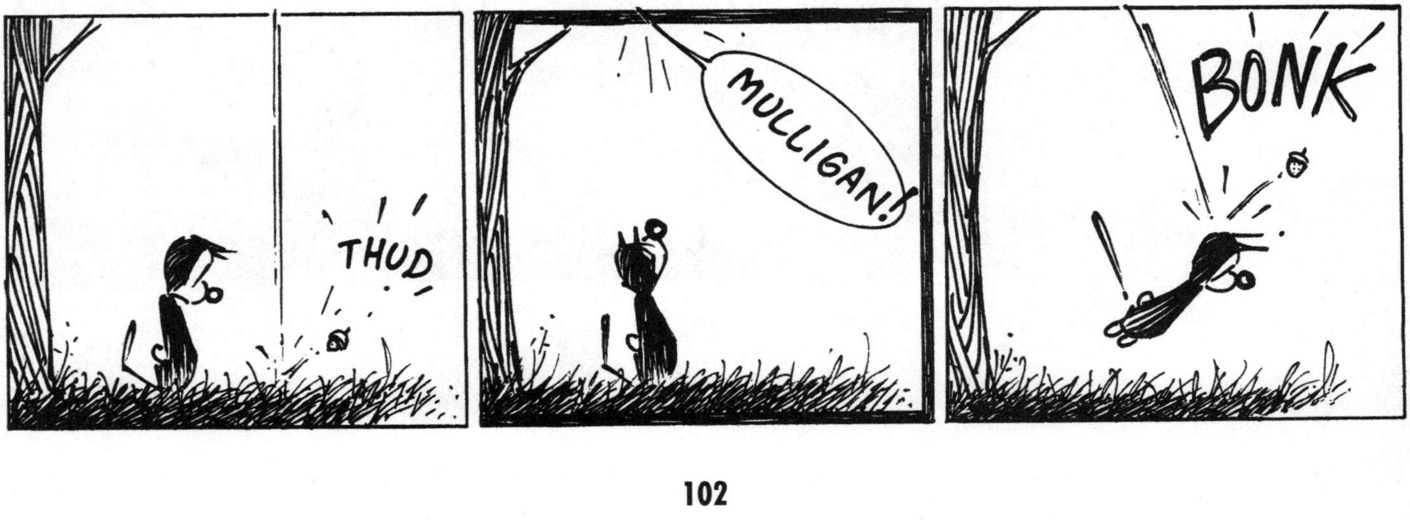
THUD
MULLIGAN!
BONK

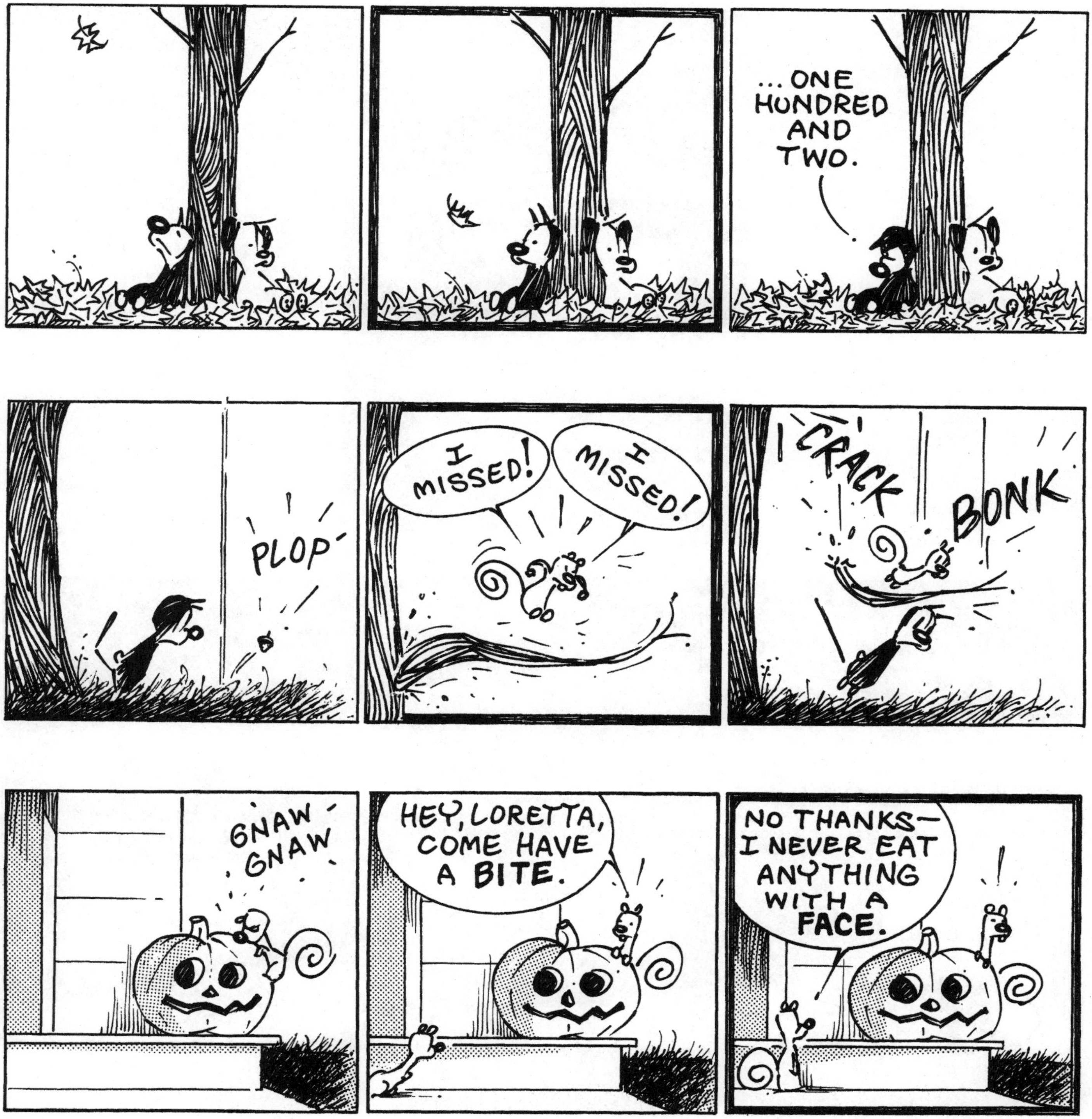
...ONE HUNDRED AND TWO.
PLOP
I MISSED!
I MISSED!
CRACK
BONK
GNAW GNAW
HEY, LORETTA, COME HAVE A **BITE**.
NO THANKS— I NEVER EAT ANYTHING WITH A **FACE**.

THE MUTTS...

AACK! THE VEGETABLE PEOPLE!
EARL!
THEY'RE ALL OVER THE PLACE! SHTARING AT ME!
PUMPKINS!!! SQUASHES!!! WHERE DOES IT SHTOP!?! CARROTS!?! CABBAGES!?! RUTABAGAS!!?! PRUNES!?!
...I CAN'T DEAL WITH PRUNES...
♫ TRICK OR TREAT ♫
OH, NO! THE VEGETABLES ARE DANCING!
WHAT A PUMP-KIN.
THIS GENETIC ENGINEERING THING IS OUT OF CONTROL!

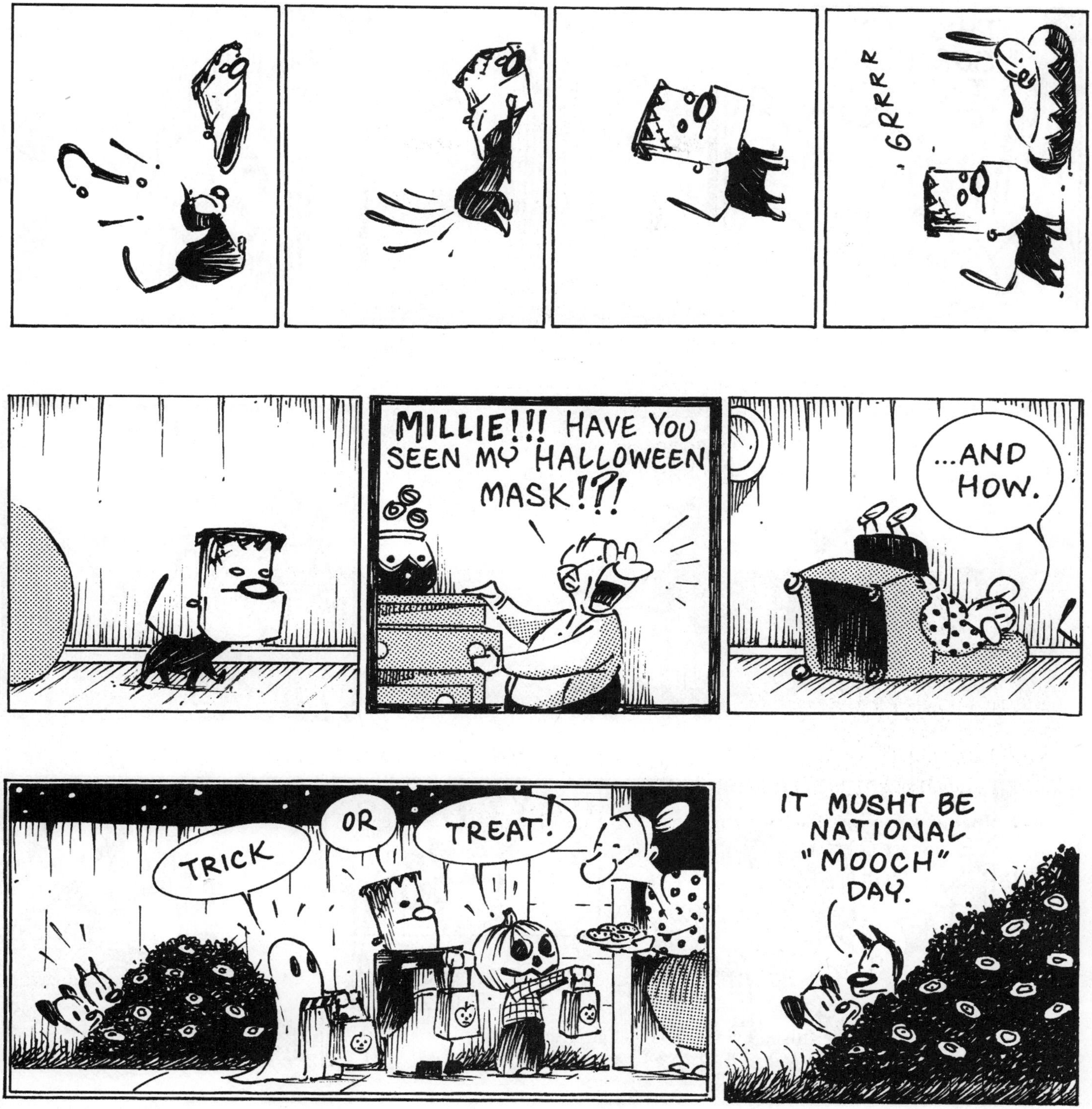
GRRRR
MILLIE!!! HAVE YOU SEEN MY HALLOWEEN MASK!?!
...AND HOW.
TRICK
OR
TREAT!
IT MUSHT BE NATIONAL "MOOCH" DAY.

THIS ISN'T "CORN" CORN— THIS IS— "CANDY" CORN !?!
!
BONK
BONK
SWEET.
HE LOVES TO PLAY BALL.
I'M IN A PICKLE.
FATTY SNAX DELI

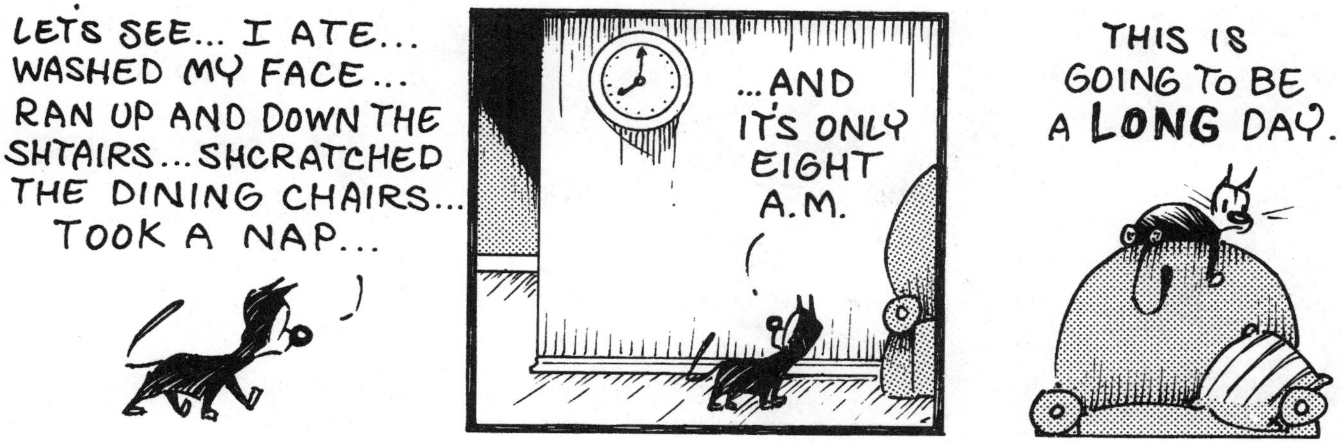
LET'S SEE... I ATE... WASHED MY FACE... RAN UP AND DOWN THE SHTAIRS... SHCRATCHED THE DINING CHAIRS... TOOK A NAP...
...AND IT'S ONLY EIGHT A.M.
THIS IS GOING TO BE A **LONG** DAY.

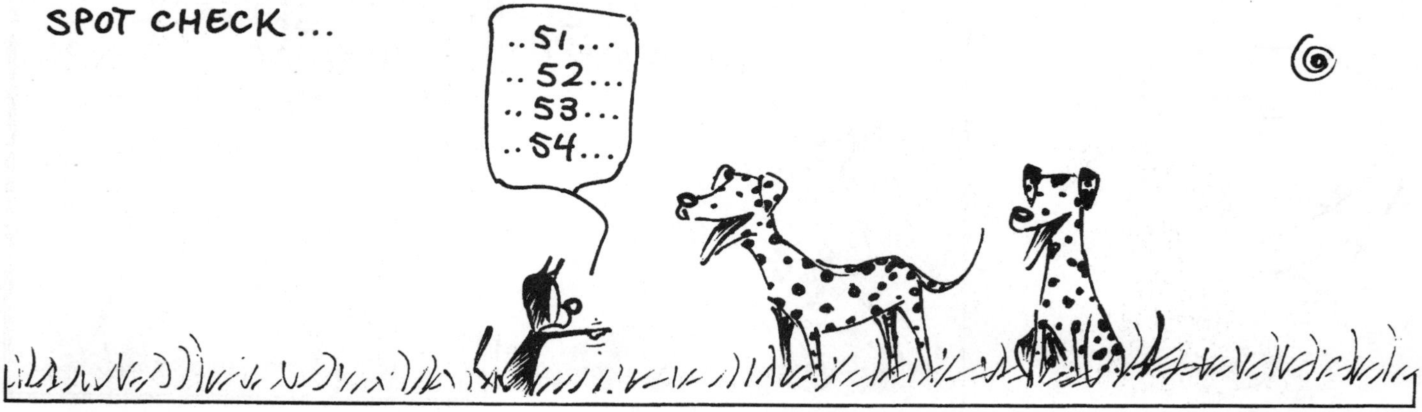
SPOT CHECK...
..51... ..52... ..53... ..54...

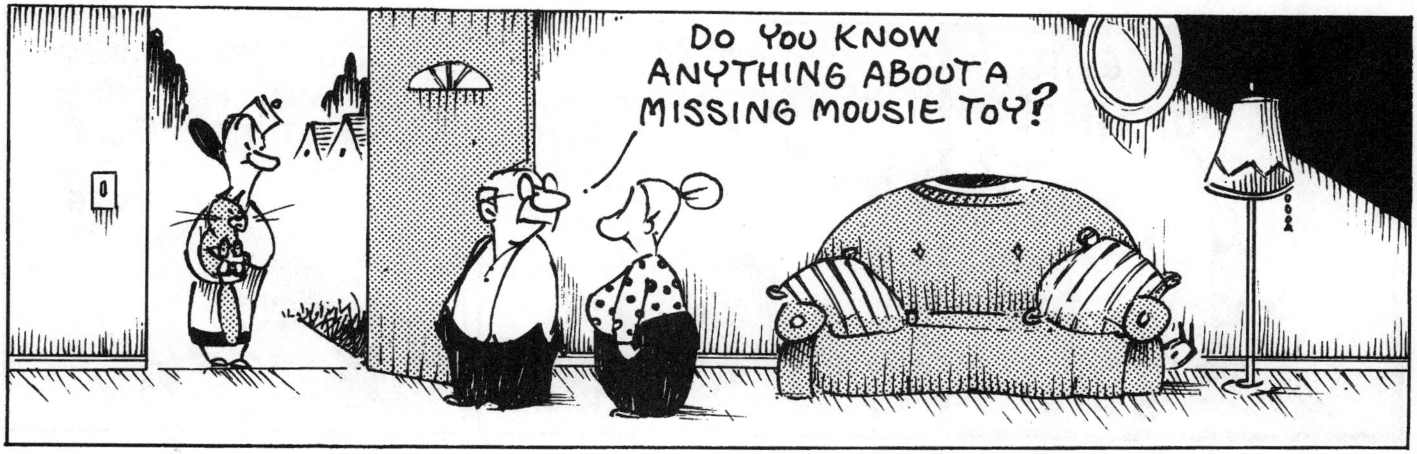
DO YOU KNOW ANYTHING ABOUT A MISSING MOUSIE TOY?

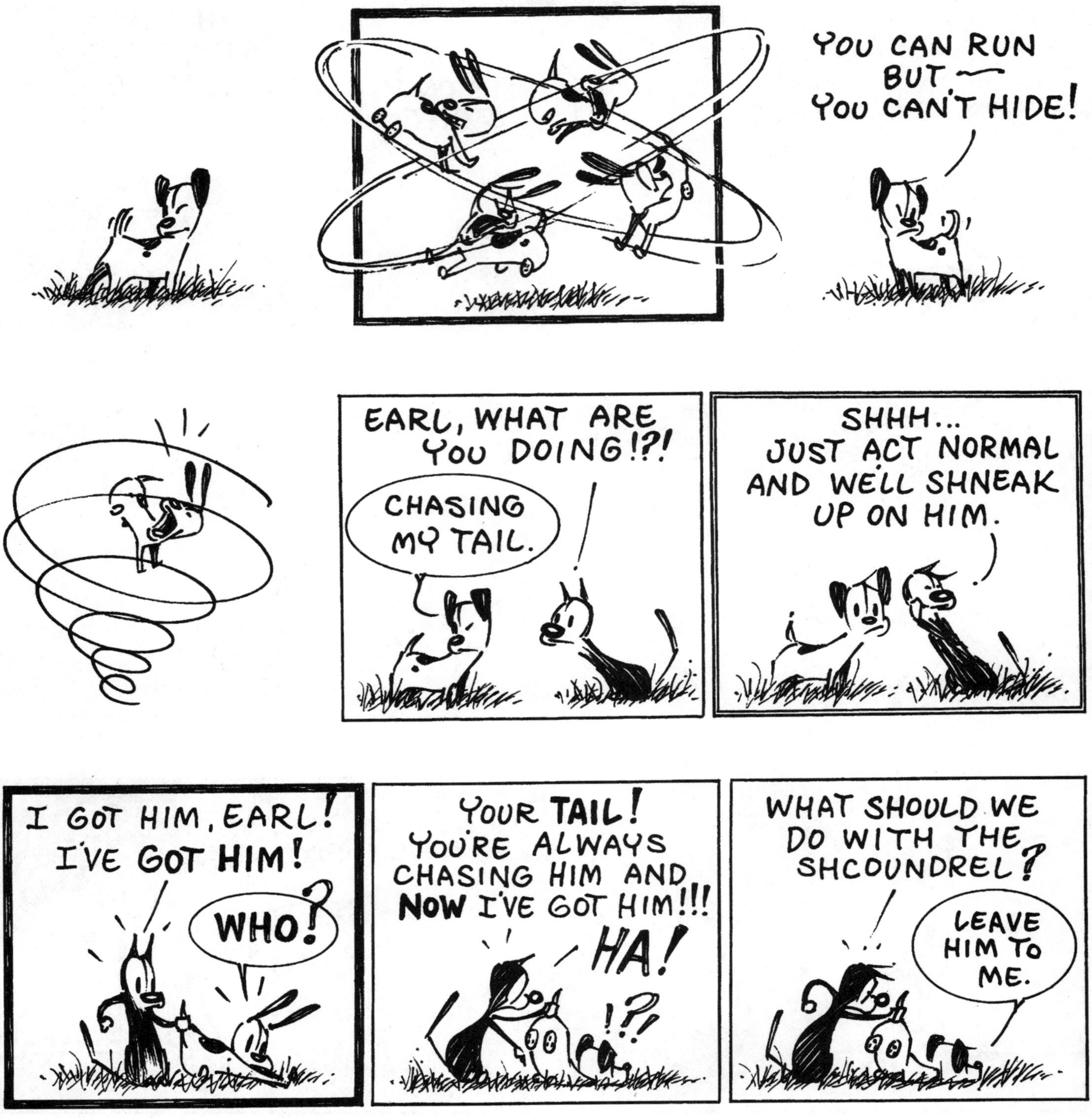
YOU CAN RUN BUT~ YOU CAN'T HIDE!
EARL, WHAT ARE YOU DOING!?!
CHASING MY TAIL.
SHHH... JUST ACT NORMAL AND WE'LL SHNEAK UP ON HIM.
I GOT HIM, EARL! I'VE GOT HIM!
WHO?
YOUR TAIL! YOU'RE ALWAYS CHASING HIM AND NOW I'VE GOT HIM!!!
HA!
!?!
WHAT SHOULD WE DO WITH THE SHCOUNDREL?
LEAVE HIM TO ME.

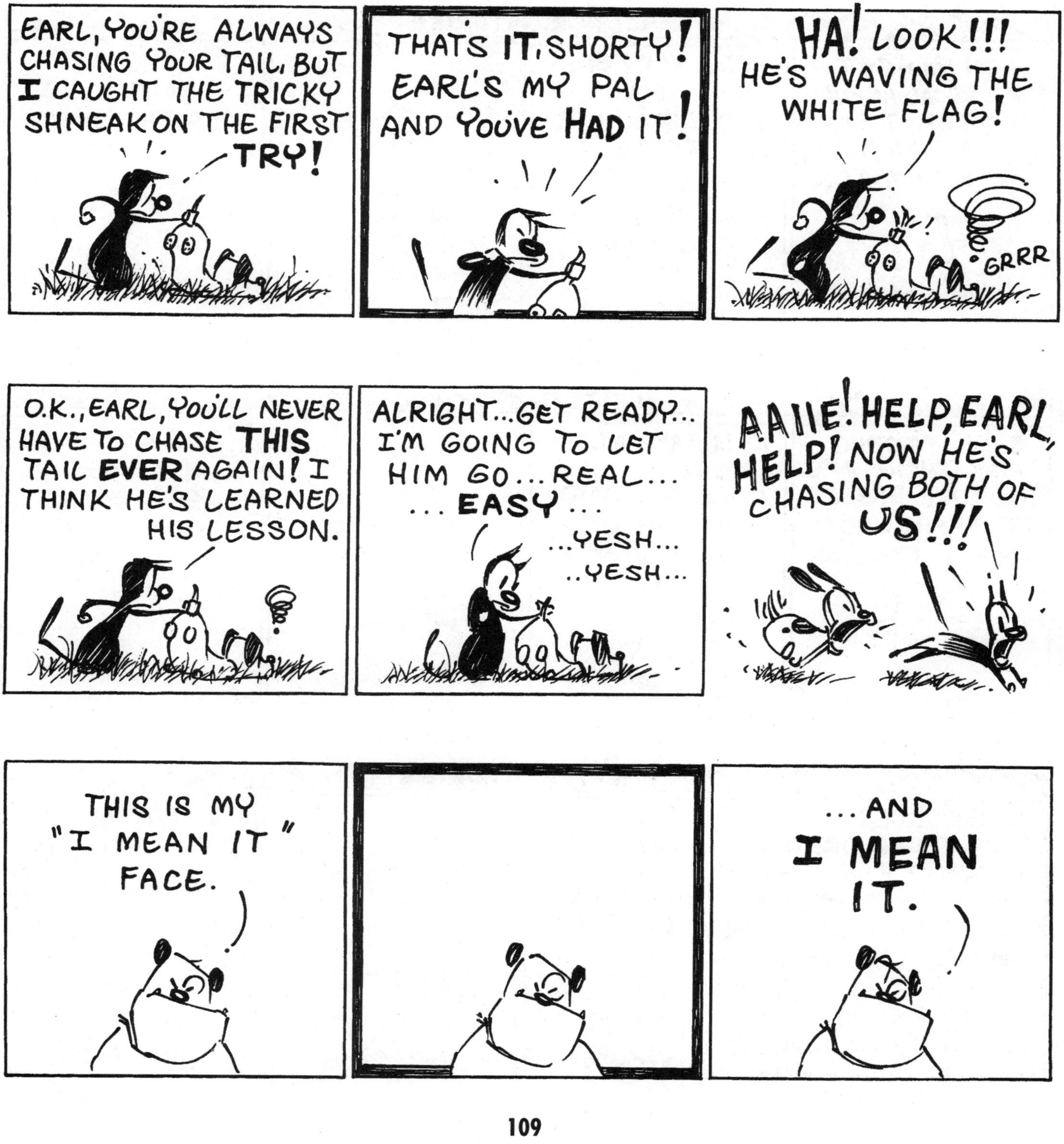
EARL, YOU'RE ALWAYS CHASING YOUR TAIL, BUT I CAUGHT THE TRICKY SHNEAK ON THE FIRST TRY!
THAT'S IT, SHORTY! EARL'S MY PAL AND YOU'VE HAD IT!
HA! LOOK!!! HE'S WAVING THE WHITE FLAG!
GRRR
O.K., EARL, YOU'LL NEVER HAVE TO CHASE THIS TAIL EVER AGAIN! I THINK HE'S LEARNED HIS LESSON.
ALRIGHT... GET READY... I'M GOING TO LET HIM GO... REAL... ...EASY...
...YESH... ..YESH...
AAIIE! HELP, EARL, HELP! NOW HE'S CHASING BOTH OF US!!!
THIS IS MY "I MEAN IT" FACE.
...AND I MEAN IT.

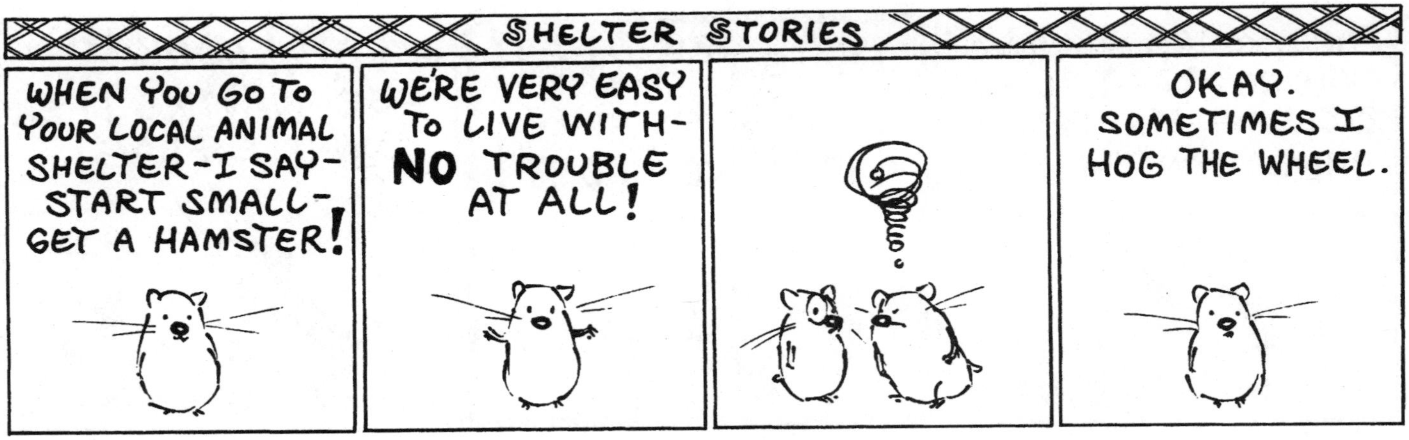
SHELTER STORIES
WHEN YOU GO TO YOUR LOCAL ANIMAL SHELTER–I SAY–START SMALL–GET A HAMSTER!
WE'RE VERY EASY TO LIVE WITH–NO TROUBLE AT ALL!
OKAY. SOMETIMES I HOG THE WHEEL.

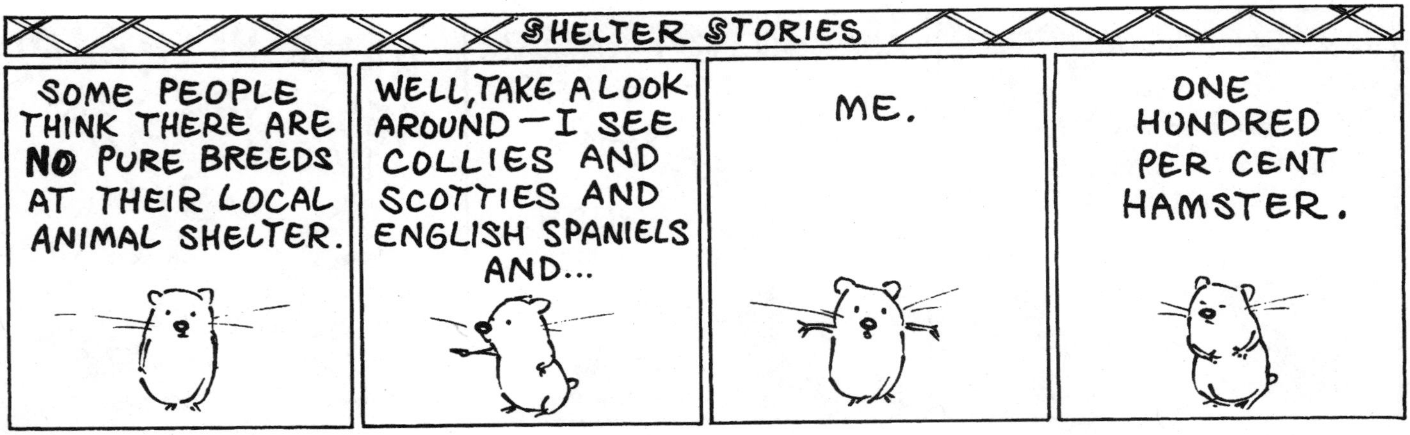
SHELTER STORIES
SOME PEOPLE THINK THERE ARE NO PURE BREEDS AT THEIR LOCAL ANIMAL SHELTER.
WELL, TAKE A LOOK AROUND–I SEE COLLIES AND SCOTTIES AND ENGLISH SPANIELS AND...
ME.
ONE HUNDRED PER CENT HAMSTER.

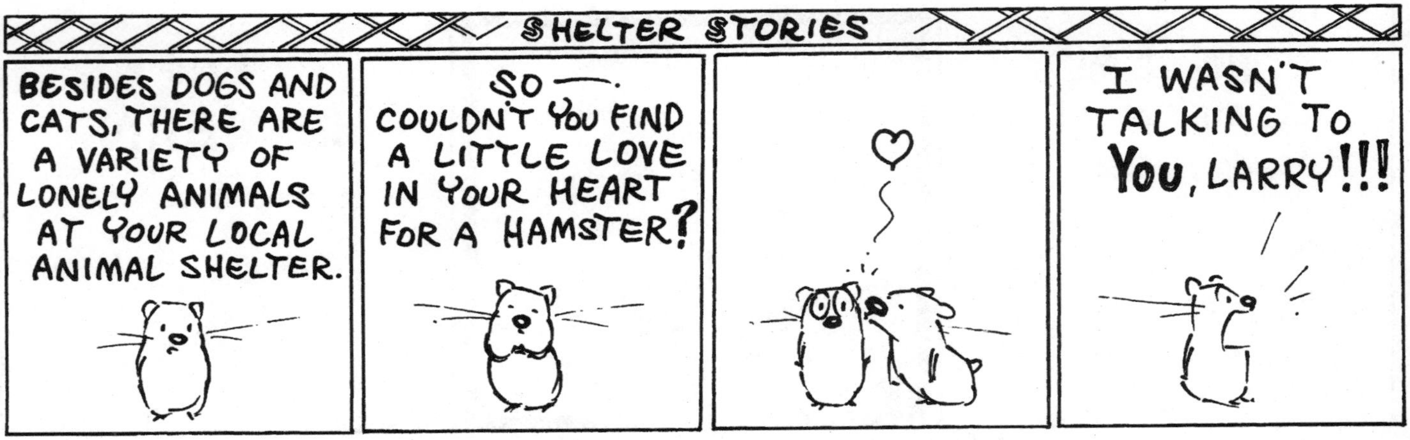
SHELTER STORIES
BESIDES DOGS AND CATS, THERE ARE A VARIETY OF LONELY ANIMALS AT YOUR LOCAL ANIMAL SHELTER.
SO– COULDN'T YOU FIND A LITTLE LOVE IN YOUR HEART FOR A HAMSTER?
I WASN'T TALKING TO YOU, LARRY!!!

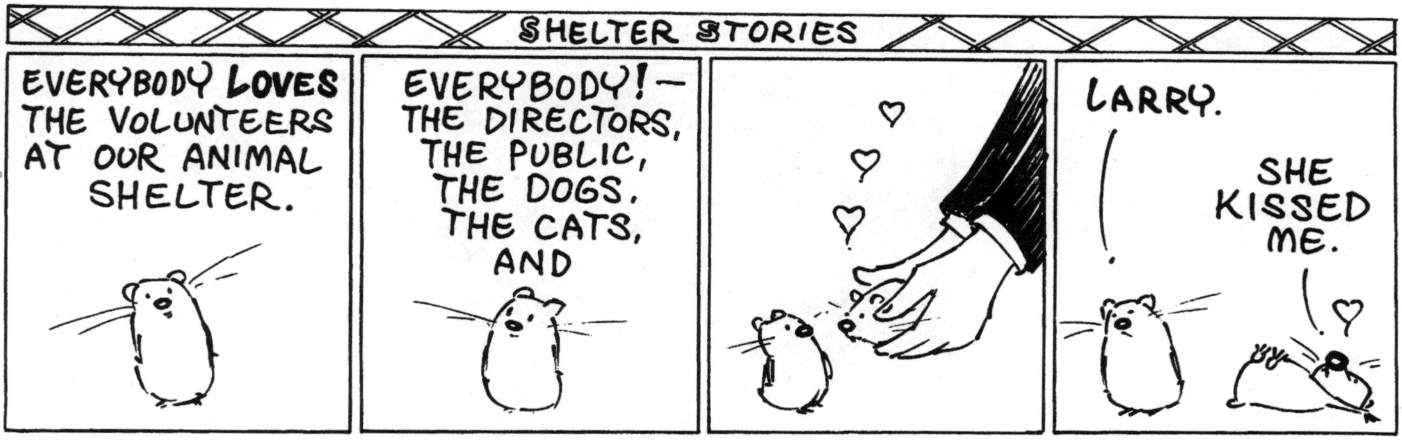
SHELTER STORIES
EVERYBODY LOVES THE VOLUNTEERS AT OUR ANIMAL SHELTER.
EVERYBODY! — THE DIRECTORS, THE PUBLIC, THE DOGS, THE CATS, AND
LARRY.
SHE KISSED ME.

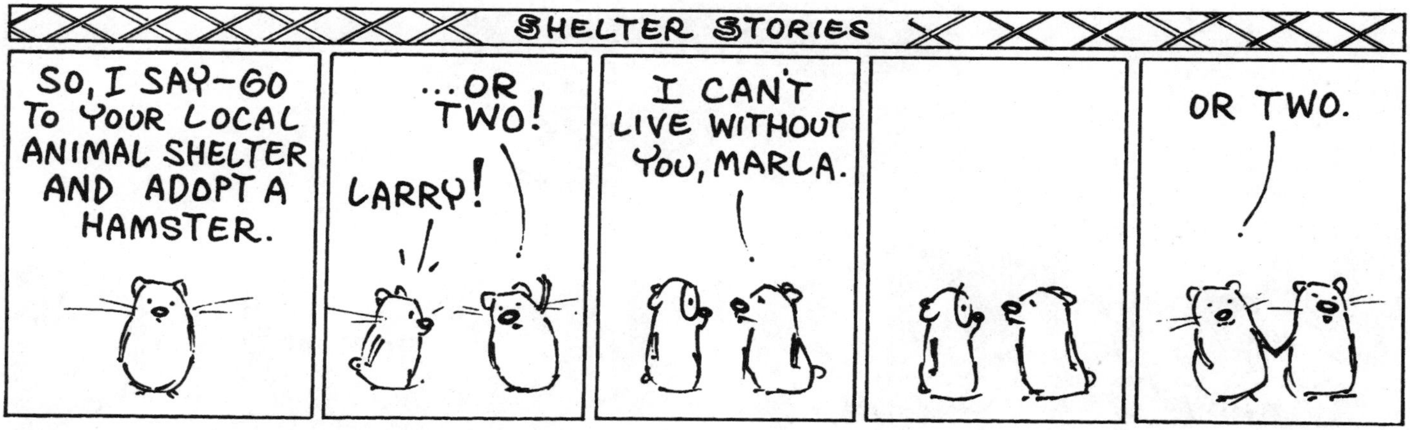
SHELTER STORIES
SO, I SAY–GO TO YOUR LOCAL ANIMAL SHELTER AND ADOPT A HAMSTER.
LARRY!
...OR TWO!
I CAN'T LIVE WITHOUT YOU, MARLA.
OR TWO.

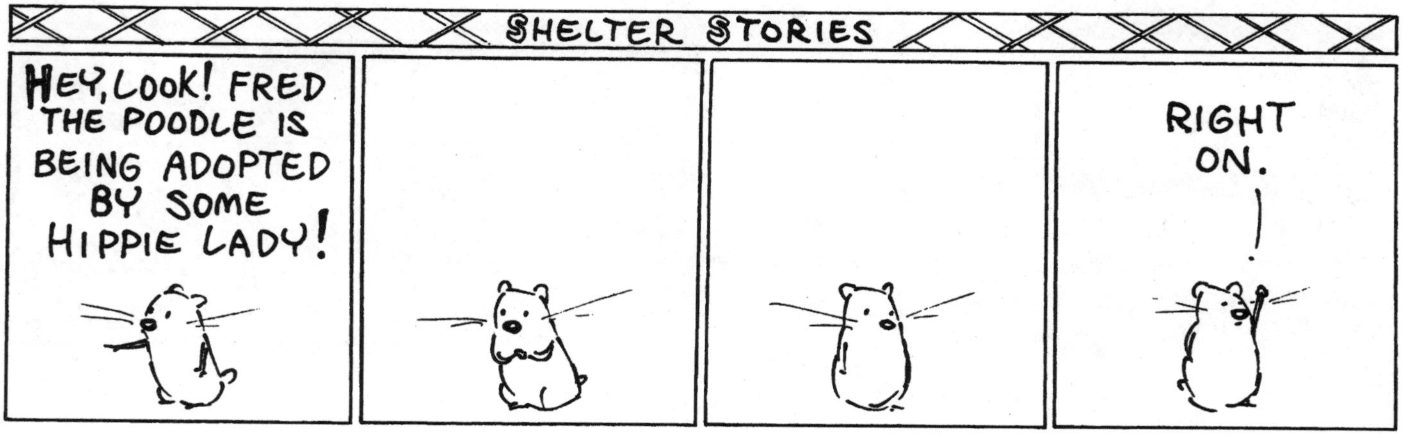
SHELTER STORIES
HEY, LOOK! FRED THE POODLE IS BEING ADOPTED BY SOME HIPPIE LADY!
RIGHT ON.

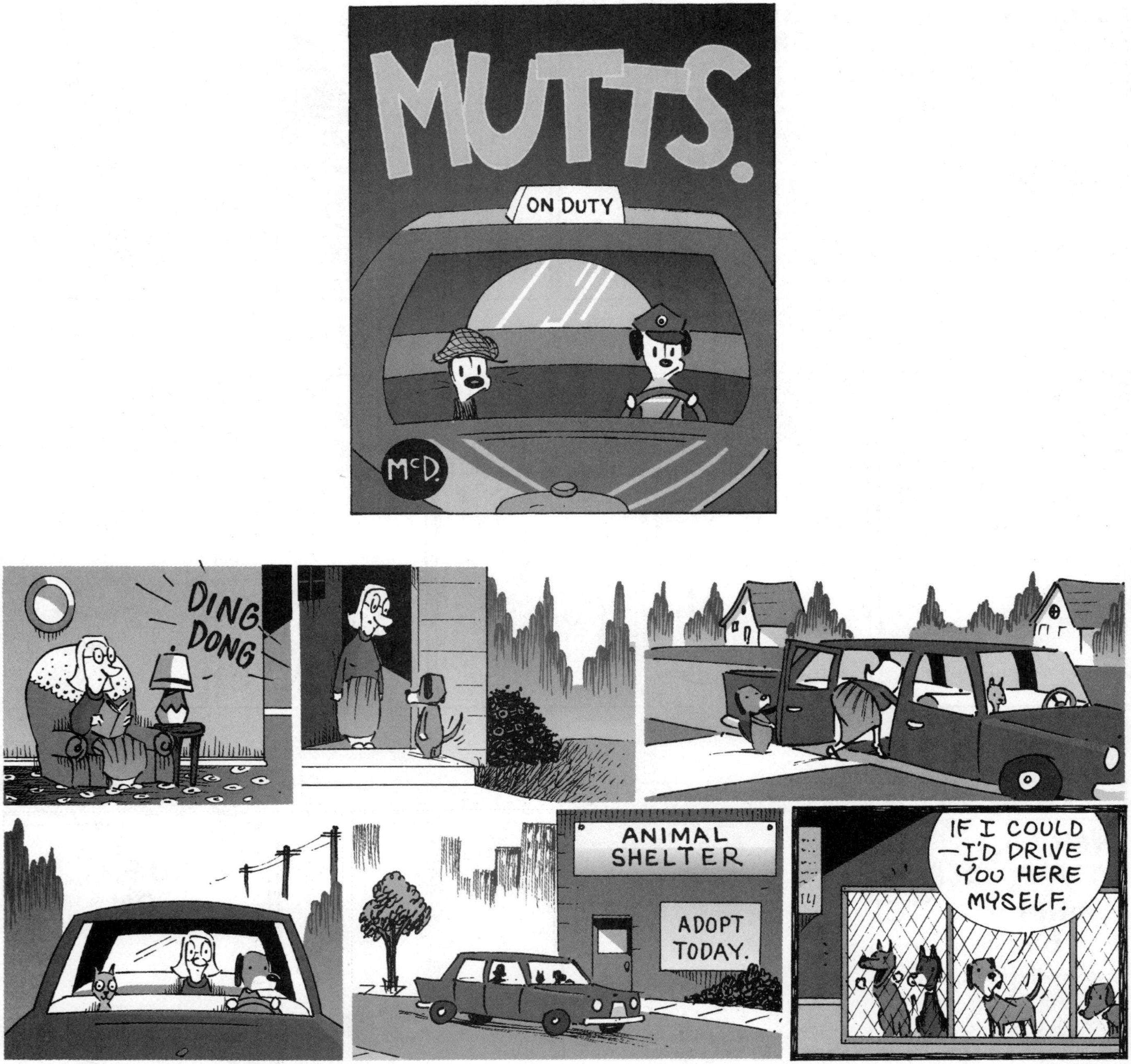
MUTTS.
ON DUTY
McD.
DING DONG
ANIMAL SHELTER
ADOPT TODAY.
IF I COULD —I'D DRIVE YOU HERE MYSELF.

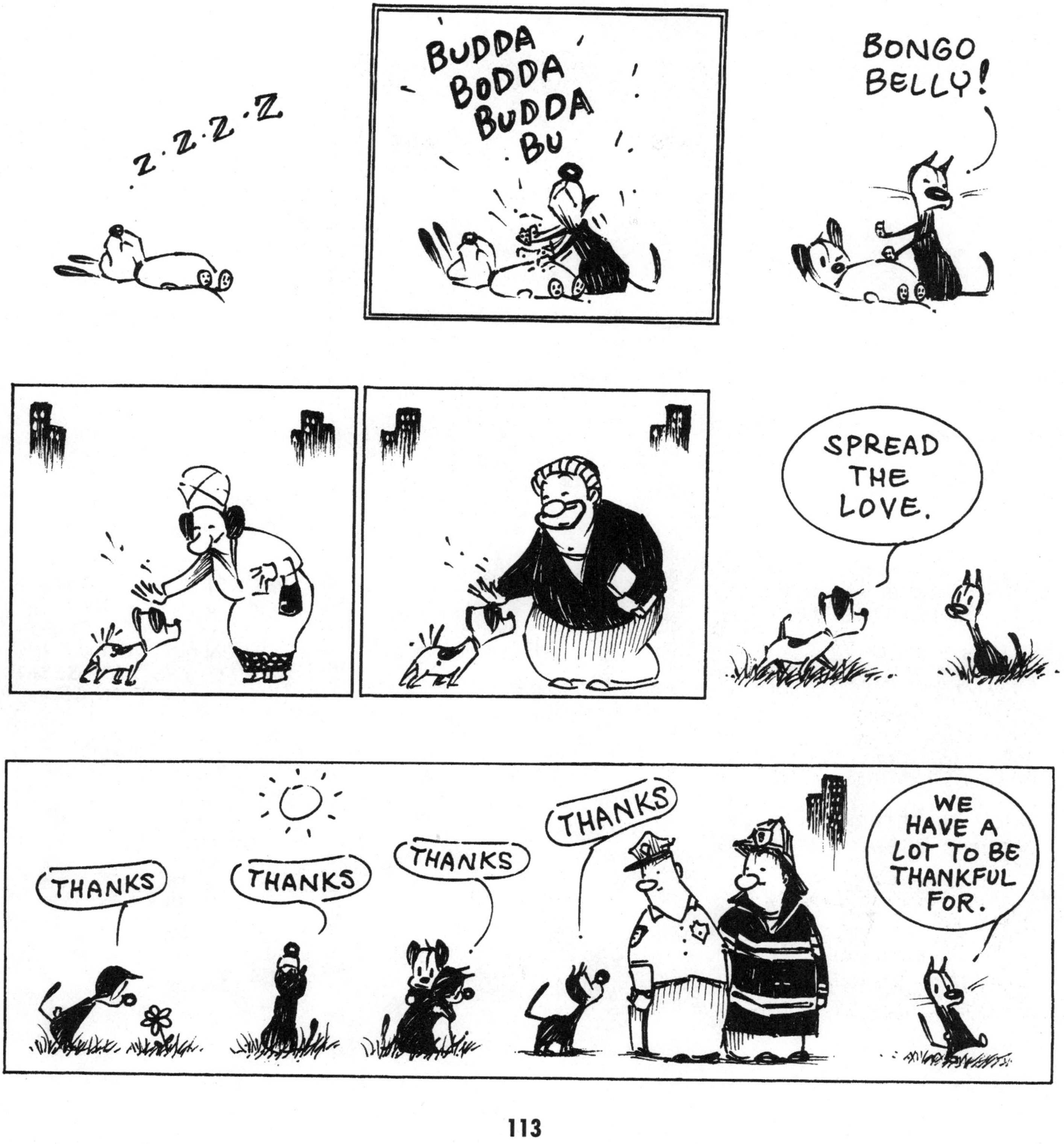
Z·Z·Z·Z·Z
BUDDA BODDA BUDDA BU
BONGO BELLY!
SPREAD THE LOVE.
THANKS
THANKS
THANKS
THANKS
WE HAVE A LOT TO BE THANKFUL FOR.

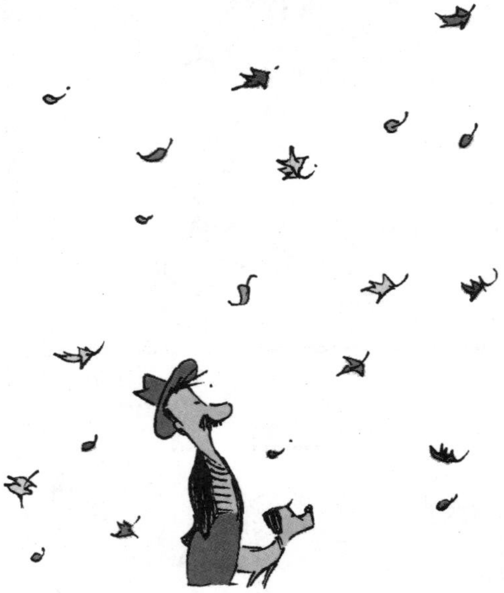

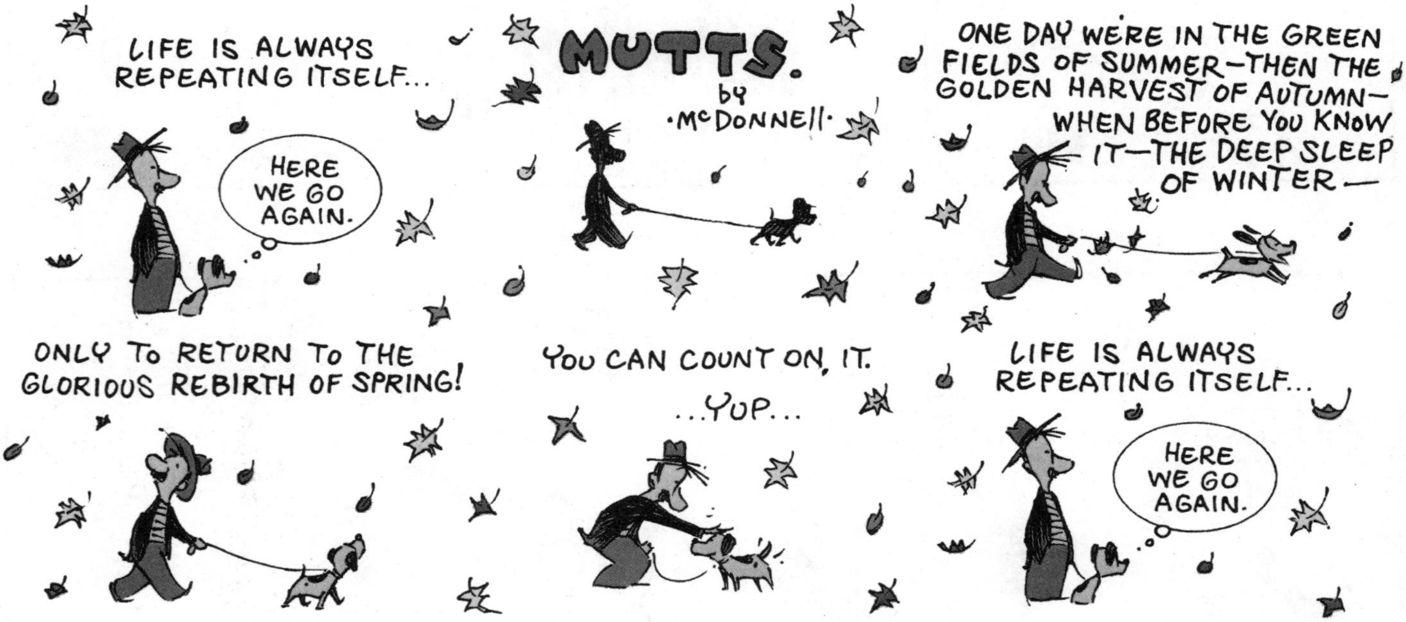
LIFE IS ALWAYS REPEATING ITSELF...
HERE WE GO AGAIN.
MUTTS.
by ·McDONNELL·
ONE DAY WE'RE IN THE GREEN FIELDS OF SUMMER—THEN THE GOLDEN HARVEST OF AUTUMN—WHEN BEFORE YOU KNOW IT—THE DEEP SLEEP OF WINTER—
ONLY TO RETURN TO THE GLORIOUS REBIRTH OF SPRING!
YOU CAN COUNT ON IT.
...YUP...
LIFE IS ALWAYS REPEATING ITSELF...
HERE WE GO AGAIN.

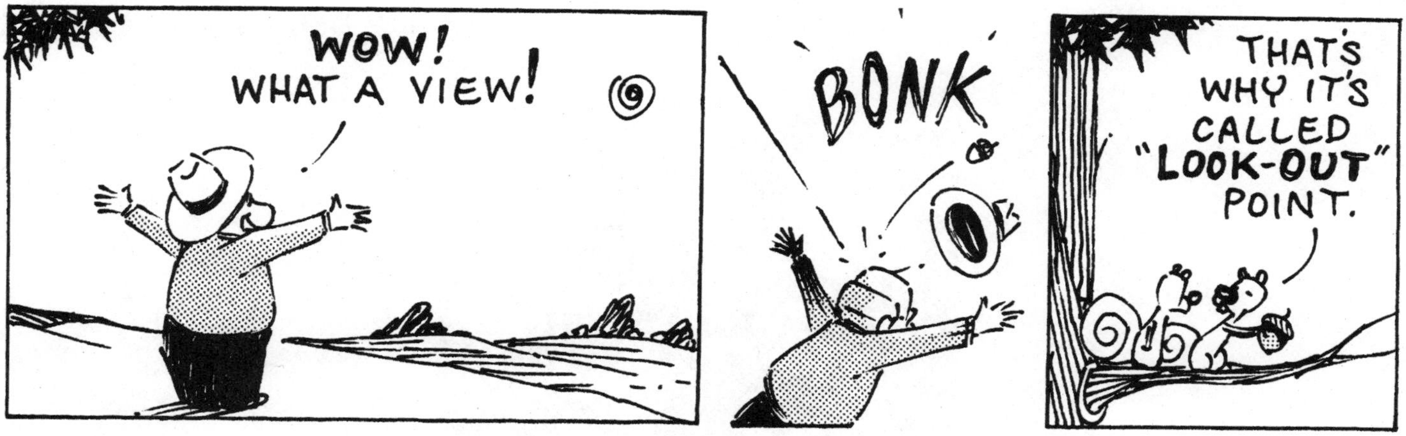
WOW! WHAT A VIEW!
BONK
THAT'S WHY IT'S CALLED "LOOK-OUT" POINT.

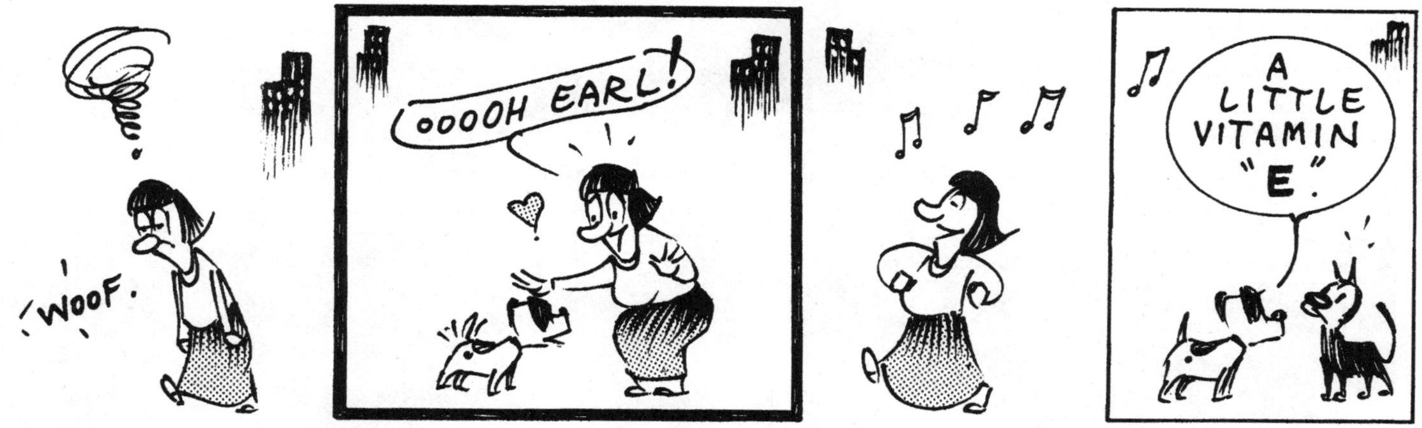
WOOF.
OOOOH EARL!
A LITTLE VITAMIN "E".

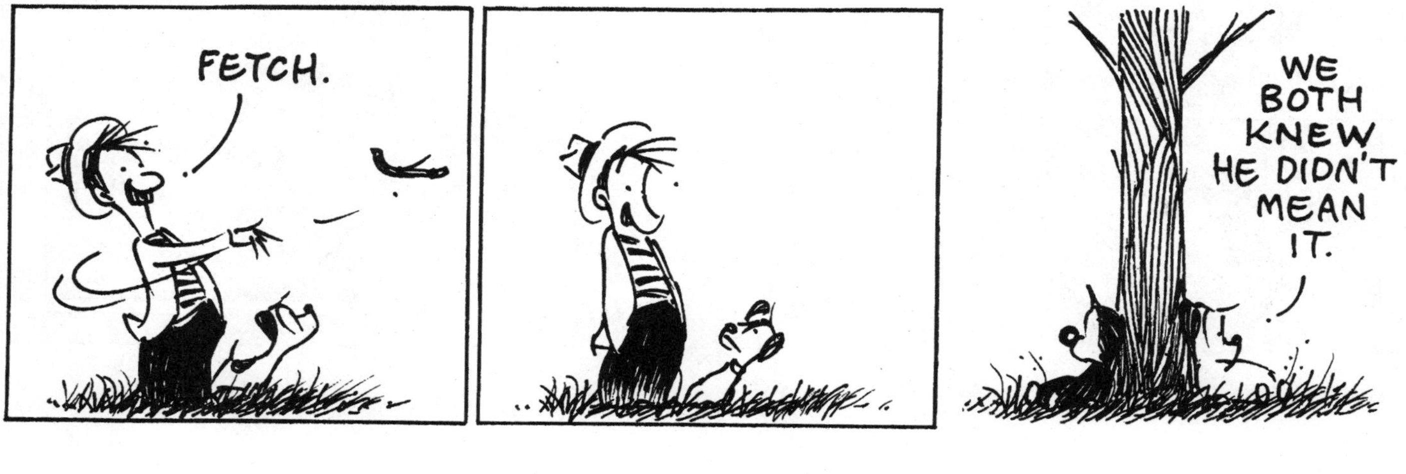
FETCH.
WE BOTH KNEW HE DIDN'T MEAN IT.

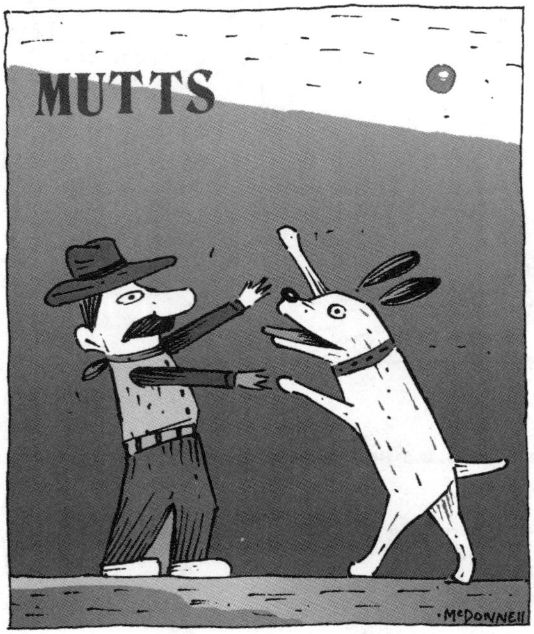
MUTTS
McDONNELL

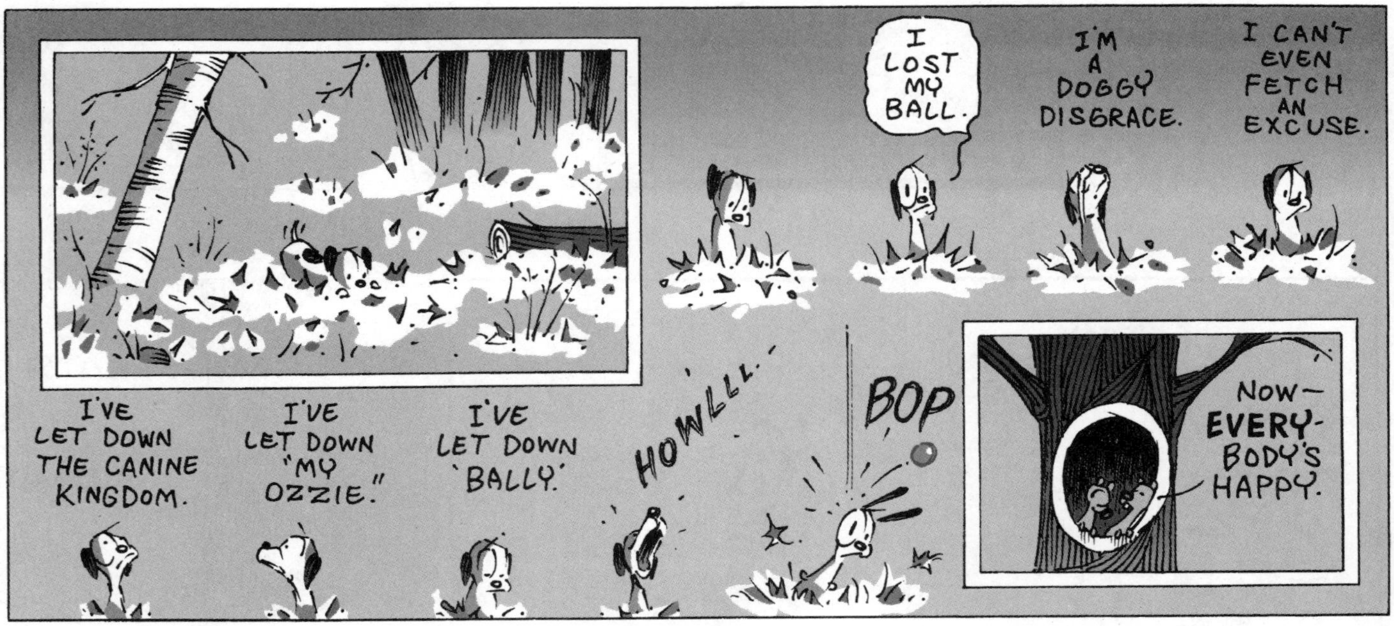
I LOST MY BALL.
I'M A DOGGY DISGRACE.
I CAN'T EVEN FETCH AN EXCUSE.
I'VE LET DOWN THE CANINE KINGDOM.
I'VE LET DOWN "MY OZZIE."
I'VE LET DOWN 'BALLY.'
HOWLLL
BOP
NOW— EVERY-BODY'S HAPPY.

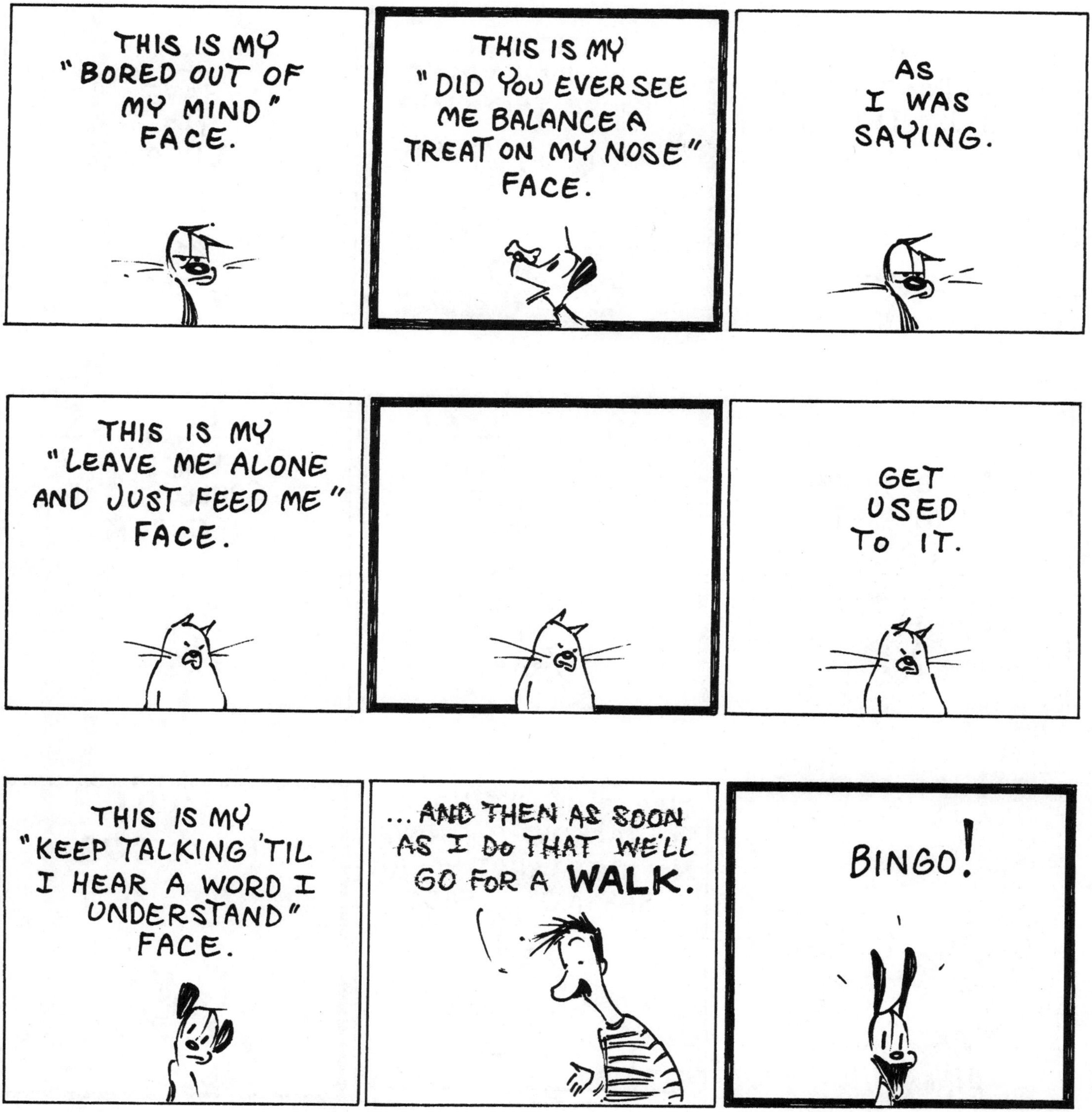
THIS IS MY "BORED OUT OF MY MIND" FACE.
THIS IS MY "DID YOU EVER SEE ME BALANCE A TREAT ON MY NOSE" FACE.
AS I WAS SAYING.
THIS IS MY "LEAVE ME ALONE AND JUST FEED ME" FACE.
GET USED TO IT.
THIS IS MY "KEEP TALKING 'TIL I HEAR A WORD I UNDERSTAND" FACE.
... AND THEN AS SOON AS I DO THAT WE'LL GO FOR A WALK.
BINGO!

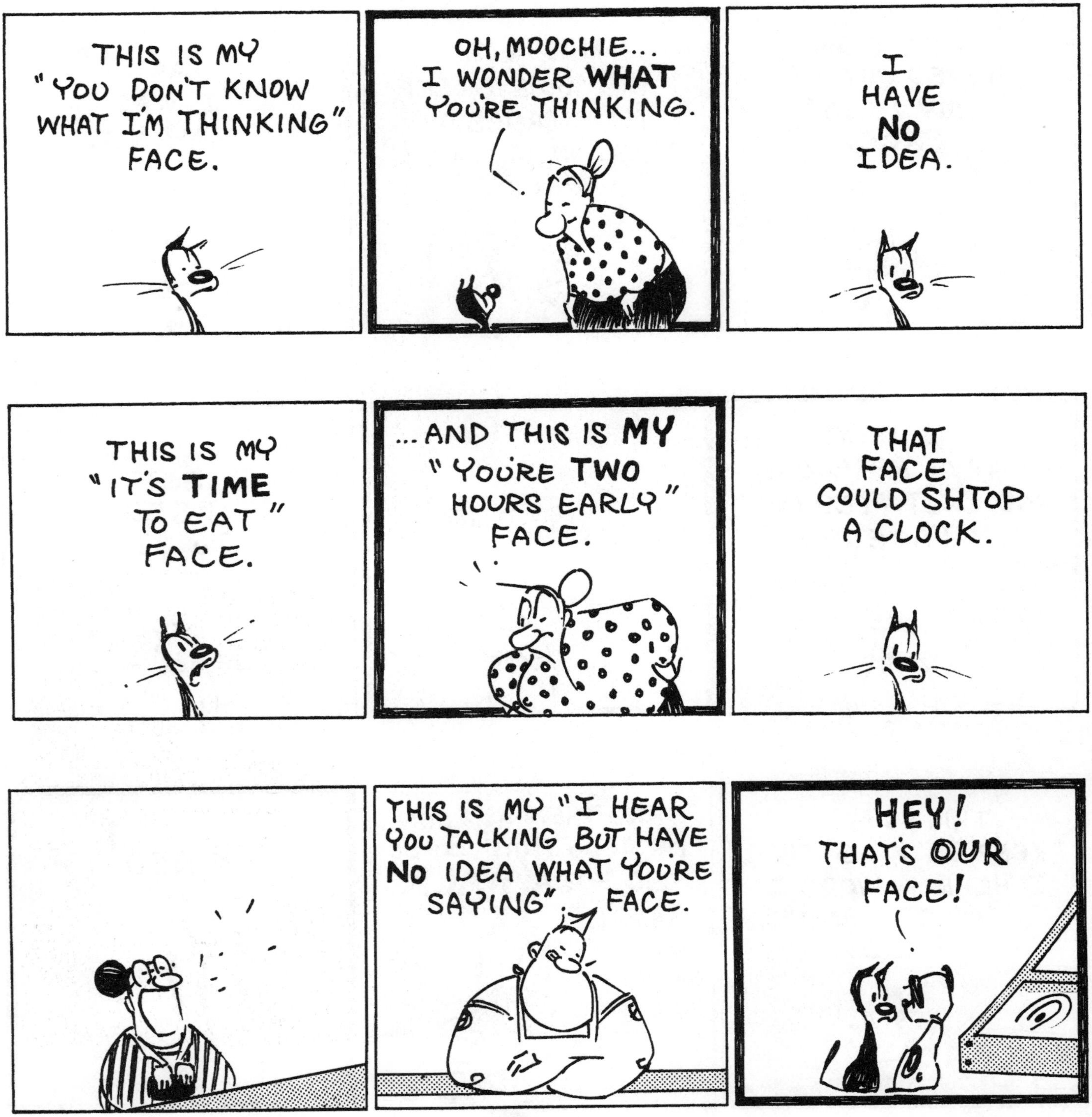
THIS IS MY "YOU DON'T KNOW WHAT I'M THINKING" FACE.
OH, MOOCHIE... I WONDER **WHAT** YOU'RE THINKING.
I HAVE **NO** IDEA.
THIS IS MY "IT'S **TIME** TO EAT" FACE.
...AND THIS IS **MY** "YOU'RE **TWO** HOURS EARLY" FACE.
THAT FACE COULD SHTOP A CLOCK.
THIS IS MY "I HEAR YOU TALKING BUT HAVE **NO** IDEA WHAT YOU'RE SAYING". FACE.
HEY! THAT'S **OUR** FACE!

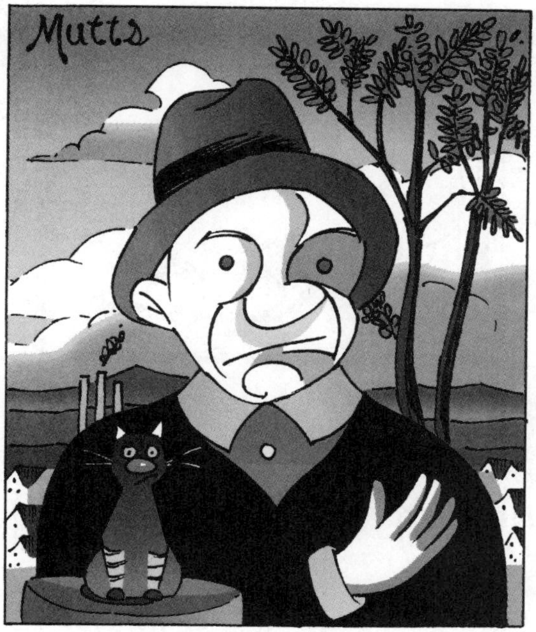
Mutts

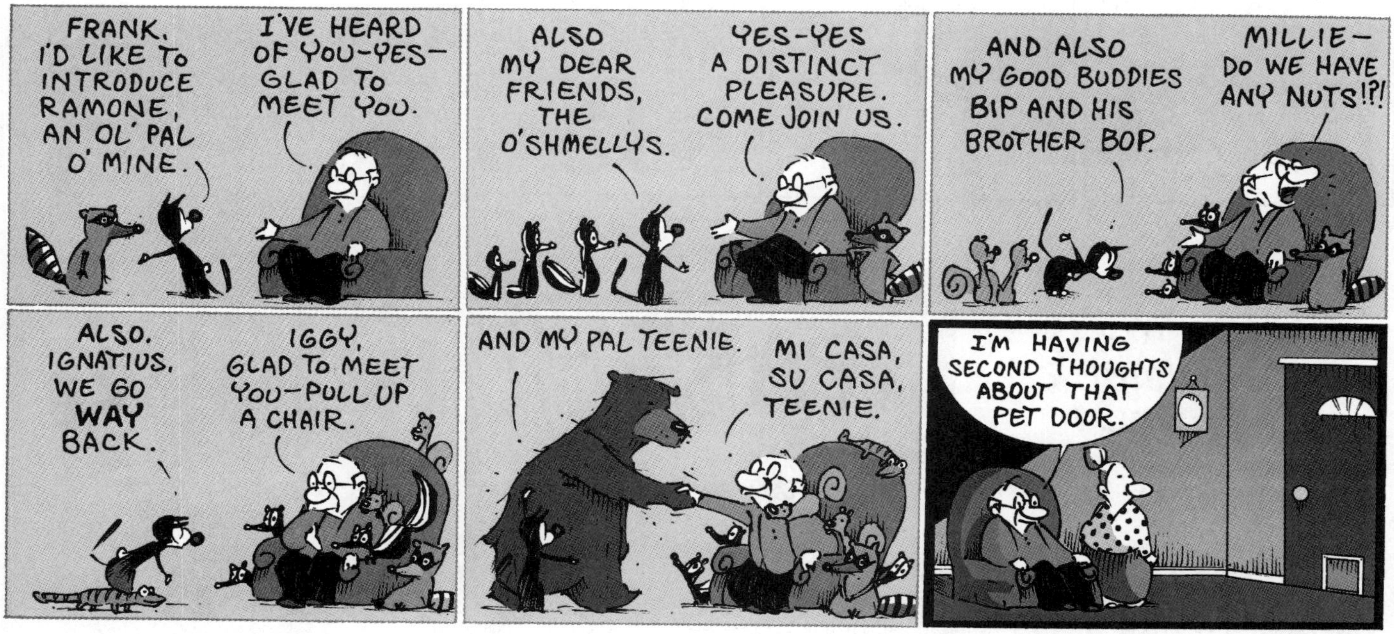
FRANK. I'D LIKE TO INTRODUCE RAMONE, AN OL' PAL O' MINE.
I'VE HEARD OF YOU-YES-GLAD TO MEET YOU.
ALSO MY DEAR FRIENDS, THE O'SHMELLYS.
YES-YES A DISTINCT PLEASURE. COME JOIN US.
AND ALSO MY GOOD BUDDIES BIP AND HIS BROTHER BOP.
MILLIE-DO WE HAVE ANY NUTS!?!
ALSO. IGNATIUS. WE GO WAY BACK.
IGGY, GLAD TO MEET YOU-PULL UP A CHAIR.
AND MY PAL TEENIE.
MI CASA, SU CASA, TEENIE.
I'M HAVING SECOND THOUGHTS ABOUT THAT PET DOOR.

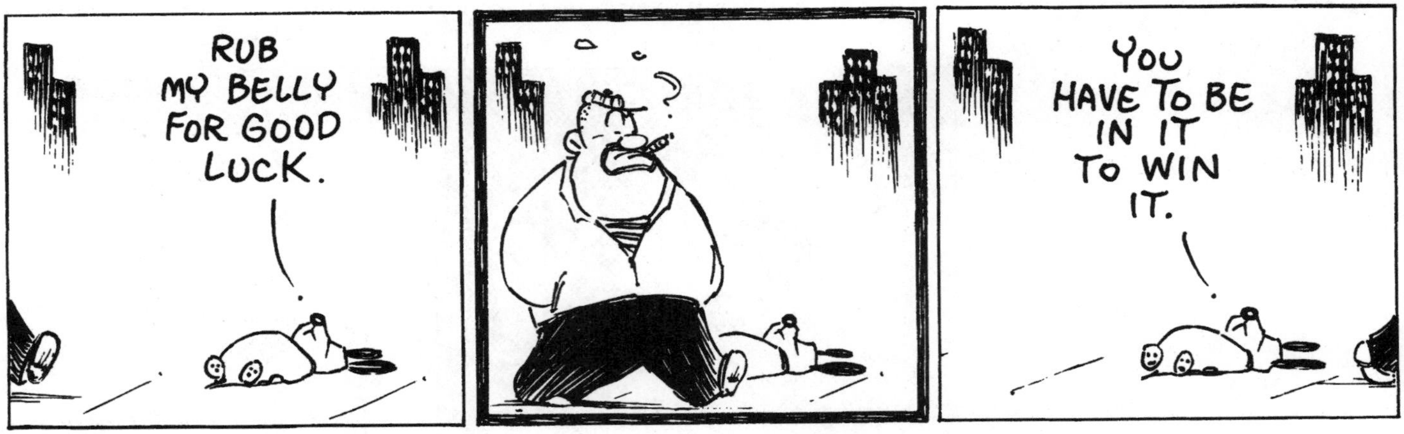
RUB MY BELLY FOR GOOD LUCK.
YOU HAVE TO BE IN IT TO WIN IT.

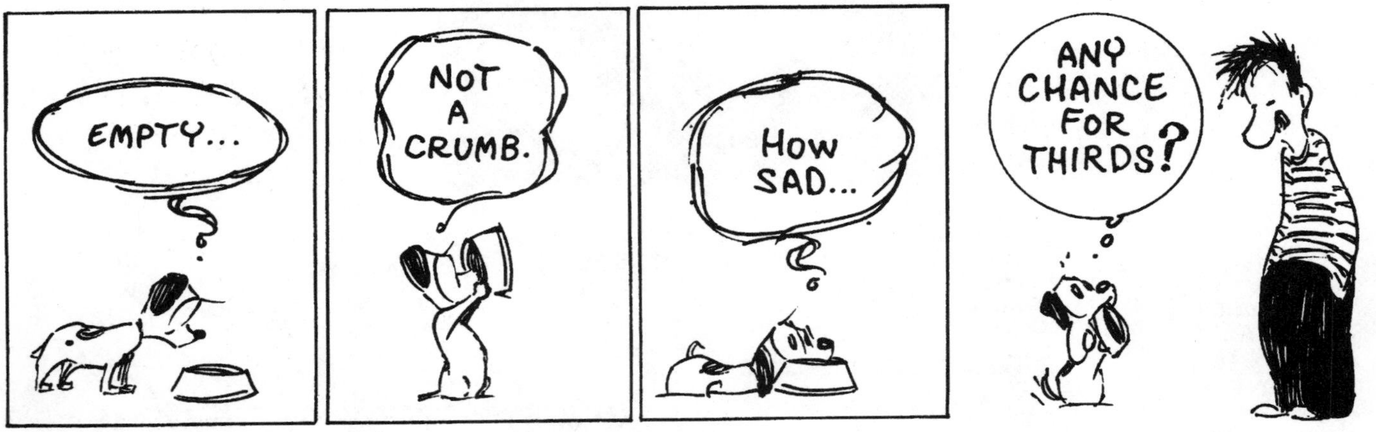
EMPTY...
NOT A CRUMB.
HOW SAD...
ANY CHANCE FOR THIRDS?

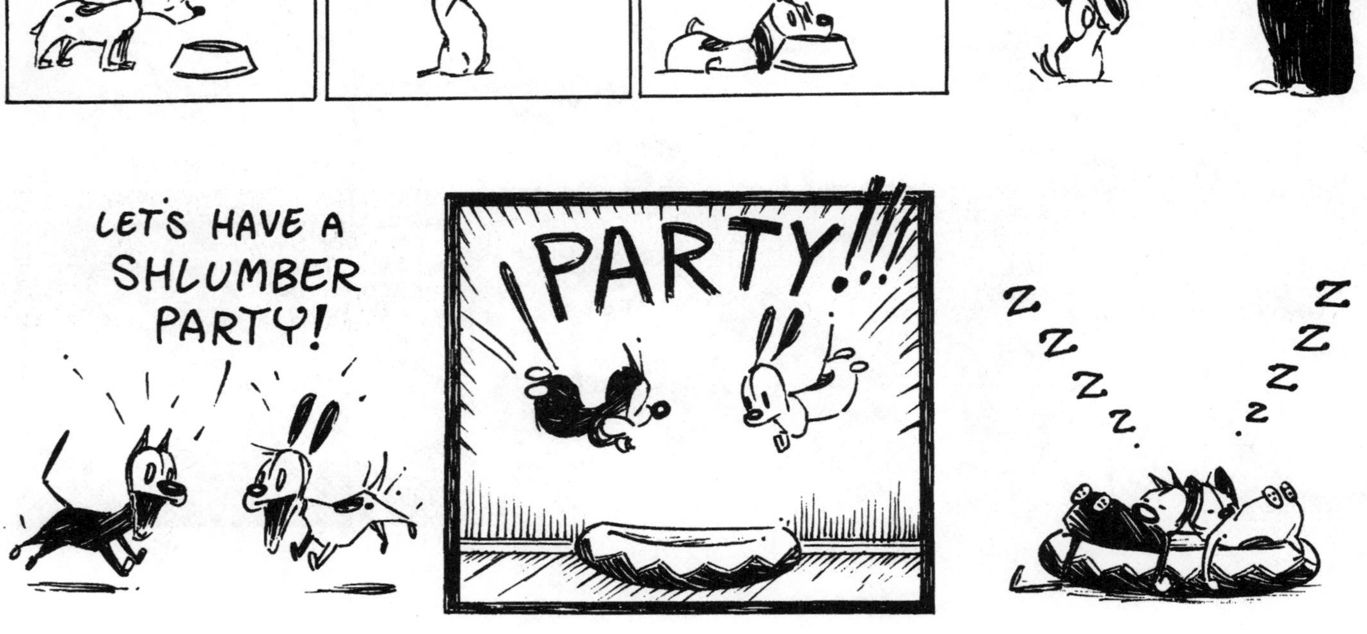
LET'S HAVE A SHLUMBER PARTY!
PARTY!!!
Z Z Z Z Z.
Z Z Z Z Z

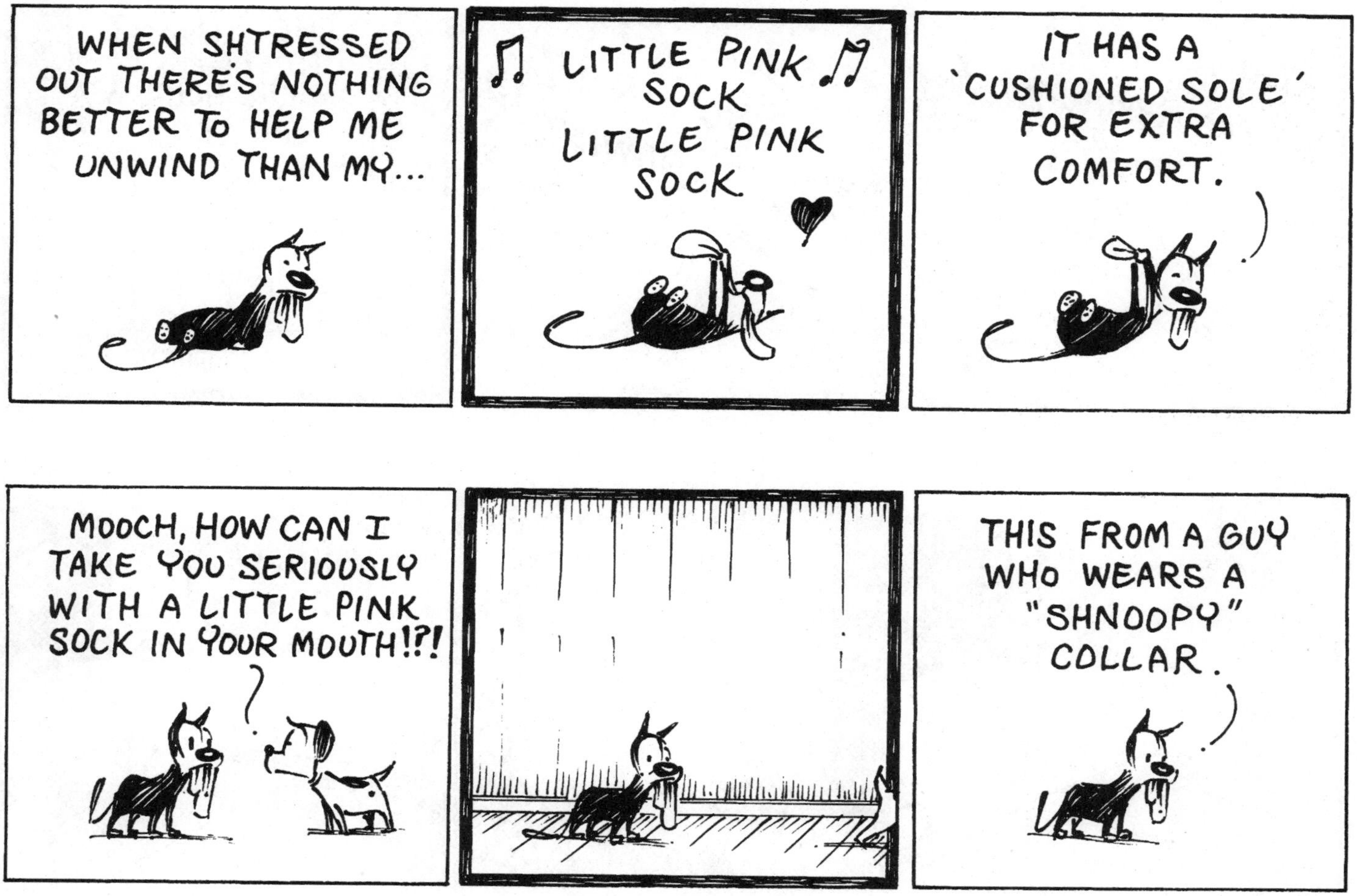
WHEN SHTRESSED OUT THERE'S NOTHING BETTER TO HELP ME UNWIND THAN MY...
♫ LITTLE PINK SOCK LITTLE PINK SOCK ♫
IT HAS A 'CUSHIONED SOLE' FOR EXTRA COMFORT.
MOOCH, HOW CAN I TAKE YOU SERIOUSLY WITH A LITTLE PINK SOCK IN YOUR MOUTH!?!
THIS FROM A GUY WHO WEARS A "SHNOOPY" COLLAR.

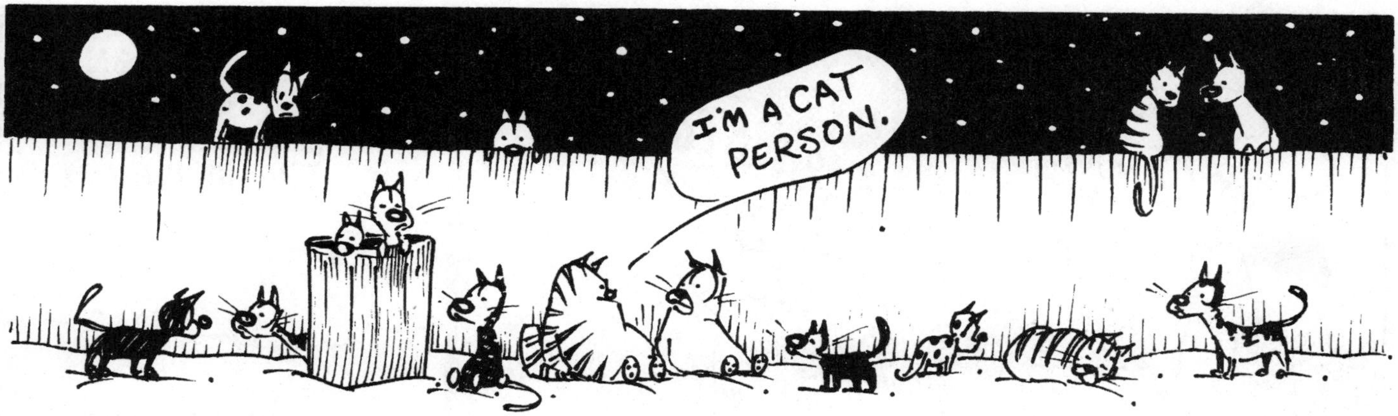
I'M A CAT PERSON.

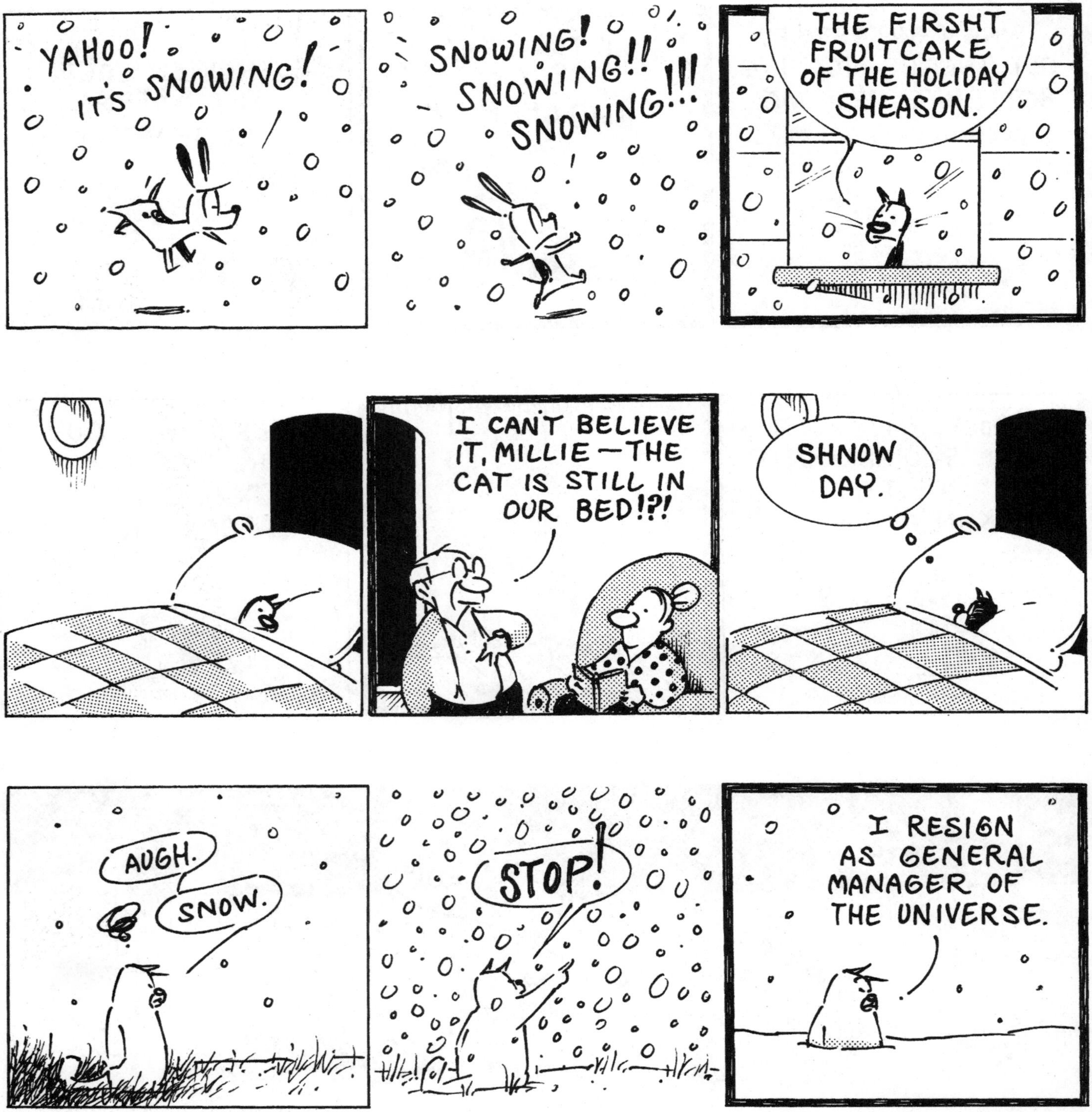
YAHOO! IT'S SNOWING!
SNOWING! SNOWING!! SNOWING!!!
THE FIRSHT FRUITCAKE OF THE HOLIDAY SHEASON.
I CAN'T BELIEVE IT, MILLIE—THE CAT IS STILL IN OUR BED!?!
SHNOW DAY.
AUGH.
SNOW.
STOP!
I RESIGN AS GENERAL MANAGER OF THE UNIVERSE.

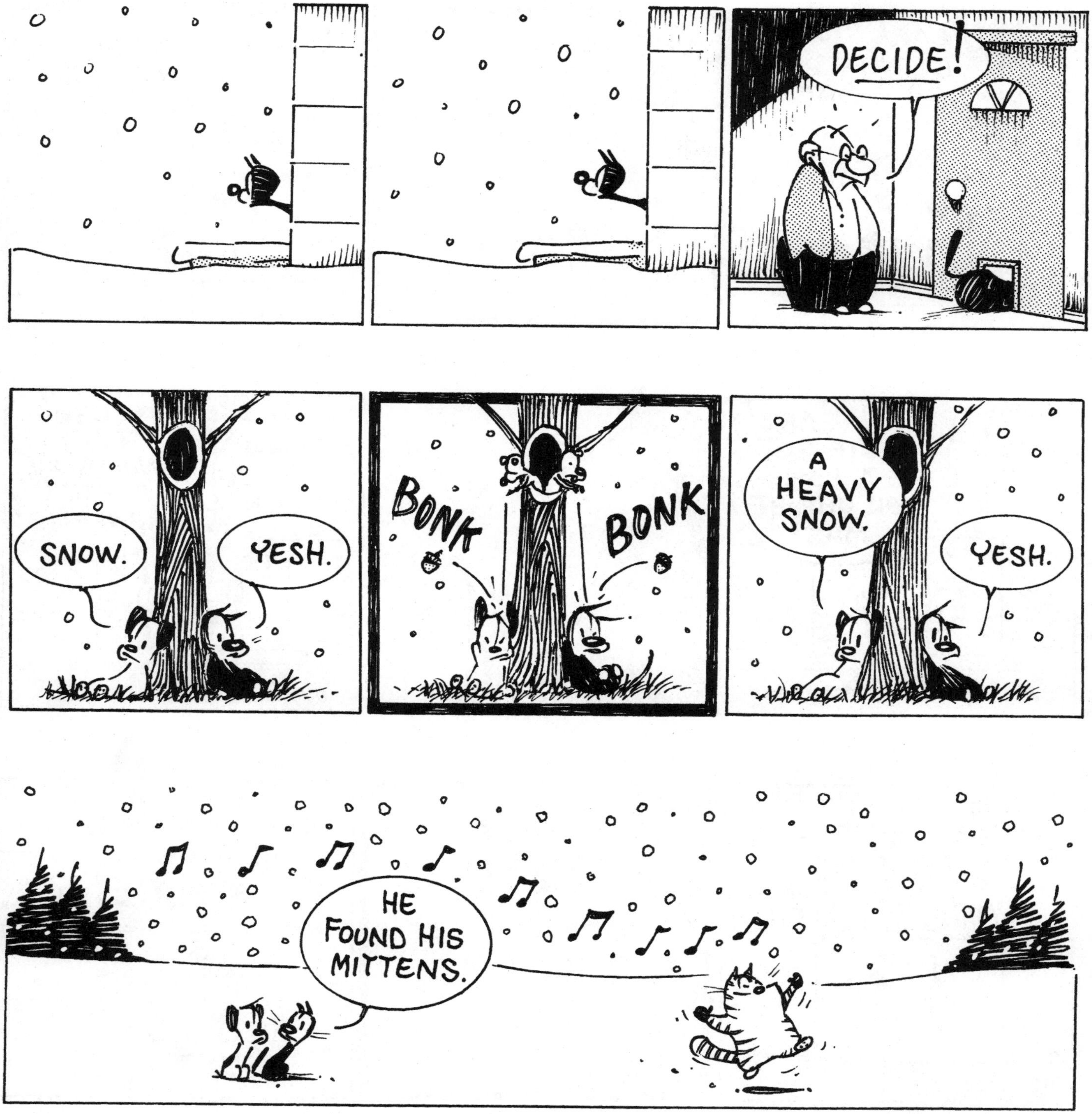
DECIDE!
SNOW.
YESH.
BONK
BONK
A HEAVY SNOW.
YESH.
HE FOUND HIS MITTENS.

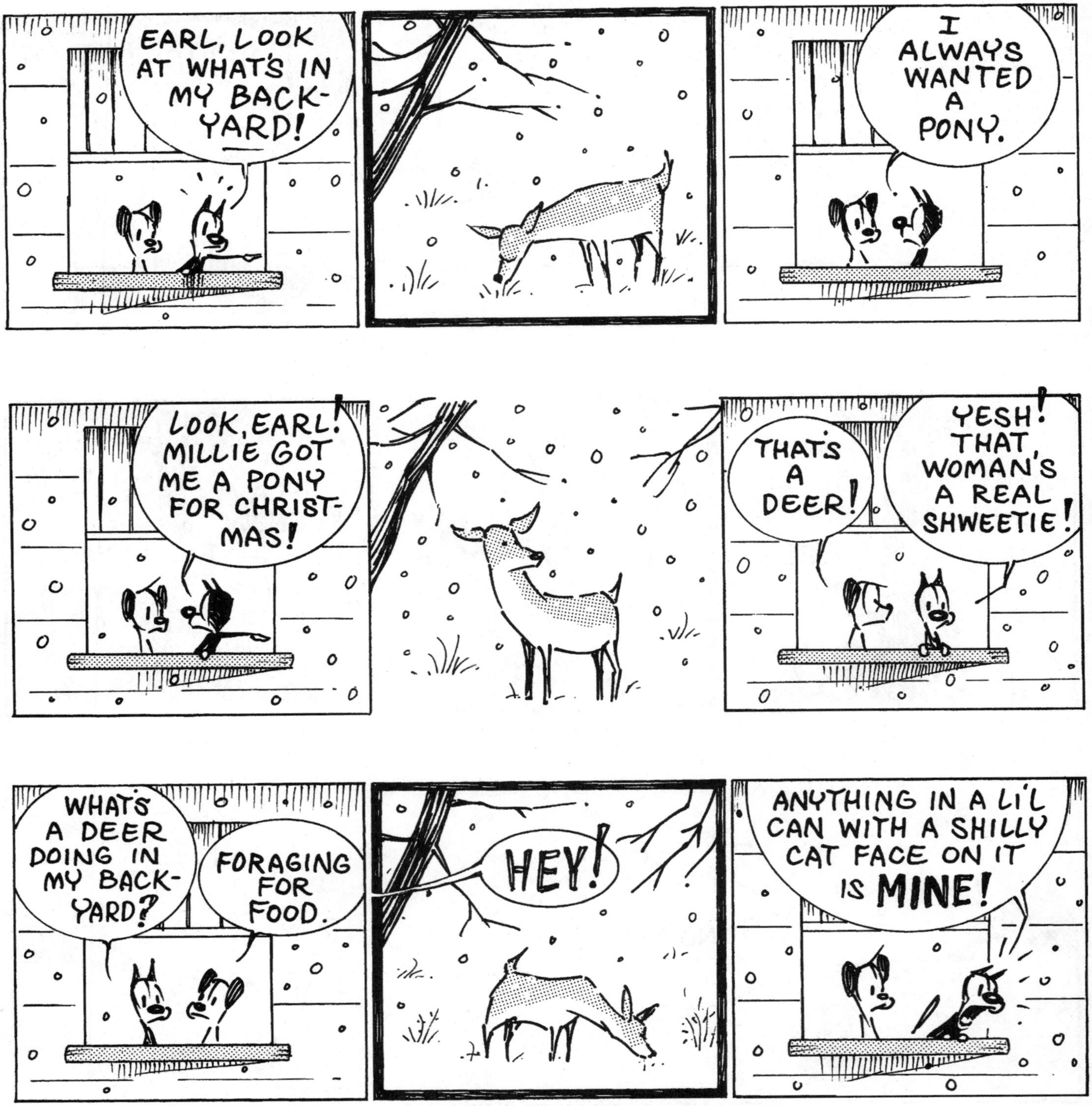
EARL, LOOK AT WHAT'S IN MY BACK-YARD!
I ALWAYS WANTED A PONY.
LOOK, EARL! MILLIE GOT ME A PONY FOR CHRIST-MAS!
THAT'S A DEER!
YESH! THAT WOMAN'S A REAL SHWEETIE!
WHAT'S A DEER DOING IN MY BACK-YARD?
FORAGING FOR FOOD.
HEY!
ANYTHING IN A LI'L CAN WITH A SHILLY CAT FACE ON IT IS MINE!

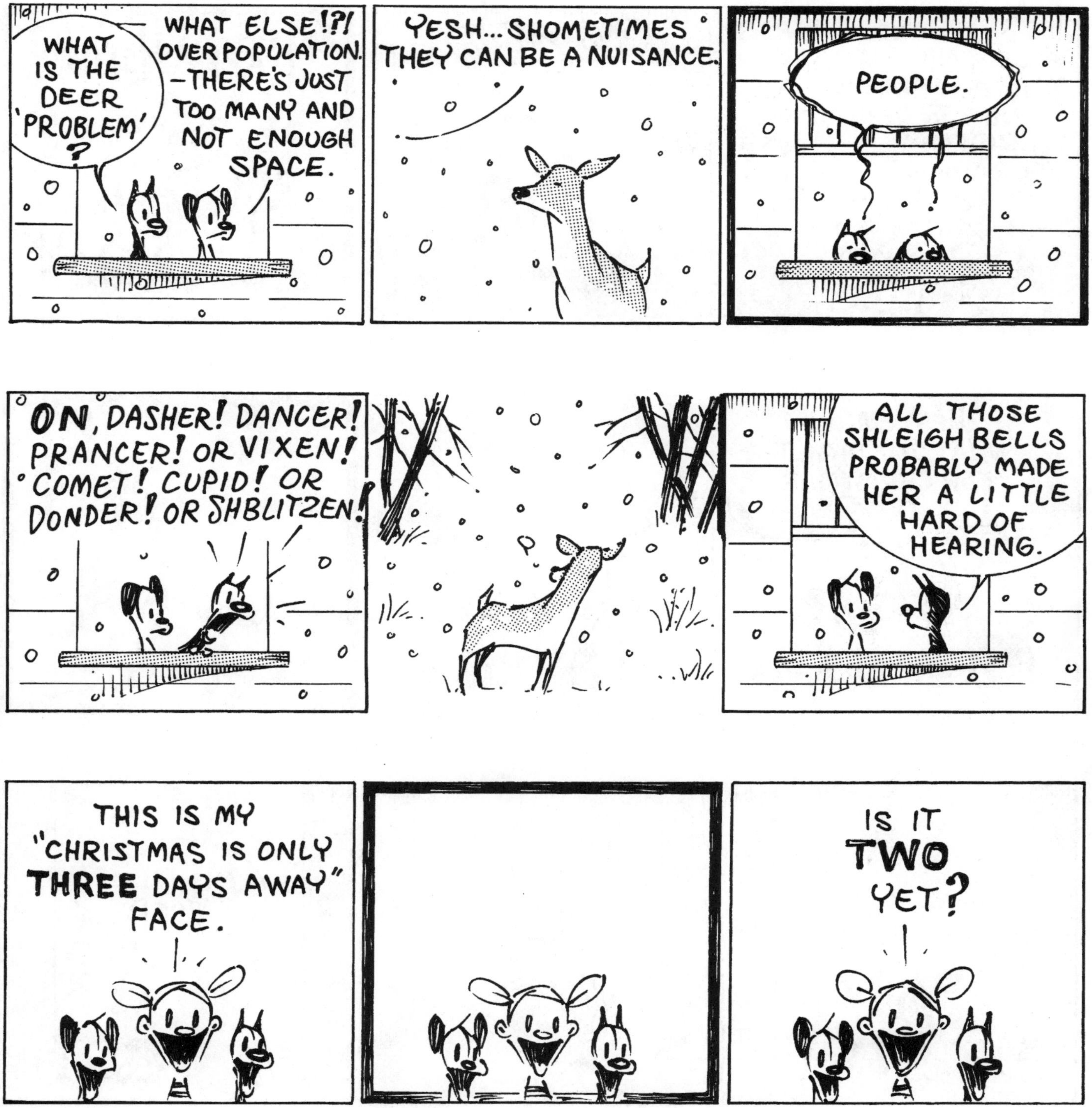
WHAT IS THE DEER 'PROBLEM'?
WHAT ELSE!?! OVER POPULATION. —THERE'S JUST TOO MANY AND NOT ENOUGH SPACE.
YESH... SHOMETIMES THEY CAN BE A NUISANCE.
PEOPLE.
ON, DASHER! DANCER! PRANCER! OR VIXEN! COMET! CUPID! OR DONDER! OR SHBLITZEN!
ALL THOSE SHLEIGH BELLS PROBABLY MADE HER A LITTLE HARD OF HEARING.
THIS IS MY "CHRISTMAS IS ONLY THREE DAYS AWAY" FACE.
IS IT TWO YET?

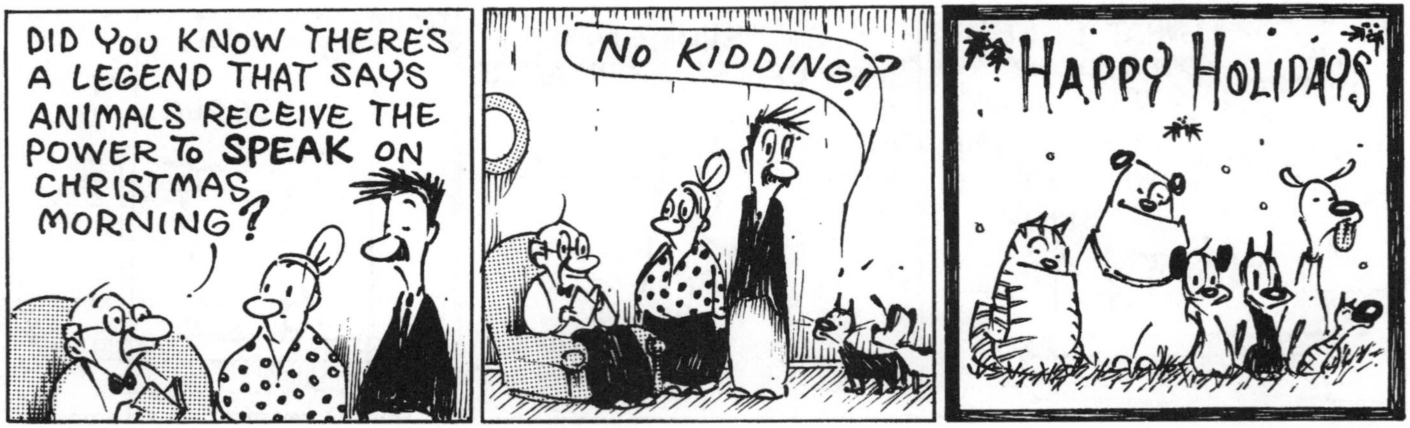
DID YOU KNOW THERE'S A LEGEND THAT SAYS ANIMALS RECEIVE THE POWER TO SPEAK ON CHRISTMAS MORNING?
NO KIDDING!?
HAPPY HOLIDAYS

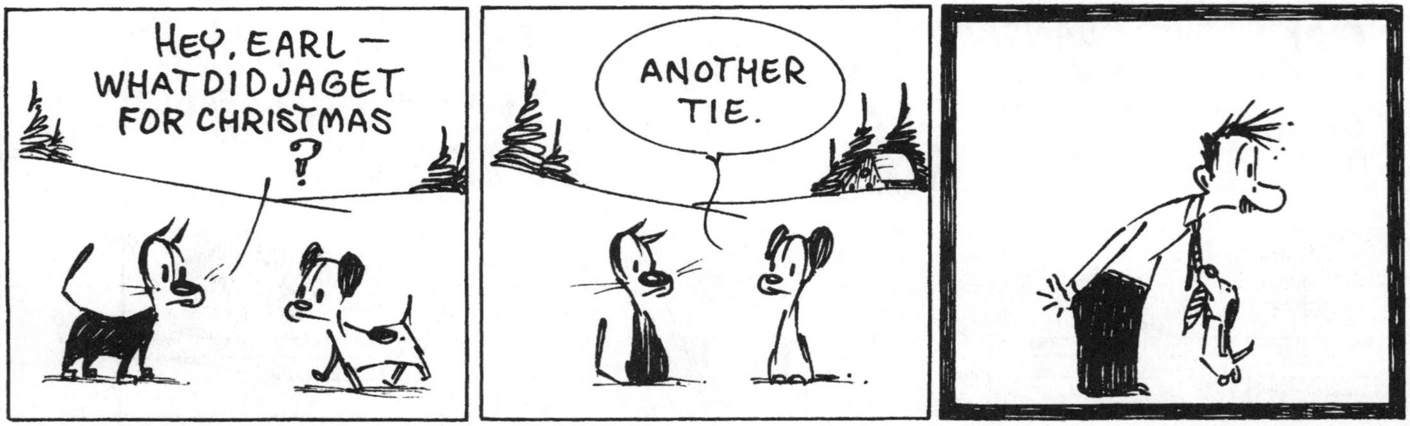
HEY, EARL — WHATDIDJAGET FOR CHRISTMAS?
ANOTHER TIE.

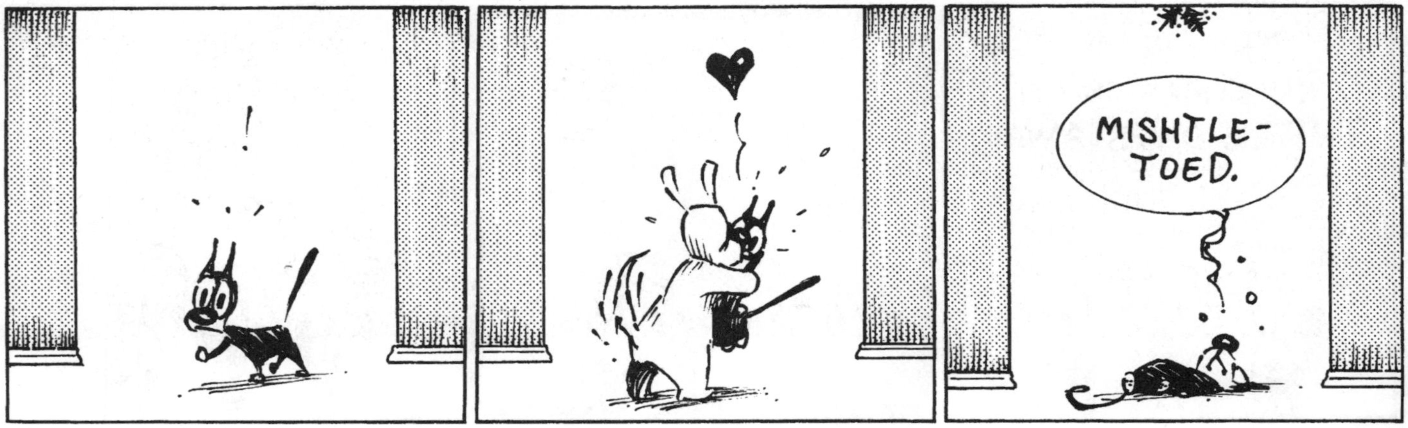
MISHTLE-TOED.

PATRICK McDONNELL

The Little Mutts

STILL TRYING TO SAVE ENDANGERED TIGERS, SHTINKY?

OH, YES, **SAVE** THE TIGER!

...AND SAVE THE SNOW LEOPARD! SAVE THE GIANT PANDA! SAVE THE GORILLA! SAVE THE CHIMPANZEE! SAVE THE ELEPHANT! SAVE THE BLACK RHINOCEROS! SAVE THE TIBETAN ANTELOPE! SAVE THE SUMATRAN RABBIT! SAVE THE BLUE WHALE! SAVE THE MANATEE! SAVE THE TREE HOLE CRAB! SAVE THE GREVY'S ZEBRA! SAVE THE CRESTED IBIS! SAVE THE YELLOW SPOTTED TREE FROG! SAVE THE SANTA MONICA SHELLBACK KATYDID! SAVE THE GOLDEN TOAD! SAVE THE YELLOW-EARED PARROT! SAVE THE

SEEMS LIKE THE WHOLE WORLD NEEDS SAVING.

...PHEW... OH, YES...

AND WE MUST ALL RISE TO THE OCCASION AND START SAVING **NOW!**

WELL, I'LL CERTAINLY TRY TO DO **MY** BEST.

SAVE THAT THOUGHT!

GOOD DOG!
ANOTHER SUCCESS-FUL DAY.

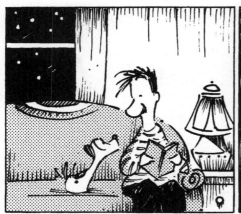

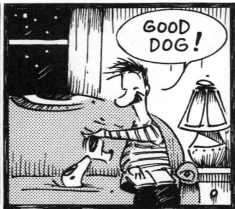

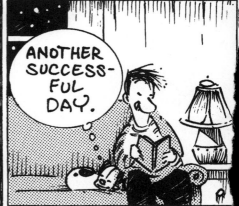

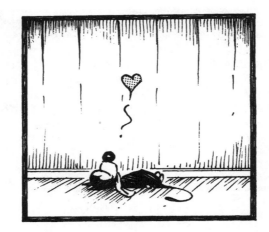